Protestant Nurture

PROTESTANT NURTURE

An Introduction to
Christian Education

by

HARRY C. MUNRO

Brite College of the Bible
Texas Christian University

Englewood Cliffs, N. J.
PRENTICE-HALL, INC.
1956

Preface

A philosophy of Protestant Christian education today must deal with a number of searching questions:

What is the real nature of the crisis that confronts western Christian civilization? What responsibility have Protestant Christians in meeting that crisis? What kind of education will enable Protestant Christians to achieve the real genius of their spiritual heritage, and thus qualify for such a responsibility?

How do recent developments in American theological thinking affect our conception of Christian nurture? How do developments in the psychology of personality and the theory of character bear upon our interpretation of Christian education? What reconstruction of Protestant churches from within is required to qualify them for their present educational and social responsibility?

How can we preserve the American principle of religious freedom and still prevent our educational system from promoting complete secularism? What are the essentials of a total educational program that will meet our needs? What are the next steps in home, church, and community toward such a program?

It is the purpose of this book to help its readers find the answers to such questions and to assist ministers and lay leaders in Protestant churches to clarify policies and improve procedures in the development of effective Christian nurture for our time.

HARRY C. MUNRO

Contents

10. What Are the Growing Edges of the
    Movement? *(Continued)*

Protestant Nurture

CHAPTER 1

What Is Our Human Problem?

In spite of the unprecedented statistical and institutional growth of religion in America, our generation is insecure, fear-ridden, and neurotic. What is wrong with us? The challenge of Communism as a rival faith, our moral and spiritual "lag" with respect to vast technological and material progress, the hysterical retreat from democracy to authoritarianism around the world, confusion and frustration under the claims of rival sovereignties: these are all superficial aspects of a problem with deeper roots. They are symptoms of a basic corruption of the faith of our fathers. We have erected one or another form of human self-sufficiency into an absolute and then substituted dependence upon it for trust in the true God. The original principle and motive of the Protestant faith is the solution to this problem. Protestant nurture must reinstate this basic principle as the means of launching a new Reformation within Protestantism itself.

There are many outward signs of a widespread religious revival in American life. Church membership is growing two and a half times as fast as population.[1] Protestant church contributions have doubled in ten years. Our church building budget exceeds one-half billion dollars a year.

Yet, the First Report of the Advisory Commission for the Evanston Assembly of the World Council of Churches in 1954 stated, "Our churches are sick. The sickness is shown in their

[1] Benson Y. Landis (ed.), *1954 Yearbook of American Churches* (New York: National Council of Churches, 1954).

1

being at home in the world and conformed to the world's standards. At the same time the churches are sick in that they are isolated from the world and failing to speak to it."

The officers of the National Council of the Churches of Christ in the U.S.A., in their Message on the State of the Church to the Council's Assembly in December 1954, said, "When we consider how little it costs to be counted among the church members in our country today, we are troubled. There is not much strict discipline in any of our constituent churches. The average church member is not conspicuously different from the average non-member. The average church is so much conformed to the world that people are surprised if it sharply challenges the prevailing behavior of the community. Consequently Christianity is regarded by many as a 'harmless adornment of a comfortable life.' "

Furthermore, the evidences of a vital religious faith seem to be steadily declining. Our generation is fearful, insecure, confused, and frustrated. We are so neurotic that over half the beds in our hospitals are said to be occupied by persons who have only "functional disorders," diseases which originate in the mind and emotions. Instead of moving confidently forward with all our unprecedented resources and powers to possess some glorious future, we seem to be retreating into a new dark age of fear, repression, cruelty, and human slavery. We have seen hundreds of millions of our fellow men frightened and harassed into bartering their economic and political freedom for the false promise of security under totalitarian regimes. In our hysterical preparation to defend ourselves against some ominous threat to the values we cherish, we have invented and stockpiled enough lethal weapons to depopulate the earth. Seemingly we are powerless to extricate ourselves from wars, either cold or hot, though we seek nothing so much as to be let alone to pursue our cherished American way of life. How is this paradox between the expansion of organized religion and the decreasing fruitage of a vital religious faith in our generation to be explained?

The challenge of a rival faith

The expansion of Communism as a way of life and of economic and political organization, and particularly as an enemy of and substitute for historical religion, is the most obtrusive cause of our dismay and insecurity. Since Communism is avowedly committed to the use of force and violence in effecting its conquests, we seem to have no choice but to prepare to meet it in corresponding terms. Though we are a peace-loving people, detesting violence and war, sheer survival in this case seems to demand such means, or at least the readiness to use them. We are preparing for war because we believe that "peace is for the strong," rather than because we want war. "It is the real threat of Communism rather than any lack of faith in God that dictates our policy," we say.

Very well. But whereas we may take shelter behind military power and the threat of its use, it should be obvious that we must use the respite gained thereby to work out a quite different kind of defense. The final battle for the souls of men will not be one of bombs and blockades, but one of ideals and motives. Are we morally and spiritually equipped for this kind of struggle? Will we be able to find in our Christian faith the resources to qualify us for a contest at this level? If we are to develop the kind of educational program which will qualify us and our children for this kind of encounter, we will need to have a clear understanding of the relevant essentials of our Christian faith. For example, we will have to face humbly and courageously the question of why generations of loving and sacrificial Christian missions in China were seemingly submerged within months by a conquering rival faith.

What is the power of Communism which appeals to so many millions? It promises salvation to the hitherto "silent billion" of the masses of the world's population who are hungry, sick, exploited, and miserable. It offers them immediate help in their struggle against poverty, destitution, political corruption, oppression, imperialism, inequalities, and war. We live in a

world which technology has shrunken to the size of a neighborhood, and in which a majority of our neighbors have discovered
that they eat too little, live too wretchedly, and die too young
while the privileged minority fare well. Any voice which offers
these masses hope will be heard. Communism is such a voice.
Does the Christian faith, as we understand, teach, and live it,
have an equally clear and confident answer? It was no Communist who stood up in the synagogue and read, "The Spirit of
the Lord is upon me, because he has annointed me to preach
good tidings to the poor. He has sent me to proclaim release
to the captives and recovery of sight to the blind, to set at
liberty those who are oppressed, to proclaim the acceptable
year of the Lord." (Luke 4:18, 19, RSV). But does the faith
we profess and practice have any such specific relevance to the
human needs which Communism professes to meet?

John Macmurray, in the early days of Russian Communism,
attempted a comparison of Christianity and Communism [2] and
thus stated his basic problem: "The difficulty of the task lies
in our inability to give any satisfactory account of what we
mean by Christianity. That is the crux of the problem. Until
we can define what Christianity means, at least as clearly as
the Communist can define what he means by Communism, it is
quite useless to compare them. It is impossible to say whether
they imply alternative solutions to the urgent problems of social
and economic reconstruction."

Similarly Elton Trueblood recently defined our frustration in
dealing with contemporary Communism: "Even after we agree
that the world conflict is basically a conflict in values, we are
confused when we try, with any precision, to say what these
values are." [3] He goes on to observe that the Communists have
a definite and clear philosophy, a well-defined program telling
them just what the next move is, and a passion dedicating them
fanatically to their cause. Most temporary Christians have none
of these.

[2] John Macmurray, *Creative Society* ("World Problems Series," No. 21 [New
York: Eddy and Page]), pp. 7, 8.

[3] Elton Trueblood, *The Life We Prize* (New York: Harper and Brothers,
1951), p. 27.

It is not that we lack formulations of Christian doctrine. It is, rather, that those we have are vague and irrelevant with respect to the crucial issues of our contemporary life. Is the social and ethical essence of Christianity to be defined primarily as the contrasts between the customs, morals, and institutions of our western social order, which has had Christianity as its principal religion, and those of peoples whose dominant religions have been other than Christianity? If our Christian faith is thus to be identified with the things we like best and value most about our western civilization, what is the difference between a Christian and a non-Christian among us? What can I expect a Christian to do about the pressing needs of our tension-ridden society that I cannot expect from any decent and cultured person who makes no profession whatever of Christianity?

Many sincere Christians are inclined to identify Christianity with "our American way of life," particularly in its traditional economic and social patterns. This is a consequence of our failure to invest the term Christianity with any clear and relevant meaning. In the absence of such explicit definition it is inevitable that those who consider themselves Christians should attach to the term meanings which are derived from their own experience, upbringing, and personal interests. This is their only way of relating Christianity to the concrete activities and concerns of daily living. But the result of thus associating Christianity with what we like best about our western culture is merely to use whatever authority and emotional power our religion may have to support the status quo, rather than as a basis for either personal or social regeneration. Christian education becomes under these conditions a means of preserving the status quo and of conforming growing persons to it.

When we attempt, however, to define just what Christianity means with respect to the problems of our social, economic, and international order, we are in confusion. Some sincere Christians believe that religious faith has authority and relevance only with respect to our personal living, but others reply that personal living is inseparable from our behavior and our relationships in all these social institutions and activities. There is no clear consensus of judgment among Christians as to whether our chief concern should be to defend and stabilize the status quo, inducting growing persons into it, or to undertake its reconstruction into an order of society more consistent with Christlike ideals of love, service, and brotherhood. What, then, is the Christian answer to the challenge of this new and aggressive rival, Communism?

Our moral and spiritual lag?

In spite of the unprecedented expansion of organized religion, of a multitude of character building agencies and programs, and of increasing emphasis upon moral and spiritual values in public education, we are warned on all sides that our basic problem is one of moral and spiritual retardation. Our moral and spiritual growth lags behind our physical and material development so that we are continually prostituting our powers and resources and relationships for unworthy ends. Of course religion has always been seeking to direct man's attention and energies toward purposes more worthy of his true nature and destiny. But in our day the voice of the preacher is more than matched by the exhortations of the philosopher, the historian, the statesman, the military leader, and the scientist. They join in warning us of the wrath to come unless this lag in man's moral and spiritual life can somehow be overcome.

Even before the dawn of the Atomic Age, the French philosopher, Henri Bergson, author of *Creative Evolution,* likened modern man to a physical giant with but the pigmy soul of his medieval ancestors. Sorokin [4] diagnoses our civilization as a "sensate culture," incapable of survival as such. Woodrow Wilson, at the close of the First World War, warned that "our civilization cannot survive materially unless it be redeemed spiritually." General MacArthur, in accepting Japan's surrender at the close of the Second World War, defined the problem of our age as basically "theological," since "There must be a re-

[4] Pitirin A. Sorokin, *The Crisis of Civilization* (New York: E. P. Dutton and Co., 1942), p. 13.

generation of the spirit if we are to save the flesh." General Omar N. Bradley has declared: "Humanity is in danger of being trapped in this world by its moral adolescence. Our knowledge of science has already outstripped our capacity to control it. . . . We have grasped the mystery of the atom and rejected the Sermon on the Mount. . . . The world has achieved brilliance without wisdom, power without conscience. Ours is a world of nuclear giants and ethical infants." [5] After the first use of the atomic bomb, the very scientists who produced it became the most ardent advocates of a warless world lest man's misuse of his newly found powers should literally destroy his earthly home and himself with it.

This fact—that our technology has produced resources, powers, and contacts far in excess of our moral and spiritual competence to use and control them for worthy and justifiable ends—seems too obvious to need supporting argument. This is not to say that there has been moral and spiritual deterioration, that modern man is the degenerate offspring of a nobler ancestry. Quite the reverse. There have been significant moral and spiritual gains. The point is that the rapid multiplication of man's material resources and powers and contacts produced by modern technology has not been accompanied by a corresponding acceleration in his moral and spiritual life. There has always been moral and spiritual retardation, a lag between man's material development and his spiritual maturity. What confronts modern man with tragic potential catastrophe is that this lag or retardation has dangerously increased because of the phenomenal acceleration of technological achievements. This increasing moral and spiritual lag at least in part defines the task or problem of religious education in our day.

The retreat to authoritarianism

We Americans had, in the early years of this century, the naïve faith that democracy would soon become worldwide. Though we detested militarism, we were willing to fight one

---

[5] Henry P. VanDusen, *God in Education* (New York: Charles Scribner's Sons, 1951), p. 18.

last "war to end war" and "to make the world safe for democracy." At mid-century, almost with our backs to the wall, we
face worldwide resurgence of authoritarianism. Our worst
frustration is the seeming necessity to compromise our own
ideals of freedom and democracy in seeking adequate means
of curbing the aggression of authoritarian regimes. May we,
too, come to value the promise of security more highly than the
exercise of freedom and, so, disqualify ourselves for democratic
living? The preservation of democracy against authoritarian
trends may be a more basic issue in the long run than the in-
filtration and expansion of Communism within our social order.
Even though Russia and the whole Communist movement were
to be removed from the face of the earth tomorrow, we would
still find ourselves deeply involved in the conflict between two
ways of life which seem to be struggling for control of our
social, economic, political, educational, and religious conceptions and ideals. Although conflict is not new in our age, it is
today critically dangerous because of the weaving of the whole
human family into a neighborhood by the lines of communication laid by modern technology, and because of the vastly increasing potential destructiveness of warfare.

These contrasting ideologies compete for dominance in the
aims, methods, and content of religious education. If Protestant
nurture is to make its indispensable contribution to the solution
of this problem, those who plan and conduct it must understand
the issues involved. How, though, can we get beyond the pre-
conceptions associated with the terms democracy and authoritarianism into the essential contrasts between them? The following interpretations define the terms for the purposes of
this discussion:

The driving motive of democracy is the freedom or liberation
and full self-realization of responsible persons. The driving
motive of authoritarianism is security and avoidance of individual responsibility. The retreat into authoritarianism is often an
escape from the dangers and risks of a daring and precarious
existence on the frontiers of thinking, ethical conduct, and

unfamiliar relationships. While the promise of security which authoritarianism holds out is often unfulfilled, it always looks safer than the uncertainties of freedom.

From the democratic viewpoint each person is of infinite potential worth and, so, is the measure of all other values. Every person normally has capacities of great potential range and power so that, in the directions which these capacities indicate, he is capable of almost infinite "becoming." Each person is endowed with certain inalienable rights and their corresponding responsibilities. Individuals constitute the indispensable unit of any social organism. Each person is always an end to be served rather than a means to be used or exploited by other persons or by institutions.

From the authoritarian standpoint, the common man is of little value. The worth and rights of persons are believed to depend upon the class they are in; humanity is naturally divided into such categories as rulers and subjects, freemen and slaves, bourgeoisie and proletariat, white and colored, nordic and semitic, saints and sinners, elect and damned. One group of individuals may be regarded as the appropriate and legitimate means for the accomplishment of another group's ends.

The democratic concept of institutions is that they are always means for the service and enrichment of all the persons involved. The institution must never become an end in itself, using persons arbitrarily for the accomplishment of institutional objectives. The authoritarian view of institutions is that they are the means by which the "properly constituted authorities" control the masses and use them for the self-perpetuation and aggrandizement of the institutions and, incidentally, of the privileged ruling class. Whenever institutions become ends in themselves or are used primarily to control rather than to serve people, they become authoritarian.

The democratic attitude toward knowledge or truth is expressed in the phrase "the public nature of truth." No individual or group or institution has a monopoly on truth. Every person is free to challenge any accepted truth and try to supplant it with a more valid and better attested truth. All truth is consistent within itself so that conflicts are to be resolved by the discovery of a yet higher truth with which what is valid in conflicting views becomes synthesized. So-called "revealed truth" is an integral part of universal truth and ultimately must justify itself in human experience. Science is regarded as a way of extending and testing human knowledge and, so, of enabling mankind the better to understand and control his environment and his own behavior.

The authoritarian attitude toward human knowledge rests upon a certain body of a priori assumptions which are not open to examination or question. This may consist of a doctrine such as that of the divine right of kings or the natural superiority of the white race or the Marxian dogma of class conflict and the ultimate triumph of the proletariat. It may be a literally inerrant Bible or the decree of a church council or a particular creedal formulation. Or it may be the encyclicals of a pope or the basic tenets of fundamentalism. Even the self-styled liberal or the scientist is not always free from such dogmas. The possessor of this special truth, whether individual, special class, or institution, has a monopoly on truth in its field of knowledge. All persons must come to this possessor for it, and any who deny it are classified with either the deluded or the damned. Any new accessions of human knowledge must be brought into harmony with this truth or be repudiated as false and dangerous. Science may be encouraged and used but it must not raise questions in the field covered by this authoritarian truth.

Democracy does not mean the absence of authority. That would be anarchy. Democracy means the administration and use of authority for the benefit of and in the best interest of all the people. It means that every person has a voice in determining who shall administer the authority under which he lives and the laws under which it will be administered. Authoritarianism means the arbitrary, despotic, imposed use of authority. Either view may assume that ultimate authority rests in God. In the authoritarian concept, certain arbitrarily selected human agents have become the administrators of God's authority. They speak his truth with finality and announce his terms of salvation. When rival agents disagree, they wax all the more authoritarian. In the democratic concept, all men are equal before God. His laws are written in the moral order of the universe. Here human experience encounters them. All men are equally responsible for living according to their best understanding of these laws. This does not mean that the Kingdom of God becomes "the democracy of God." (He is a sovereign ruler. He does not stand for re-election periodically. He would still be the Ruler of this universe and of mankind even though no man believed in him or accepted his kingship.) What this concept demands is that under God's authority men treat each other as equals and administer any authority entrusted to them reverently, conscious of their own finiteness and fallibility.

As we explore further the issues involved in a Protestant nurture which is relevant to the crucial issues of our generation, we will see the basic implications of the authoritarian threat to our Protestant faith.

One World — divisive sovereignties

Until our own day the human family was separated into relatively independent fragments by such barriers as geographical distance, economic self-sufficiency, cultural differences, and lack of effective intercommunication facilities. Under these conditions the existence of many independent sovereignties was inevitable. Completely sovereign nationalism, economic systems which were self-sufficient and self-contained and considered by those they served to be ideal, class and race stratifications which were supposedly either biologically or divinely ordained, and religious faiths each regarded by its adherents as exclusively and absolutely the final truth: these parallel and independent sovereignties governed human behavior and supposedly determined human destiny. These sovereignties were consistent with a view of the world which regarded it for all practical purposes not as a universe but as a multiverse, and with a conception of humanity in which differences were played up as far more significant than similarities.

With astonishing historic suddenness, however, the old isolation of nations, peoples, and cultures has given way to the fact of One World. It was the function of a sovereign nation to protect its citizens from each other and from any invading danger. In One World it can no longer do that, for the resulting international anarchy exposes every citizen to the danger either of being conscripted into military service in the futile attempt to provide security, or of being blown to smithereens by an atomic invasion. It was the function of the economic order to provide its participants with livelihood and some measure of economic security. But in One World rival economic orders are bankrupting themselves in a struggle for survival through world domination. The effective meeting of basic human needs has become a secondary consideration. Race and class were believed to correspond to and preserve basic qualitative differences in human kind. In One World these surface differences are lost in the evidence that mankind is actually a closely interrelated family whose common stock embodies similarities of vastly greater significance than all the differences which have been culturally and environmentally conditioned. Each religious faith, designating its own adherents as God's Chosen People and the adherents of other faiths as either deluded or damned, sets up the terms of an exclusive salvation and bases its intolerance upon the will of God. In One World, elements of truth are apparent in all the great faiths of mankind, and no denomination or religious system bears so plenteously the fruits of the spirit that its claim to exclusive validity can be justified.

But these sovereignties persist. Each seeks to serve and protect its adherents in terms of the outmoded fragmentary world. Rivalry among these sovereignties shatters the individual's integrity by divisive loyalties and threatens the very survival of the human family itself. For mankind itself is left defenseless and without an advocate or a protector among these warring sovereignties. This is the point made so effectively by Norman

Cousins in his able plea for world government, *Who Speaks for Man?*[6] (He is referring to a spark of common human recognition and fellowship which flashed between himself and a Chinese sentry who was challenging his entry into Red China and to whom Cousins tossed a pack of American cigarettes): "Months later I kept thinking of the Chinese sentry and the circumstances that made it possible for two creatures to build on their essential mutuality. Both of them shared the fabulous gift of human existence, both of them were dependent upon the same natural bounties for well-being, both of them were part of the same mixture, part of the same potential.

"In that sense—the sense of having something in common more vital than the differences officially assigned to us—we were members of a leaderless and unrepresented group. Belonging to a nation, we had a nation that could speak for us. Belonging to a religion, we had a religion that could speak for us. Belonging to an economic or political order, we had an economic or political order that could speak for us. But belonging to the human race, we were without a spokesman. Indeed, we could hardly speak to each other."

From one aspect the basic human problem of our day is that of replacing these divisive and rival sovereignties, which are tearing the human family asunder, with a sovereignty sufficiently inclusive to protect humanity from self-destruction. Such an inclusive sovereignty is an inevitable corollary of the achievement of One World. The question is, will it come in time?

Faith in human self-sufficiency

A deeper analysis of our situation reveals that our fear of Communism, our seeming moral and spiritual lag, our retreat into authoritarian attitudes, and our involvement with conflicting sovereignties are symptoms of a basic corruption of the faith by which we live. Expansion of human knowledge and

6 Norman Cousins, *Who Speaks for Man?* (New York: The Macmillan Company, 1953), p. 149.

extension of man's control over the forces of the physical universe have so increased our human pride and self-sufficiency that our faith as a people has gradually transferred from an infinite Creator, Ruler, and Determiner of Destiny to our own finite human genius and self-sufficiency. Of course this is but to restate the age-old problem of Sin. Man's undoing has always been his tendency to enthrone outcomes of his own Godlike potentialities, finite though they are, as a substitute for surrender to, and worship of, the true God.

What makes faith in human self-sufficiency so dangerous in our day is that man's technological success has so vastly increased the evil results of his self-worship. Each of the foregoing aspects of our human problem roots in the tendency to erect into an absolute some humanly devised and enforced system or power or doctrine. Self-sufficient finitude is the basic evil. In a human world so interdependent as ours its destructive power is enormous.

Communism is the erection of a humanly devised economic and political system into an absolute. Its philosophy of history makes inevitable the final dominance of this system in human society. The Communist believes that his cause aligns him with the "process of history" so that the cause cannot ultimately fail. Consequently his cause has the qualities and the driving motivation of a religious faith. This faith cannot be destroyed by argument or stopped by force. It can be overcome only by a stronger and more valid faith. Such a faith must be something more than a rival, self-sufficient finitude such as our "American way of life," functioning as an absolute. We rightly fear Communism because the faith by which we actually live may be just another form of human self-sufficiency.

We have used the atom bomb once. We are afraid we will use it again. This dreaded, fatal misuse of our powers might be due to moral and spiritual immaturity or lag. Our troubled consciences, however, indicate that, in some measure at least, we know what we are doing and how evil it is. Our self-justification is that, in the case of this particular enemy, there is no alternative. We have to respond to them in the only language they understand, the threat of force and violence. This means that we as a people have lost faith in any other kind of resistance. We want to win peace at the conference table rather than on the battle field, but, since "peace is for the strong," we will go to the conference table only armed to the teeth. Since the faith of our enemies is of the same character, what chance has the conference table? Of course we think we trust in God. But the God in whom we actually trust is one who works through bombs and blockades. Our national policies are dictated not by faith in the God of Jesus Christ but by trust in the self-sufficiency of a man-made security. We are suffering not merely from spiritual retardation but from spiritual perversion.

The principles of democracy as we have defined them are based upon the dignity and worth of the individual person as a child of God. It is doubtful whether democracy can be achieved and maintained on any basis other than this religious view of the worth of human personality. Democracy is essentially a way of regarding persons, and this regard is due to the relationship of the individual to God. The forms of democracy may continue after some human absolute has usurped the place of God. But the essence of democracy is gone. Whenever a human absolute, be it scientism or state or economic system or church, replaces God or stands between the individual and God, democracy is doomed, for the erection of a human absolute, either in the place of God or as the official and authorized embodiment of God's sovereignty, is authoritarianism. Even the medieval doctrine of the divine right of kings was less authoritarian than modern political authoritarianism because it was exercised within the frame of reference of God's ultimate sovereignty and the responsibility of the king as well as the subject to God himself. If the modern democratic state operates within a totally secular frame of reference, it will tend inevitably toward authoritarian practices and attitudes.

Authoritarianism in religion arises when a church or prelate or an official religious body or a dogma becomes an absolute to which persons are subject, or through which they must approach God. Authoritarianism arises and spreads for two reasons. First, those to whom responsibility and power are delegated are easily corrupted thereby, and tend to extend their control over their fellow men through exalting their human offices and institutions into absolutes. Second, to masses of people, the security and irresponsibility of submission to such a human absolute seems preferable to the spiritual exercise and responsibility of direct encounter with God. Organized religion always faces the hazard of becoming, itself, a human absolute.

The rival sovereignties which have been outmoded by the achievement of One World, are one form in which some human absolute is thrust between the individual and his God. The achievement of world government sufficiently powerful and well-implemented to protect individuals and the human family as a whole from divisive political and economic sovereignties is the indispensable next step in enabling the human family to go on living in One World. But on a purely human and secular basis, World Government might itself become just another human absolute erected in the place of God. On this basis it cannot solve our human problem because it does not deal with the whole of human life. It overlooks man in his highest and most significant relationship, his relationship to God.

Prophetic religion has always asserted that God is one, that he is the creator, sustainer, and ruler of the universe, and that he is universal in his relationship to mankind. He is the Father of all mankind and not just of a Chosen People. It is this concept of the Universal God, who is the one Absolute and to whom all human agencies, institutions and forces are subject, that can give spiritual reality and validity to One World. The establishment of any sovereignty, be it national, race, class, denomination, or sect, attempts to fragmentize this God as it fragmentizes humanity. The solution to our human problem is essentially religious. It calls for a religious principle which will relate the individual directly to God and, on the basis of that relationship, to the entire family of God, the human race.

Protestant Christianity, not in its organized forms, but in its original principle and motive, is the specific solution to our human problem as here outlined. It was a revolt against the human absolutes of doctrine, of priesthood, and of ecclesiasticism, which had usurped the place of God in the Christian religion. It was a reassertion in New Testament terms of the utter insufficiency of man to extricate himself from his predicament by merely human resources. It was a declaration of his utter dependence upon God. It was a reaffirmation of the readiness and the all-sufficiency of God to reconcile man to himself, not through any merit or worthiness on man's part, but through man's penitence for his self-exaltation and self-sufficient pride and through faith in the redemptive mission of Christ, through whom man knew and appropriated the love and forgiveness of God. It was an emphasis upon the worth and dignity of the individual person as based upon his direct filial relationship with God. It was an Emancipation Proclamation for the mind and the spirit of man.

In the measure that this basic Protestant principle has worked out during the Protestant Era, mankind has experienced a new age of freedom, of enlightenment, and of human achievement. Our human problem, as we have been defining it, is due largely to our failure as Protestants to apply this principle more fully in our ecclesiastical, political, economic, educational, and social life and institutions. A partial application is not enough. So far as the Protestant Era consisted in this partial application of its basic principle, it is at an end. Our only salvation is in a new Reformation within Protestant Christianity itself, which will go much farther in the working out of this principle in terms of modern life. The task of Protestant nurture is to implement this new Reformation with a program of Christian education which, in its aims, its content, its method, and its spirit, is thoroughly consistent with this mission. What will such a program be like?

CHAPTER 2

What Is the Faith We Teach?

Christian faith is faith in a person. To follow this faith is to risk living one's life upon the basic assumptions by which Jesus lived — his assumptions about God, about man, about love, and about the future. The Protestant principle relates the individual directly and personally to God through Jesus Christ, in an experience of surrender, reconciliation, dedication, and filial love. This relationship gives meaning and power to his life and guides his behavior. Such a faith cannot be merely passed on. It must be achieved by each growing person for himself. It must be passed on by each generation. An education of authoritarian indoctrination is subversive of this faith. Its propagation requires a religious nurture of testimony, and of creative and democratic sharing of experience.

How shall we define Christianity?

A program of Protestant nurture relevant to our basic human problem must be derived from a clear understanding of the essence of the Christian faith. Obviously one must approach the task of formulating such a statement in deep humility, knowing that the results are bound to be unsatisfactory to a majority of his readers even as they are to the writer himself. Anyone confident of his ability to capture within the network of words and phrases the essential meaning of the Christian faith would thereby exemplify the sin of self-sufficient finitude. Perhaps no one has interpreted Christianity more clearly for the modern mind than Dr. Harry Emerson Fosdick. Yet, in answer to the question "What is Christianity?" he begins with this paragraph:

"Starting in Galilee nearly two thousand years ago, it [Christianity] has run an amazing course. Diverse ages, races, and temperaments have played upon it. In it can be found all the dominant types of religious experience and expression known to mankind. Upon it mystics, metaphysicians, and moralists of many sorts have left their mark. It has become stark asceticism in some, and in others it has assumed the pomp of ecclesiastical autocracy. It has been pacifist in the Quaker, and militarist in the Crusader. It includes within its historic movement many kinds of theology, from the frontiers of pantheism to the borders of polytheism, and many sorts of sacramental theory from magic up. What is Christianity? The more one knows about it, the more difficult the answer becomes." [1]

History reveals all sorts of human error and wrongdoing wearing the mask of Christianity and claiming the authority of Christ. In a historical study of "Christian" beliefs and practices, Kirby Page sets Jesus over against the historical movement which bears his name in a succession of glaring contrasts in his book, *Jesus Or Christianity, A Study in Contrasts.*[2]

An understanding of the Christian faith involves attention to at least four sources of information and insight: the specific actions of God in human history through which he has made himself known to men and has sought to bring them into responsible and filial relationships with himself; the coming of Jesus of Nazareth into the life of mankind as the Incarnation of God and the revealer of God's character and will; the continued life of the Risen and Living Christ as Savior and Redeemer of mankind; the meanings which the Christian faith has accumulated through the experiences of those who have sought to live by it during the centuries of Christian history. The relative importance attributed to each of these four sources varies greatly

1 Harry Emerson Fosdick, *As I See Religion* (New York: Harper and Brothers, 1932), pp. 33, 34.
2 Kirby Page, *Jesus or Christianity, A Study in Contrasts* (Garden City, N. Y.: Doubleday, Doran and Company, Inc., 1929).

among Christian theologians. While recognizing that all four of them must be considered, we frankly confess that, for the purposes of defining the Christian faith as a basis for a program of Protestant nurture, we intend to give the greatest weight to the second in the series, Jesus Christ as revealer of God's character and will.

This means that, so far as our sources enable us to know and understand Jesus as a historic person, we will approach our understanding of God's dealings with mankind, and man's experience in trying to understand and live by the Christian faith, through Jesus himself. We see Jesus appearing upon the plane of history as the beneficiary, along with his Jewish contemporaries, of a rich spiritual heritage reflecting the dealings of God with his people, and incorporated in the complex and varied literature of the Old Testament and in contemporary religious institutions. This heritage embodied the conflict between the nationalistic, legalistic, priestly, institutionalized Jewish religion and the universal, ethical monotheism of the prophets. Though the prophetic movement had seemingly been dormant for more than two hundred years, since the appearance of the remarkable allegory of Jonah, Jesus took his stand clearly in the line of the prophets. He carried to its climax their interpretation of a universal ethical monotheism in terms of a Father-God of all mankind.[3] He pressed his views so vigorously and uncompromisingly, in a highly unfavorable religious climate, that his human career was cut short by the opposition of the religious authorities before those who had responded to his leadership had more than glimpsed its deeper and more far-reaching implications. It was their experience of his resurrection and continued spiritual presence with them that gave these disciples the courage and the wisdom to continue their faith in him and to incorporate this faith in a missionary movement and in the formation of churches wherever they went. The literature of the New Testament, which is the source of our information

---

[3] Leroy Waterman, *The Religion of Jesus* (New York: Harper and Brothers, 1952), chap. v.

about the historic Jesus and his continued influence as the Risen Christ, is a legacy from these early missionary endeavors.

Now the Christian faith is not faith in a historic personage only, but in the Eternal Christ. It is the death and resurrection of Christ that give eternal and saving significance to his earthly life and teachings as the Incarnation and the Revealer of God; but it is also his earthly life and teachings as the Incarnation and the Revealer of God which give redemptive significance to his death and resurrection. We propose to emphasize the life and example of Jesus, with the insistence that this in no way disparages the redemptive significance of his death and resurrection. In seeking to understand the meaning of the Christian faith as a basis for a program of Protestant nurture, let us begin, therefore, with Jesus himself.

Jesus said, "I am the way, the truth, and the life." (John 14:6.) In the records of his followers in the Book of Acts, they are called those of "the Way." The essence of early Christianity was a kind of living, a quality of life, an experience of confident and victorious living based upon Jesus' example, his teachings, the quality of his life, the conviction that God was in Christ reconciling the world to himself, and the confidence that his living presence empowered his followers to do all things involved in loyal discipleship. Enthroning Christ and his will means dethroning self and all self-sufficiency. Christianity began as an inner experience of personal relationship with Jesus Christ which qualified and controlled all other relationships.

But Christian faith is more than merely "following Christ" in terms of imitating his behavior. In its full sense Christian faith is the response to God of the whole person in his thinking, his judging, his feeling, and his actions, when God is confronted by accepting Jesus Christ as the Interpreter of God and as the Lord and Savior of the individual. The resulting relationship between the individual and God is due in part to the seeking, forgiving, reconciling approach of God through Christ, and in part to the response of the individual to this approach. In so far as this response is an act of will on the part of the individual, it consists of surrender or commitment to Christ in loyal discipleship. If this discipleship is to be something more than an attempted imitation of Christ, in what does it consist?

Attempting to imitate the behavior of Christ provides inadequate guidance for such discipleship. The situations in which Jesus lived were very different from those which we face. Our limited records of his life give but occasional glimpses of how he faced even these situations. We do know the impressions which he made on others. The glimpses of his earthly life which we have give us the basis for sensing the quality, the temper, the driving motives, the dynamic of his life. We can discover some of the basic assumptions, the axioms of behavior, underlying his actions, his attitudes, and his relationships. These assumptions, these most important facts which he took for granted, constituted the faith by which he lived. To have faith in Christ, in so far as it is an act of the will, then, might mean to base one's life upon the conviction that he was right about these basic axioms of behavior by which he lived and for which he died.

So defined, faith in Jesus Christ would demand a willingness to risk our lives on the conviction that he was right about God. He never argued or even reasoned the existence of God. He assumed God as the central fact of the universe and of human experience. God as he knew him was a God of love, best understood in terms of fatherhood. But his is a fatherhood raised to a degree so high above the best human fatherhood we know that he is to be contrasted rather than compared with a human father. (Matt. 7:11, Luke 11:13.) To be sure, he is a sovereign God. He is a King. His government is an inescapable fact. As Dr. Weigle [4] has phrased it, however, "God is for him (Jesus) not the sort of a father that a king would be; he is the sort of king that a father would be."

This universe and the controlling conditions of human life and relationships derive their character from this fatherly God who is at their center. Since he is love, his universe supports

[4] Luther A. Weigle, *Jesus and the Educational Method* (New York: Abingdon, 1939), p. 90.

and works with love as a way of life, as the controlling force in human relationships, as the arbiter of human destinies. Men were made and meant to be brothers, not competitors or enemies. And the only reasonable way to treat an enemy, to avoid the worst injury he can inflict, is to love him and so to help him overcome his enmity. Undiscourageable, patient, forgiving love is the only real solution to all problems of human relationship. To have faith in Jesus Christ is to base our lives on the conviction that he was right about love as the essential nature, the controlling power, the moral order of this universe.

Jesus made revolutionary assumptions about human personality. His regard for persons underlies the whole democratic principle. Dr. Fosdick regards it as the distinguishing characteristic of Christianity as a religion:

"In what terms, then shall we describe that quality which gives peculiar flavor to Christianity so that when it is absent Christianity is not Christian at all? This differential seems to reside in one major matter, discoverable elsewhere, to be sure, but so emphatic in Christianity, so dominant in the Founder's message, so inescapable in the ethic of the movement which succeeded him, that from it as from a fountain flows the result which makes Christianity Christian.

"The genius of Christianity lies in reverence for personality.... Were one to select the special contribution which Jesus of Nazareth himself has made and is making to man's thought, one could do no better than to call him the champion of personality." [5]

The key idea in Dr. George Albert Coe's notable answer to the question "What Is Christian Education," is his assertion that the creative principle in Christianity is the principle of the worth of persons. Contemporary religious education is self-deceived and ineffective, he contends, because this principle of the worth of persons is in an undeveloped condition. The "Coda" with which the book closes is:

"What, then, is Christian education? It is the systematic,

---

[5] Harry Emerson Fosdick, *As I See Religion* (New York: Harper and Brothers, 1932), pp. 40, 41.

critical examination and reconstruction of relations between persons, guided by Jesus' assumption that persons are of infinite worth, and by the hypothesis of the existence of God, the Great Valuer of Persons." [6]

Both Dr. Fosdick and Dr. Coe proceed to show how the Christian conception of a personal God rests back upon this principle of the infinite worth of persons. Granted that principle, we have no higher terms in which to conceive of Supreme Being than in terms of personality.

This personality principle accounted for Jesus' insistence that persons are always ends to be served while institutions are means to the serving of persons. "The Sabbath was made for man, not man for the Sabbath." (Mark 2:27.) The final conflict with the authorities which brought him to the cross was his condemnation and defiance of institutions which were exploiting persons. His sense of mission to cause social conditions and institutions to serve the welfare of persons rather than to exploit them is revealed by his choice of the text for his offending sermon at Nazareth. (Luke 4:18, 19.) He depicts the Last Judgment (Matt. 25:31-46) as based upon the principle that the service or the neglect of God is identical with the service or neglect of one's fellow men.

These attitudes and emphases of Jesus were based upon his assumptions regarding persons. He assumed that each person is a child of God, that this relationship endows him with Godlike potentialities, and that he is consequently of infinite worth. He may have fallen far below these possibilities; he may be lost from his Father's house and his family circle; he may be in rebellion against his Father; he may have enthroned Self as the ruler over his life. But he is redeemable, and his Father in loving forgiveness seeks his penitent return. No person can wander beyond the Father's loving concern and outreaching care. Regardless of race, color, age, or social status, each person

---

[6] George Albert Coe, *What Is Christian Education?* (New York: Charles Scribner's Sons, 1929), p. 296.

is the object of his seeking and redeeming love. Having faith in Jesus Christ means living by the conviction that he was right about mankind and treating one's fellow men accordingly. To have faith in Christ means to believe that human nature, in spite of its well-known weaknesses and perversities, will support his faith in its Godlike potentialities, and in its redeemability.

He who has faith in Christ bases his living upon the hopes and expectations of Jesus. Jesus anticipated a life of fulfillment beyond this earthly life for every child of God; and he expected the triumph of God's reign in human affairs. But in his hopes two diverse strains are intertwined. Sometimes he contemplates an indefinite continuation of history on the plane of which God's will is to prevail increasingly in human affairs. The Kingdom of God, already a fact of human experience, is to grow toward a consummation for which his followers were taught to pray, "Thy Kingdom come; Thy will be done upon earth as it is in heaven." Intertwined with these hopes are prospects of a seemingly sudden and cataclysmic end of human history, a last judgment through intervention on God's part independent of human action or expectancy. Nineteen centuries of history seem to have disappointed the first of these hopes and invalidated the second; but they may only have shown that God is neither in a hurry nor subject to human time tables.

Each of these strains is too deeply embedded in our sources to be discounted as a misinterpretation of Jesus by his followers. We must try to analyze them for their basic ideas as the source of our own hopes. There are three main ideas:

1. The Kingdom of God means the kingship of God. He exercises his authority in accordance with his character, which is that of an infinitely loving and wise father. He has given man freedom as the condition of moral character and responsibility. But he has not abdicated. Unless man's exercise of his freedom is in accordance with the nature and laws of the universe which embody God's will, man will frustrate and destroy himself in his attempted defiance of them. Every human act and institu-

tion is under God's judgment. God's rule is a present fact as well as a future consummation.

2. Man's part in the Kingdom is to "receive" it or to "enter into" it or to "seek" it. When man adjusts himself to God's government and exercises his freedom in the light of it, he lives abundantly. He may suffer at the hands of men who defy God, but he is at peace with God. He is in the Kingdom.

3. The climax of history will be the fulfillment of God's Kingdom or rule. Through human co-operation or in spite of human perversity, God will finally give his Kingdom in its fullness to the faithful. History moves at a rate beyond human calculation toward this final consummation, which will include the return of Christ to the earth and the Last Judgment.

Faith in Christ, then, gives confidence in the future. The long range outcome is not in the hands of a man with the H-bomb or the C-bomb. Men may do vast harm to each other in defiance of God's law of love. But the Last Judgment is in God's hands. We may not know what the future holds. But we know Who holds the future, and we are not afraid.

Obviously most so-called Christians base their daily living, attitudes, and relationships upon assumptions quite different from these. Christians through the centuries have been dominated by motives and interpretations many of which bear little resemblance to these basic assumptions or convictions which seem to constitute the faith by which Jesus lived. This observation should give us both warning and guidance. We must have some principle of discrimination in determining what Christianity shall mean for us. We can find such a principle in the proposal that we make a vivid acquaintance with the historic Jesus central and that, for us, the essence of Christianity involved in a program of Christian nurture shall be interpreted as a way of life based upon the assumptions by which he lived. This is at least a starting point for understanding the Christianity which we teach. It will guide us in appropriating the other sources which have indispensable contributions to make to our understanding of our faith.

Does such a faith have driving power?

Basing your life on the assumptions by which Jesus lived is more than a mere working hypothesis for life, to be discarded when you find a better one. Of course the Christian is ever a truth seeker. He believes that to act upon the truth he already has will lead to fuller truth. He takes Jesus at his word, "If any man's will is to do his will, he shall know whether the teaching is from God" (John 7:17) Like any truth seeker he acts upon the testimony of those of his predecessors in whom he has the greatest confidence. The Christian faith is a quest for wholeness of truth. But it is more than that.

The Christian believes that in Jesus he has the supreme source of religious truth. Jesus, for him, was not a mere experimenter with life. He is the Master of life and of death and of the eternal future. He is the answer to the human quest for the truth about God, about man, and about the universe. The Christian is a seeker, not for a fuller and more reliable source of truth, but for a fuller comprehension and appropriation of the truth which is already available in Jesus Christ. So the truth which he has already understood and appropriated from Jesus is not a mere working hypothesis; it is a driving conviction. He is convinced that it will be validated fully in his experience. Living the Christian life is basing your life on this truth and believing that in the long run it will never let you down.

It is common Christian experience that this commitment to Christ releases power in the life of the Christian enabling him to surmount difficulties, to perform tasks, and to endure sacrifices which lie far beyond ordinary human capacity. Paul defined such commitment as the power of God unto salvation. Such surrender charges the Christian's life with the "grace of God" which enables him to achieve a unity and singleness of purpose, an integrity which brings conduct into conformity with ideals, a harmony with God and the universe, so that he enters upon a whole new kind of living. With Paul he says, "It is no longer I who live, but Christ who lives in me; and the life I now live in the flesh I live by faith in the Son of God, who loved me and gave himself for me" (Gal. 2:20). Christianity is both a way of living and power to live that way.

Is this just a new authoritarianism?

When we interpret Christian faith in these terms and commit ourselves to the principle of making the assumptions, the experience, and the example of Jesus normative for our own life and thought, have we not merely set up for ourselves one form of authoritarianism? Is there any real difference between the authoritarianism exerted by a historic person and that of a living priest or church or sacred book? Jesus "spake as one having authority," and in the final commission to his followers he said, "All authority has been given unto me in heaven and on earth." If we are to be truly democratic can we set up even the authority of Christ in such terms as we have described? Many liberal Protestants would say, "No. Authoritarianism is authoritarianism by whomsoever exerted."

But is this just another form of authoritarianism? Jesus is regarded by the Christian as an altogether unique person. We accept as a part of his own assumptions and as a part of the Christian faith the fact that in a peculiar sense he was God's son, the revealer of God, God Incarnate in a human life. We recognize God the Creator and Sustainer of the universe as the ultimate source of authority, as Jesus did. We believe that the relationship which Jesus sustained to God made him the agent of God's authority in an altogether unique way. Consequently, recognizing the authority of Jesus over our lives is the most definite way of recognizing our responsibility to God. This is not authoritarianism because it is not the substitution of a human absolute for God. It is the surest way of putting God himself at the controlling center of our lives.

As we have seen, democracy does not mean the absence of authority. That would be anarchy. In democracy authority is not imposed upon those living under it, but is accepted by them voluntarily and administered on their behalf by persons of their own choosing. Ultimate authority is conceived as residing in the very nature of things, in a moral order which man did not create and does not control, but which is based upon the infinite worth and the inalienable rights of persons who are directly responsible to the Supreme Person, God the Creator and Ruler. As man individually and as mankind collectively conduct their lives in accordance with this moral order under God they get along well. They live orderly successful lives. To ignore or defy this moral order of the universe, which we believe to have been incarnate in the attitudes and assumptions of Jesus, is to confront ultimate frustration and disaster.

One's commitment to Christ might be authoritarian under any of these conditions: if he were coerced by fear or social pressure into making the commitment; if his life and conduct thus came under the arbitrary control of a church or priest or teacher who wore the reputed authority of Christ as a mask for human domination; if a slavish literalism or legalism obscured the great underlying assumptions and purposes of Christ with inconsequential, irrational, or irrelevant imitation.

Authority in a democratic order, be it domestic, educational, or ecclesiastical, consists in the weight or influence which a free person gives to the experience and the rights of others in controlling his own. When a free person commits himself to Christ and enthrones Christ as the self-chosen authority in his life he gives supreme weight or influence to the experience of Christ as it is known to him, and to the claims of Christ upon him in controlling his own experience. His commitment to Christ in the first place is voluntary. His acceptance of Christ's influence in controlling his life still leaves him free, for he himself administers this control. It is not imposed upon him. He is not coerced into it. He experiences the paradox of the "glorious liberty of the children of God." As the familiar hymn of George Matheson has expressed it:

> "Make me a captive, Lord,
>   And then I shall be free.
> Force me to render up my sword,
>   And I shall conqueror be."

Though Jesus' own faith and life are not only in harmony with the democratic viewpoint but are actually the principal source of it, he lived, and did his teaching, and died in an authoritarian world. His principles were a revolutionary attack upon much of the status quo. In such an authoritarian climate, it is perhaps inevitable that the authoritarian spirit soon began to develop among his followers. The historic movement known as Christianity has been on the whole characterized more by the authoritarian than by the democratic spirit and ideal. Consequently the theological formulations of doctrine about God, the universe, man, salvation, the church, and human society, have tended generally more toward the authoritarian than the democratic spirit and viewpoint. Those who oppose the liberal and democratic trends in Christian thinking and in Christian education lament the great importance given to the historic Jesus. [7] We justify it as a necessary corrective to the dominance of authoritarianism in the whole history of Christianity.

Why are we Protestants?

We are concerned with Christian nurture in Protestant churches. Having explored the assumptions and attitudes of Jesus for guidance in defining the relevance of Christianity to our modern world situation, what account shall we take of the historic Christian movement in gaining further guidance? What is the relationship between our Protestant faith and original Christianity?

Most of us are Protestants because our parents were and we grew up in Protestant families. Probably our parents and grandparents were Protestants for the same reason. But somewhere a dozen generations back we would find ancestors who were not Protestants. These spiritual ancestors of ours broke with the past, like Abraham of old leaving Ur of the Chaldees, to follow the leading of God's spirit into a new faith of their own. Their spiritual adventure and its outcomes are our spiritual

[7] H. Shelton Smith, *Faith and Nurture* (New York: Charles Scribner's Sons, 1941), pp. 17-26.

heritage. This faith of our fathers which lived and spread "in spite of dungeon, fire, and sword" was a venturing, pioneering faith. What is the essence or genius of it which we should seek as a spiritual heritage? Is this heritage basically a body of religious beliefs which must mean exactly the same thing to us as they did to them in order for us to enter into this heritage? Can their faith be inherited, or must it be achieved anew by each generation? Can it be reproduced without being reborn? What is the genius of our Protestant faith?

To place this spiritual adventure in its historic setting we should realize that it was a part of a fourfold revolution which ushered in the most creative and brilliant period in human history, the Protestant era. The Protestant Reformation climaxed the Renaissance in an *intellectual revolution* which freed the mind of man from medieval repression and opened the way for free inquiry, research, and the whole scientific method and viewpoint. The long range outcomes were the development of technology and our brilliant western material civilization. Technology, applied to the production and distribution of goods and services, produced an *economic* or *industrial revolution* which gradually transformed feudalism and hand craftsmanship into the mass machine production of modern industry. The birth of free sovereign nations out of the old Empire, and the gradual beginnings of political democracy during this period constituted a *political revolution* which reached its climax in our own American democratic government. But fundamental to all these revolutionary processes were the basic principles and motives generated through a *religious revolution*, dramatized by a revolt, led from within its own priesthood, against the medieval Church. Our primary concern here is with these religious principles. We have already noted that the basic principle of the Protestant revolt was the fallacy and irrelevance to man's salvation of any human absolute, be it dogma, priest, church, or even human righteousness. Paul Tillich interprets this as "a special historical embodiment of a universally significant principle. This principle, that the divine 'No' is spoken against every finite claim of finality, that man is not God, has been demonstrated in all periods of history, in every religion of mankind; it was powerfully pronounced by the Jewish prophets; it is manfest in the picture of Jesus as the Christ; it has been recovered time and again in the life of the Church; it was the sole foundation of the Churches of the Reformation; it challenges those Churches whenever they leave their foundation." [8]

This principle may be further interpreted through several basic doctrines or derived principles characteristic of original Protestantism.

What are the basic doctrines of Protestantism?

The first doctrine was "justification by faith." According to this principle, man cannot earn his salvation or justify himself before God by any amount of "good works." He cannot be good enough to merit God's favor. But he has no need to, for salvation through faith in Jesus Christ is the free gift of God to every believing person. Salvation is gained by throwing oneself in complete surrender upon the mercy of God, accepting his forgiveness, and effecting filial reconciliation with him through Jesus Christ. This principle repudiated the elaborate system of meritorious works such as doing penance, contributing to the church or to charity, repeating prayers, fasting, abstaining from meat at certain seasons and on certain days, attending mass, and making pilgrimages. It was the exploitation of these works of merit through selling indulgences and preying upon the fears of the ignorant and credulous that occasioned the revolt of our Protestant ancestors.

Justification by faith, by a personal filial relationship with God, does not divorce faith from good works or righteous and devoted living. It does change the motivation. The Christian who feels himself to be a redeemed child of God will refrain from wrong doing and fill his life with service and brotherly

---

[8] David Wesley Soper, *Major Voices in American Theology* (Philadelphia: Westminster Press, 1953), p. 125.

love, but not to earn or to maintain his status with God. As a child of God he is assured of that status. His brotherly love and high ethical living are a natural and wholehearted expression of his filial relationship with God. Conscious that the most important fact about him is that he is a child of God, he spontaneously lives like one. St. Augustine summarized the principle in his admonition, "Love God, and do as you please."

The second doctrine or principle, "Every Christian is his own priest," cut through and repudiated the whole elaborate and often corrupt system of priestcraft based on the assumption of "apostolic succession." Through Jesus Christ, our "great High Priest," every believer has direct and immediate access to God. He needs no human professional mediator. Or if one does lose touch with God and seems unable to re-establish this personal relationship, a brother Christian may help him find the way back. So every believer is not only his own priest; he is also his brother's priest when his own testimony can be helpful in finding or restoring a lost soul. But this is a lay and temporary service. Unlike the professional priest who remains permanently as the necessary mediator between the believer and God, the pastor or lay brother who serves in this priestly way steps aside as soon as the relationship has been established and the person so helped can become his own priest.

The third doctrine or principle deals with the question of authority. Briefly stated, it is to the effect that the authority of Christ is mediated through the Bible rather than through the church. Our spiritual ancestors repudiated an authoritarian insitution on the democratic principle of the inherent right of each person to deal directly with God as known through Jesus Christ, acting as his own priest on the basis of his own personal experience of God. These democratic principles were embraced in a strongly authoritarian climate and in defiance of a powerful authoritarian institution. Inconsistent though it was, a rival authoritarianism was invoked in this conflict. In order to exalt the authority of the Bible itself over that of the Church, the reformers carried over the medieval doctrines of the "verbal inspiration" and the "inerrency" of the Bible. Thus they were able to proclaim an "infallible Book" as superior to an "infallible Church." So this principle in its actual application set the Bible itself up as the only authoritative rule of faith and practice, rather than as the means through which the authority of Christ is mediated to the individual.

The fourth doctrine, "the right of private judgment," is a declaration of religious liberty. Because the first and second doctrinal principles emphasize Christian faith as a personal, inner experience, in some sense unique for each individual, the freedom of each person to experience this faith in his own way, and to bear his own unique testimony to it, inevitably follows. When the source of one's authority is in his personal relationship to Christ and is also in a sense unique, the fourth principle is consistent with the other three. Unfortunately our spiritual ancestors (and, alas, most of their descendents) have been much more eager to grasp this right of individual freedom for themselves than to grant it to others.

A corollary of this principle of religious freedom is the principle of the public nature of truth. All truth is God's truth, whether it be historical, scientific, aesthetic, philosophic, or religious. And all truth, including religious truth, is equally open to all seekers after truth. No institution or priestly order or scientific society has a monopoly on any of God's truth. The traditional attitude of most denominations has been inconsistent with this principle. In their bigotry and attitude of superiority to other Christian groups, they have usually implied a monopoly on certain truth which no other group had, and to which no one could gain effective access except as he came to them for it.

This denial in practice of the public nature of religious truth is not to be confused with the Protestant privilege and responsibility of testimony. The Protestant is properly a witness to his own personal and unique experience of God. His testimony is given for the enrichment and encouragement of his fellow man and not as a standard to which others must conform. It is only when the unique experience or insight of an individual or a group is imposed on others as a condition of their salvation, and of their inclusion in the Christian fellowship, that the principle of the public nature of truth is violated. This erection of a human opinion into an absolute, in complete violation of the basic Protestant principle, is Protestantism's greatest sin.

There were, of course, other differences between the "faith of our fathers" and the medieval church from which they separated. There was a different conception of the church and of the relationship between the church and the state, and a different interpretation of the sacraments. But the four principles which emphasized the inner, personal, spiritual nature of the Christian religion and which related every person directly to God through Jesus Christ with no intervening institution, priesthood, or outward test, define our essential spiritual heritage.

These principles embody and produce a religion of inner, personal, spiritual experience, a religion of direct relationships between the individual and God, in sharp contrast with the institutional, priest-dominated religion of the medieval church. These principles underlay the free, creative, deeply spiritual, and personal religion of first century Christians. They accounted for its dynamics, its self-propagating motivation, its disturbing power "to turn the world upside down." Those same principles, fully operative in the life of twentieth century Christians, could reproduce in us the spiritual quality and life-changing dynamics of early Christianity.

The very word "Protestant," in its root meaning, further emphasizes this personal and unique experience of each individual as essential Christianity. From the Latin verb "testari" (to affirm; to aver, to testify or bear witness), and the prefix "pro" (for) the meaning "to testify for" or "to bear witness on behalf of" is clear. A protestant is one who has a testimony to give, a witness to bear. He has an inner experience of God, uniquely his own, to affirm, to witness to, to share with others. The negative word implying antagonism and intolerance is "contestant." Unfortunately far too much of our potentially glorious Protestant testimony has degenerated into this negative attitude.

The very genius of our Protestantism, when it has been true to its principles, has been the diversity, the richness, the courageous pioneering which always characterizes the human spirit when it is free. The genius of authoritarian religion is uniformity and exclusiveness; the genius of free democratic religion is diversity and contributiveness.

The scientific study of religious experience justifies this individual uniqueness of each person's faith, and shows that the uniformity assumed by the authoritarian as the proper goal of religious teaching is in fact an impossible goal. Dr. Gordon W. Allport summarizes his findings in this respect as follows:

"The conclusion we come to is that the subjective religious attitude of every individual is, in both its essential and non-essential features, unlike that of any other individual. The roots of religion are so numerous, the weight of their influence in individual lives so varied, and the forms of rational interpretation so endless, that uniformity of product is impossible. . . .

"This conclusion, I know, . . . will disturb some historians and sociologists who like to think that the individual cannot help but mirror the cultural model offered to him as a guide to his development. It will be unpalatable likewise to those theologians and churchmen who deceive themselves by thinking their followers are safely and entirely within some particular ecclesiastical fold."[9]

These conclusions are quite in harmony with the principles and assumptions both of New Testament Christianity and original Protestantism.

The relationship of these principles to democracy is obvious. Each asserts in a different way the worth, the dignity, the rights, and the responsibilities of the common man. They justify the high value which democracy places upon all persons regardless

[9] Gordon W. Allport, *The Individual and His Religion* (New York: The Macmillan Company, 1950), pp. 26, 27

of their inequalities by asserting their filial relationship to God. Democracy is reasonable only on the basis of this Christian view of personality. Persons are sacred or of supreme worth because of their potential Godlikeness. This religious regard for persons is both the justification and the dynamics of democracy.

It is for this reason that we are justified in considering the religious revolution as basic to the intellectual, economic, and political revolution in the total Protestant Reformation. This whole upsurge of democratic idealism had as its motive the new regard for persons as spiritually akin to God. The success of the whole Reformation, then, in achieving its democratic aims was dependent upon the realization of democratic principles in religious life. If these basic principles could be made really operative in organized religious life they could operate throughout all of life. It was of momentous importance that Protestantism hold to its principles then. It is perhaps of even greater moment that those principles be made operative in the Protestantism of our own day.

Because these democratic principles of Protestantism, like the corresponding principles of early Christianity, were projected into an authoritarian world, their application or operation in human affairs has been only partial. They have probably been best embodied in the intellectual realm. The repudiation of medieval repression and dogma, the freeing of the mind to question, to doubt, to explore and inquire, to investigate and experiment, launched the whole scientific movement. Free enterprise in thinking has produced the brilliant technology of the Protestant era.

These principles have had revolutionary significance in political life. The old authoritarianism yielded reluctantly and resisted stubbornly. It is currently staging a comeback in great areas of the world. Nationalism, which was a first outcome, has now became an obstacle, and only the achievement of democratic world government seems to promise any security for the future. This is a goal to which our own American experiment in democracy commits us.

Free enterprise in economic life, based upon Protestant individualism, has produced a material abundance unprecedented in history, but with unsolved problems of distribution and with conflicts among authoritarian power blocs which are a denial and negation of democracy. A democratic solution to these problems seems to be the only alternative to the threat of a completely authoritarian economic life.

How well have these principles worked out in our Protestant religious life? Unfortunately they were almost at once compromised by an authoritarian use of the Bible. There of course arose disagreements in interpretation of the Bible, and each of the Protestant groups began the formulation of creeds to set forth their positions on controversial issues. These creeds were used to exclude nonconformists and to identify those of the "true faith" so that both the principle of religious freedom and the unity of the fellowship of believers were violated. In fact, each Protestant group became itself a "church." This church as an institution began to formulate its doctrines of scriptural truth into tests of membership. Since most of the original Protestant churches were "established," or state, churches, they could and did exert powerful pressures on nonconformists, even to the extent of persecution and death. As a result, Protestant churches became about as authoritarian as the Roman Catholic Church and retreated from their original democratic principles into a new regime of authoritarianism. What was wrong with their application of this principle of authority?

Diverse interpretations of the Bible are inevitable, for it is not the simple "flat" book, all parts being equally the authoritative word of God for guidance in present-day living, which the medieval dogmas implied. It represents a long development in religious concepts and ideals from primitive and naïve levels to the climax in Jesus Christ himself. Its various portions must be read with historical perspective and interpreted in the light of some valid principle of evalution. Consequently, Protestants have had to restudy this principle of authority to find a sounder and more unifying basis than this divisive and irrational theory about the Bible. This basis is found in Jesus Christ himself. He is the authoritative interpreter of the Bible and of the Way. The primary and indispensable relationship of the Christian is a personal relationship to Christ himself. Vital union with Christ, not agreement with an official formulation of beliefs, is the basis of the Christian's authority, and of unity among Christians. One who is in union with Christ is in union thereby with everyone else who is in union with Christ. The question is not "what do I believe?" but "Whom do I believe?" The true Protestant faith is faith in a Person.

It is obvious that this principle of seeking a basis of authority in Christ as a Person, rather than in the whole Bible as a book, has not yet succeeded in unifying Protestants. It is so far accepted only among liberal Protestants. Even we who accept it find it difficult to avoid interpreting Christ as an external authority to be imposed on others in the terms in which we have accepted and experienced him for ourselves. It is for this reason that a thorough mastery of the principles and procedures of a genuinely democratic and creative education is so indispensable for Protestants.

The great contribution of this Protestant period of free enterprise in religion has been the richness and variety of the total religious experience of Protestants. The ecclesiastical or institutional forms which this rich diversity of experience has taken constitute the unsolved problem of Protestant Christianity.

What then is our Protestant responsibility?

To reproduce the reforming and creative power of original Protestantism, then, is not merely to reassert the creedal formulations from which liberal Protestantism has drifted away. Nor is it to substitute the vague and inclusive generalities of a liberalism which makes what one believes a secondary matter. It is first of all to recover and make operative in our religious practices the repudiation of "every finite claim of finality" which interposes between the individual and his God any humanly devised creed, or church, or mediator, or performance. The only true function of any of these aids to religious life is to bring the individual into a direct personal encounter with God. The democratic principles of original Protestantism must be invoked to prevent the erection of any human absolute, whether it be science, nationalism, philosophy, creed, church, or self-righteousness, into the place of God, either in the life of the individual or in society.

If Protestant Christianity is to meet the deep human problem of our day, its hope lies in making the Protestant principle the basis of a new and thorough Reformation within the Protestant churches themselves. This, then, is the responsibility of Protestant nurture: It must seek to effect a second Protestant Reformation, bringing our churches and their programs into harmony with the original democratic and God-centered principles taught and exemplified by Jesus himself and restated, but only partially followed, by the churches of the Protestant movement. It must reproduce the essential spiritual qualities of original Christianity as the solution to the desperate needs of our distraught world.

CHAPTER 3

How Is Protestant Faith Propagated?

Protestantism has motivated universal education. But it has tolerated within its own program traditional, authoritarian, and transmissive types of education which have denied rather than fulfilled its basic creative principle. So the Reformation, religiously, lost most of its power. Only by developing and making prevalent a creative, democratic, experience-centered type of religious nurture can Protestantism fulfill its destiny and mission. Such a program would be Christ-centered. It would draw upon race experience embodied in our rich spiritual heritage for guidance and enrichment, while liberating the human spirit from the dead past and invoking the guidance of the Holy Spirit for today.

How Protestant is our education?

The basic democratic principles of original Protestantism demanded universal education. The relative high degree of literacy and the universality of educational opportunity in Protestant North America reveal the effectiveness of this educational incentive. The protestant motive for education was twofold. The inborn worth, dignity, rights, and responsibilities of the individual entitled him to the development of his capacities as a free person, and without education the individual's potential worth was but an empty shell. Futhermore, if every man is his own priest, if the authority of Christ is mediated to him directly through the Bible, and if he has a right to his own interpretation of that Bible, then he must be able to

41

read and understand it for himself. It was therefore inevitable that, wherever the Protestant movement took hold,
schools for the masses were established, and some measure
of education was deemed the right of every person.

Since the motive for education was primarily religious and
the earlier Protestant churches were "established," or state,
churches, education was provided by the churches. In spite of
the democratic principles which provided the motive for universal education, the strongly authoritarian reaction which
dominated the churches in their conflicts with Rome and with
each other came inevitably to control education. Consequently,
much of the education motivated by those democratic principles was quite out of harmony with them in its spirit and
conscious objectives. Traditional conceptions of education were
adopted as the basis for interpreting its meaning and purpose
and are still dominant in practice.

According to the first of these traditional concepts the content of education is the accumulated knowledge of the race, and
its purpose is the transmission of this knowledge to the growing
generation by a process of instruction and memorization. "The
Encyclopedists," authors of the great French Encyclopedia
(1751-72), hoped so to formulate and classify human knowledge that any well-educated person could possess it all! The
ordinary school curriculum is still organized largely into bodies
of knowledge which the educated person should possess. The
job of the curriculum maker is to select from all the vast store-
houses of information that knowledge which is of most worth.
The effect of this conception of education is to fix attention
upon the past, rather than upon the present and the future; to
attempt to subject the oncoming generation largely to the control of those who select the content of such a curriculum; and
so to idealize this heritage as to secure the uncritical acceptance
of it, whether or not it qualifies one for self-realization and effective living. Such education is primarily an education of transmission or imposition.

The adherents to a second traditional conception of education regard it as discipline. Originally, supporters of this concept held that preparation for adult life calls for the training of the faculties of reason, memory, imagination, and will. These tools of efficient adult living are to be sharpened and tempered by the disciplines of education. The subject matter used is not important if it involves effort and the exercise of these faculties. No matter how the training is received, it is presumed to "transfer" to other subject matter or situations as generalized ability.

While both "faculty psychology" and the idea of "transfer" of training have generally been abandoned, the conception of education as training for adult life is still widespread. The curriculum is made up of those disciplines which will qualify one for the functions of adulthood in the present social and economic order. The appropriateness of such education in specific vocational training is obvious, although the traditional apprenticeship system was probably superior to a school. But the disciplinary or training concept is widely held in connection with character education programs and general cultural orientation as well. When the practical value of higher mathematics, language study, or memory work is questioned, their "disciplinary value" is cited as justification for their place in the curriculum.

Since the educational process centers in the supposed needs and responsibilities of adult life, the current, on-going experiences and responsibilities of the learner are regarded as of secondary importance. This creates the problem of interest and motivation in the learning activities since they are determined by adults and largely imposed upon learners. Such education is predominantly authoritarian in spirit. It makes little provision for the critical evaluation of the status quo, or for the freedom and initiative of the learners. Education as discipline remains external to the vital and dynamic experience of the learner.

Education conceived as recapitulation of the experience of the race is a third concept, more recent in origin. This conception grew out of the evolutionary theory, particularly the observation that the individual, biologically, recapitulates racial evolution. Beginning as one fertilized cell, the human organism passes through stages of development roughly parallel to the successive orders of animal life. By analogy it was assumed that the child, in the development of his personality, recapitulates the various stages of social development from a primitive savage culture to that of civilized society. The best preparation for each stage of his development, then, is to have opportunity for the full expression of the preceding stage. The curriculum should provide for orientation to and expression of these successive cultural stages.

This theory is reflected in the character education programs which center in the activities of primitive or pioneer life, using Indian lore or scouting as their source of content; it is also seen in our regard for the Old Testament with its primitive life as an ideal source of stories for children. Here again the current, on-going life experiences of the learners are regarded as of secondary importance to types of experience the past has superimposed on the present. Even this education, supposedly centering in the natural interests of children in these successive stages of development, is actually imposed by the adults who select and idealize the experiences to be imitated.

This outmoded recapitulation theory of education is not to be confused with the recently formulated conception of education as consisting primarily of successive groups of "developmental tasks." See pages 87-90.

Can authoritarian education transmit the Protestant faith?

These traditional educational concepts, applied to the specific function of Protestant nurture, have all but defeated the true genius of our faith. The prevailing Protestant educational program seems calculated to hand on intact a "faith once for all delivered to the saints." Teaching operates largely as though it were a transmissive process designed to pass packaged truths from one generation to the next. The assumption that each denomination must have its own peculiar curriculum, even though all use indentical Bible passages, supposedly safeguards the orthodoxy of the transmitted truth.

We may be Protestants, even of some particular brand, because our parents were. Our educational program may operate as though the Faith were passed on in some sort of spiritual germ cell which is unaffected by the body in which it lives. We might thus hope that the purity of the hereditary Faith may be preserved and guaranteed. Such a hope, however, would not be justified. In the case of religion, acquired characteristics exert definite influence upon the next generation. Religion is passed on in the sharing of experience, not by a mysterious process insulated from experience.

Obviously there is much of the handing-on process in all teaching. It cannot be avoided. But a teacher who is deliberately committed to imposing the "true faith" upon others is self-deceived. With his attention fixed solely or primarily upon the content which he is trying to convey, he does not see factors far more determinative of his actual results. Content, after all, is not in an insulated germ cell. Truth cannot be conveyed in sanitary packages, and even if it could, learners are not receptacles open only to such packages. Religion changes in the process of being taught because it has to pass through life and experience and personality. Several factors operate to defeat the strictly transmissive process. And these factors operate whether we think of religion primarily in terms of a sacred book, a body of saving truth, a divinely ordained institution, or set of approved behavior patterns and practices.

Teachers and teaching institutions carry on a selective process based on a stress-and-neglect principle, which makes what they pass on to the future different from what they received from the past. It is easy to see this change of emphasis in the teaching, the curriculum, and even the preaching in any denomination from generation to generation. Else why are we continually at work on new curricular materials to replace those which are "out of date"? And why is it so hard to get church schools to use undated units or courses even though they might be superior? Each generation determines for the next what of all it has received from the past, shall be passed on. In addition, it adds many new meanings which have arisen from its own on-going experience. The same Bible, the same creed, the same ceremony will be cited as authority for new and different meanings.

Dramatic changes in the conditions of life, in the climate of public opinion, and in the patterns of human relationships profoundly influence the content of contemporary religious teaching. What happens to the church's message during wartime? How does a major economic depression affect religious teaching? How does a series of race riots or an industrial controversy influence the church's testimony? To what extent are religious ideas modified by such changing and contrasting political concepts as the divine right of kings, fascism, democracy, free enterprise, communism? To ask these questions is to recognize that the religion which is taught is profoundly affected by what is happening to life as a whole in any generation. Does this mean that religion is just one of many commingling currents in our social and cultural life, taking its color from the stream as a whole? Or does religion determine the color and quality of the whole stream? Obviously it is not unaffected, however much it may exert its own influence.

A religion which is alive is growing and changing as it pulsates through human experience. It is not the inherited truth which is passed on. It is the truth which emerges, tested, modified, vitalized by the experience of the teaching generation. It may be a poorer and less valid truth. Or it may be a better and more valid truth. One thing, however, is certain. It is not precisely the same truth even though it be couched in the same phrases and represented by the same symbols.

Imposed teaching deceives itself because it overlooks the varied meanings which the same word, act, or other symbol may have for different people. The only meaning one is capable of giving to a symbol is meaning which his own experience supplies. Meanings vary as experience varies. The learner never gets the full and exact meaning from a word, phrase, ceremony, or other symbol which the teacher meant to put into it. So the lesson "learned" never equals the lesson "taught." Not only are parts of the lesson unlearned; there is always some misunderstanding of the meanings intended by the teacher, so that some meanings which the teacher never intended to teach are learned.

Furthermore, there are elements present which the teacher overlooks, but which enter into the learning process. The teacher and the institution select for attention and for acceptance or imitation, virtues, ideal qualities of heroes, the best things about the church, illustrations of noble Christian conduct. But the learners know that life is not all like that. They may choose to imitate the teacher's faults rather than his virtues. We may present a highly idealized church. But our pupils see the real one. As Dr. Coe said, "When God, incarnated in children, peers about our ecclesiastical garden, every denomination resorts to fig leaves." [1] Undesirable qualities in the hero or the villain of the story may have the most appeal. (When a group of juniors was about to dramatize the Parable of the Good Samaritan, every boy wanted to take the part of a robber!) The teacher who overlooks this discrepancy between what he wants to pass on and meanings which the learners actually appropriate is self-deceived.

This education of imposition, fixing its attention upon passing on a ready-made holy book, or body of revealed truth, or sacred institution, or set of behavior patterns, separates teaching from the kind of vital, firsthand experience which would give its content valid meaning. Even when an "application" is made to life it is usually just more verbalizing. It seldom reaches the experiencing level. This separation of religious teaching from meaningful living experience creates a dualism which devitalizes religion. It places religion in one compartment of life, while the actual experiences which would provide reli-

[1] George Albert Coe, *What Is Christian Education?* (New York: Charles Scribner's Sons, 1929), p. 30.

gion with its major field for operation and with its vital meanings are kept safely in another compartment. Most of the ethical significance of the life and teachings of Jesus is thus lost through rationalization. Christianity is effectively prevented from becoming an experienced way of living based upon the assumptions by which Jesus lived. Such religion is as impotent as an empty powder keg.

Imposed teaching overlooks or ignores the almost universal testimony that it is the teacher's character and personality rather than the content of the lesson courses which has been the dominant influence upon the learners. "The curriculum is ninety per cent teacher," is an extreme statement of this fact, but it will be denied by few experienced religious educators. The really determinative factor in Christian education is the teacher-learner relationship within the total situation conditioning this relationship. This includes, besides the teacher himself, the class or learning group, the church as a whole, the family background and situation, public school or vocational influences, and other community forces. Among all these conditioners of the learning process, the content of the lesson is only one. This content itself is more likely to be modified by the other factors in the situation than it is to be the controlling factor. The futility of the purely transmissive concept of teaching religion is so obvious that its prevalence is little short of astonishing.[2]

The whole transmissive or imposition concept of Christian education is consistent with the assumptions, the religious philosophy, the intolerance, and the authoritarianism of the medieval church. But the consequences of this interpretation of Christianity and of this method of propagating it through the centuries were the corruption and abuses within the church against which our spiritual ancestors revolted.

Clearly, one of the major sources of our failure to realize the

[2] The writer is obviously greatly indebted to Dr. George Albert Coe for this interpretation of transmissive education which is more fully treated in his book, *What Is Christian Education?* (New York: Charles Scribner's Sons, 1929).

full power of our Protestant principles is that we have failed to develop and put into operation an educational program consistent with them. Instead, we have carried over to a large extent from an intolerant, authoritarian medieval church an educational philosophy and method which is destructive of true Protestantism. Little wonder that Protestant trust in this kind of education has all but destroyed, in its best sense, the very germ of Protestantism itself.

If Protestantism is — as was original New Testament Christianity — an inner, personal experience unique to each individual, it cannot be "handed over" from one person to another. It can only be testified to and expressed in daily living as a means of helping others to achieve an equivalent, inner personal experience for themselves. True Protestant nurture consists in this sharing of spiritual experiences on the part of free, growing persons, with never an attempt to impose one upon the other or to bring some into spiritual submission to others. Leaders and learners are alike in that they are all freely experiencing and growing together. The difference between them is that the leaders have a larger and richer experience to share, and know both the resources and the methods for the most effective sharing of human experience, both contemporary and historic.

What is democratic education?

These traditional concepts of education, which subordinate present experience to the remote past and the unpredictable future, have been yielding before a "creative" or "liberal" philosophy of education which centers in the present, on-going experience of the learner. Pestalozzi with his "child-centered school" and Froebel with his "kindergarten" (a garden in which the growing things are children) were influential in launching the idea. The philosopher-prophet of this creative type of education in American has been John Dewey. In 1910 he set forth the basis of its methodology,[3] and in 1916 he propounded its

[3] John Dewey, *How We Think* (Boston: D. C. Heath and Co., 1910).

larger social and moral implication.[4] The scientific basis of this
method, rooted philosophically in "experimentalism," has been
further developed by his colleagues, Edward L. Thorndike [5]
and William H. Kilpatrick.[6]

The principal contrasts between traditional education and
education as conceived from this liberal or creative viewpoint
are:

1. The real subject matter or curriculum of education is not
"race experience" as embodied in literature, art, traditions,
codes of conduct, and institutions. Rather, it is learner experience, for it is only through experience that desirable changes
are brought about in growing persons. The value and effectiveness of this learner experience in accomplishing educational outcomes is increased in the degree that it is continuous with and
typical of normal, everyday, out-of-school experience.

2. The goals or purposes of educational activity are not determined and imposed by the teacher or the school. To be
effective they must be self-chosen by the learner. This is accomplished by the "project principle." A project, according
to Dr. Kilpatrick[7], is a purposeful activity in which the purpose
furnishes the motive or drive for the activity and guides the
process. It is therefore necessary for the school to set up the
kind of community living which will give rise to learner purposes out of which significant educational projects will develop.
Discipline, essential to all learning, need not be imposed upon
the learner, for a far more wholesome discipline will be provided by the self-discipline growing out of the pursuit of learner
purpose and adaptation to the conditions of such community
living.

[4] John Dewey, *Democracy and Education* (New York: The Macmillan Company, 1916).

[5] Edward L. Thorndike, *Educational Psychology* (three volumes), (New
York: Teachers' College, Columbia University, 1919).

[6] William Heard Kilpatrick, *Foundations of Method* (New York: The Macmillan Company, 1925).

[7] _____, *The Project Method* (New York: Teachers' College, Columbia
University, 1918).

3. Rather than conditioning the learner to accept, accommodate himself to, and pass on his social and racial heritage, this liberating type of education must function creatively. The past will be subjected to critical review by the oncoming generation. The job of education is to achieve in the life of this new generation a better social order than the present. Therefore, although the school should be a cross section of everyday life, it should also be a foretaste of life in the better social order which the growing generation is helping to achieve.

4. Traditional subject matter, while not the organizing center of the educational process, does have an essential function. It is to be utilized for the enrichment of present learner experience; for the presentation of various alternative ways of living and of meeting life situations together with appraisals of their values and outcomes, so that the learner may profit by the past experience of others; and for a better understanding of our physical and social world and the conditions of successful life therein. The organizing center of the process is the on-going present experience of the learner, with historic subject matter utilized only in the degree that it has meaning and worth for that experience.

5. In traditional education the present is entirely subordinate to the future. Schooling is "getting ready to live". Its purpose is to equip the individual with supplies of knowledge, with certain skills and disciplines, and with codes of conduct which will become useful to him in adult life and which will be taken from the storehouse of the mind and utilized as the need arises. Creative education emphasizes the worth of present experience. The best preparation of a growing person for life in our rapidly changing and unpredictable world is to live richly, happily, and skillfully at his present age and in the contemporary situation. Contrary to the old disciplinary assumption that the more distasteful an educational activity was, the more valuable it was, is the assumption that the learning value of an experience depends upon the intrinsic satisfaction provided by the experience as a whole. This brief summary makes it clear that creative

education embodies a decided shifting in its attitudes and procedures from an authoritarian to a democratic viewpoint.

Though, obviously, our whole public school system in America still reflects the traditional viewpoint more than the creative, our educational philosophers and teacher training institutions exert their preponderant influence in the direction of the liberating type of education. Disillusionment arises frequently out of efforts to embody these principles in practice; there is definite, and in some cases aggressive, reaction against them here and there. But, on the whole, the philosophy of John Dewey is the dominant single influence in American education, and the conception of education which we have briefly described is the American ideal, however short of it our practice may fall.

Can Protestant nurture become democratic?

During most of the nineteenth century while the Sunday school movement was developing, both general education and Christian education were generally authoritarian and transmissive. The public school, with its employed teaching staff, its system of normal schools, and its required standards, has been able to respond more quickly than the Sunday school to improvements in theory and technique. But Christian education, also, has had its philosopher-prophets and its liberating tendencies. A century ago Horace Bushnell rocked the theological foundations of Protestant evangelism by proclaiming that "the child is to grow up a Christian, and never know himself as being otherwise."[8] The implications of this claim were as revolutionary for Protestant nuture as were those of Pestalozzi and Froebel for general education.

At the turn of the century, Dr. George Albert Coe began outlining a democratic theory of religious education.[9] In 1917 his *Social Theory of Religious Education*[10] proposed that "the

[8] Horace Bushnell, *Christian Nurture* (New Haven: Yale University Press, reprinted 1947), p. 4.
[9] George Albert Coe, *Education in Religion and Morals* (Chicago and New York: F. H. Revel Co., 1904).
[10] _____, *A Social Theory of Religious Education* (New York: Charles Scribner's Sons, 1917), pp. 80, 82.

central fact of the educative process is a growing Christian ex‧
perience in and through the pupil's social interactions . . . now
instead of attempting to transfer to the child's mind certain
truths that we hope will enter into his experience in a vital
manner at some indefinite future time, we help him to define,
understand, and improve something that he is already doing
and enjoying. There is no longer the deadly separation of knowing from doing, or of Christian doctrine from Christian experience." In a later book, *What is Christian Education?*, Dr.
Coe pointed out the futility and self-deception of the prevalent
"transmissive" type of religious education and challenged the
churches to undertake a democratic and creative educational
program as the one way toward a revitalizing of the church and
a real revival of religion in American life.[11]

The democratic theories which Dr. Coe and others were formulating had only incidental effect upon Christian education in
the Protestant churches until, in 1922, the International Council
of Religious Education appointed a committee on the new
"International Curriculum of Religious Education." Professor
William C. Bower was appointed chairman of this committee.
The other members, like himself, were conversant with and
committed to the liberal and democratic tendencies in religious
educational theory. The committee also called into consultation
representative leaders in public education. Thus, the educational boards of the Protestant churches opened the way for a
thoroughly fresh approach to the whole theory of Protestant
nurture.

This committee developed a theory of the curriculum and a
statement of principles[12] which were adopted by the Council's
Educational Commission in 1930 and referred for their study
and use to its constituent denominational boards. The type
of curriculum contemplated seemed to be such a radical de-
parture from existing systems of lesson courses, and the publica-

---

[11] _____, *What is Christian Education?* (New York: Charles Scribner's
Sons, 1929).

[12] *The Development of a Curriculum of Religious Education* (Bulletin 101;
Chicago: International Council of Religious Education, 1930).

tion problem, involving many denominational publishing agencies, was so complex that there was reluctance to proceed to the development of an actual curriculum. Consequently the only concrete outcome of the committee's work was a series of mimeographed "International Curriculum Guides." The committee processes which were carried out, however, involving a large proportion of the employed personnel of the national denominational boards of some forty denominations, have unquestionably exerted a liberalizing influence upon Protestant nurture.

The contrasts already presented between traditional education and creative or democratic education, when applied to Christian education, indicate quite accurately the contrasts between the current Protestant nurture and the kind of program and procedure contemplated as the New International Curriculum.

The period during which the democratic, truly Protestant approach to Christian education has been seeking to become effective, has been a period of world-wide war, economic depression, and political and social revolution. Democracy has been on the defensive and actually in retreat over great areas of the world. Unprecedented insecurity and fear have been widespread, especially in those countries which have tried to preserve at least some semblance of democracy in the face of aggressive authoritarianism. The movement toward democratic, liberal, and creative thinking and attitudes in religion has been reasserting the original principles of Protestantism in terms of religious concepts which were at home in a world of scientific inquiry and intellectual freedom. But the democratic movement has received a serious setback. Fear and insecurity always tempt the timid to retreat into the seeming security of authoritarianism. The inability of the insecure masses to confront calmly the personal perplexities and individual responsibilities involved in democratic living has given totalitarian regimes their opportunity in nation after nation. Reluctance to make the spiritual adventure involved in a genu-

inely Protestant faith has caused multitudes to retreat into the
apparent security of an authoritarian faith. Liberal Protestant
nurture got under way a little too late to stem this tide of
retreat into one or another authoritarian camp.

The International Council of Religious Education, constituted by the educational boards of about eighty per cent of
Protestantism, took account of these cross currents in theological and educational thinking and their implications for
Protestant nurture, in its "restudy of Christian education."
Authorized in 1944, this "restudy" was conducted by a very
representative committee comprised of leaders from both within and outside the religious education profession, and including
both critics and advocates of the liberal tendencies in Protestant
nurture.

On its own request the Committee made its report to the
International Council, not for approval or adoption, but for is-
suance on the responsibility and authority of the Committee
itself. The report was published in a somewhat condensed and
popularized form, but with faithfulness to content and point
of view. The volume, entitled *The Church and Christian
Education,* [13] was prepared by the Committee Chairman, Paul
H. Vieth. The Report achieves in some measure a synthesis
between the views of liberal Protestant nurture and those of
traditional orthodoxy. The educational point of view is restated
in terms familiar to the theologian. In many cases, particularly
those dealing with the doctrinal foundations of Christian education, it has been necessary in the Report to recognize different
points of view which could not quite be harmonized. This
study and the resulting Report have made an important contribution to the theory of Protestant Christian education. Some of
the principal values have been these:

1. In re-thinking and re-formulating the principles of creative
Christian education with conscious reference to the doctrinal
content common to the Protestant tradition, Christian educators

[13] Paul H. Vieth, *The Church and Christian Education* (St. Louis: Bethany
Press, 1947).

have made their ideas and viewpoints more congenial to the general Protestant mind. The process has exerted a corrective influence also upon secularizing tendencies in liberal Christian education. It has helped Christian education to effect its necessary twofold orientation, to education and to Christian doctrine.

2. The contrasts between the educational concepts and the theological concepts were shown to be not as sharp as the controversial interpretations had been making it appear. Often the differences were more in terminology than in basic meanings. In true Protestant fashion, the diverse testimony was often enriching and contributory to a larger truth for all concerned.

3. Where real issues remain, they have been clarified or made explicit. For example, the Christian educator has a generally more optimistic view of human nature or of the inborn tendencies and capacities of persons than has the orthodox thelogian.[14] Both agree upon man's dual nature and his vast potentialities for both good and evil. The liberal view, however, would find the source of much of the evil which afflicts mankind in wrong social and institutional relationships which have been inherited from past generations, while the traditional, orthodox view would locate the source of all evil in the inherited tendencies in the individual.[15]

It is to be hoped that the degree of synthesis achieved by the Study Committee will provide the basis for continued development of a liberating, creative type of Christian education for Protestantism, which will be consistent with its basic principles of religious freedom and testimony.

Obviously this kind of education will not insure uniformity; nor will it guarantee the continuation of any fixed concept, practice, or institution from generation to generation. The total spiritual heritage will be tested at the judgment bar of experience by each new generation. As the living Christ is thus re-experienced by each succeeding generation we have a right to hope that he will increasingly control human life and

14 *Ibid.*, pp. 53-60.
15 *Ibid.*, pp. 234f.

human destiny. Our trust in the guidance of the Holy Spirit is put to the test at this point. Teaching by imposition always reveals a lack of trust in the Holy Spirit. Having complete faith in the Spirit's guidance, teaching by liberation dares trust the free spirit of growing persons with all the resources for the richest possible experience.

The critics of these democratic and creative tendencies in Protestant nurture have expressed much concern over their dependence upon secular sources.[16] Obviously, the findings of psychology and sociology have a deep significance for the religious educator, as for any other educator, in helping him to understand and work effectively with growing persons. Horace Bushnell was not dependent upon secular educational theory, and yet he has probably influenced Christian educational philosophy more deeply than Pestalozzi or Froebel. Dr Coe's *Social Theory of Religious Education* actually antedated some of the corresponding developments in general educational theory,[17] so that he can be credited with making a direct application to religious education of developments in psychology and the social sciences without borrowing them secondhand from public education. But the basic thrust of his theory probably came not from education at all but from the social implication of the teachings of Jesus. The principle of the inherent worth of persons, which he called the "personality principle" in *What Is Christian Education?*[18] he credited directly to Jesus. Dr. Coe was certainly familiar with progressive educational theory, but his whole orientation was to a theistic view of the universe and to a religious interpretation of personality and of the processes by which persons grow. There is correlation with general education, but there is also independence from it. It is well

[16] H. Shelton Smith, *Faith and Nurture* (New York: Charles Scribner's Sons, 1941), p. 172.

See also Frank E. Gabelein, *Christian Education In a Democracy* (New York: Oxford University Press, 1951), p. 86, note.

[17] See Harrison S. Elliott, *Can Religious Education Be Christian?* (New York: The Macmillan Company, 1941), p. 52.

[18] George Albert Coe, *What Is Christian Education?* (New York: Charles Scribner's Sons, 1929), p. 60.

that common viewpoints underlie creative trends in both general education and religious education. Co-ordinating the two systems of education in our American situation is complicated enough at best. Christian education and general education should go together as far as they can without either's basic purpose suffering from this relationship.

There are dangers in too great interdependence between public education and Christian education. But there are also dangers in too great an alienation between them. Public education in America is committed to two major ideals: democracy and science. If the prevalent religious education carried on by the churches is unscientific or in conflict with science, and if it is authoritarian rather than democratic, two dangers threaten.

The first danger is that a conflict of ideals will be precipitated in the experience of children who participate in both educational programs. This is not so bad from the democratic and scientific viewpoint, for both democracy and science assume differences and provide ways of dealing with them as a means of growth. But it is bad from the viewpoint of an authoritarian religion because authoritarianism does not have a constructive method of handling differences. In a majority of cases the influence of such religion will lose out in the conflict.

This danger is accentuated by a second danger, namely, that public education, finding the religion of the churches incompatible with its own ideals, will erect democracy and science into a humanistic religion which will be promoted as "spiritual values." This tendency of public education to forsake its supposed "neutrality" with regard to religion and vigorously to promote a religion of ethical humanism is one of the problems involved in our total American plan of education. All religious groups agree in their opposition to it, but they do not agree in the best policy for dealing with it. In the measure that the religious education carried on in the churches is contrary both to the spirit of science and the spirit of democracy, public educators see little hope that the religion taught in the churches will actually achieve and conserve the spiritual values inherent in the ideals of public education. They are moved, therefore, to ignore the place of the churches and to attempt to develop and conserve these values on a humanistic basis in public education. In the measure, however, that they see in the program of the churches their own concern for these values in the scientific and democratic approach cared for, their propagation of a secular humanism as the only means open for conserving these values will be less justified. This indicates the responsibility of Christian educators with regard both to a scientific point of view and orientation, and also to a democratic spirit and procedure.

We are not saying that Christian education should derive its philosophy, its purpose, and its content from public education. Quite the contrary! If it is to be Christian education, these must come from within Christianity itself. What we are saying is that the liberal or liberating type of Christian education, taking into account the scientific and democratic principles which actually root in Christianity itself, has developed an educational philosophy, basically Christian, and yet congenial to liberal public education as well. If this type of liberal Christian education could be made prevalent in our American churches, they would be in a far more favorable relationship to public education, both from the viewpoint of developing a comprehensive educational system in America which would give religion its proper place, and from the viewpoint of curbing the tendency within public education to erect the "spiritual values" of science and democracy into a pseudo-religion of ethical humanism.

In spite of the disappointing outcomes of the proposed new International Curriculum (the Bower Committee's work); in spite of fears and misgivings about a liberal and democratic type of Christian education for Protestants, it is our contention that the only hope for a truly Protestant Christianity in America lies in the development and widespread use of some such creative and educationally vital program as was contemplated in the "New International Curriculum."

What is a school in Protestant nurture?

The acceptance of a truly democratic and Protestant conception of Christian nurture presents problems in setting up a school for getting the job done. How much simpler the authoritarian transmissive procedure seems! Yet its simplicity is due largely to its self-deception, as we have seen. What is a school for real Protestant nurture like? It must be an arrangement for providing situations which are rich in their possibilities and incentives for experiences in the direction of Christlikeness. It must be a place where such experiencing can be concentrated, where favorable conditions for it can be provided. The situations must be those which are normal and real to the learners. They should be as representative of the real life of these learners as possible; in fact, they must be real life. They should subordinate *future* reference and preparation for some *future* responsibility, to enabling religion to function effectively *now* in the life that those of each group are living.

A class will not be a device to enable the mature to impose their ideas, convictions, prejudices, and faults upon the immature. Rather, it will be a fellowship of growing persons. Their varying stages of maturity will present an opportunity for enriched sharing. The teacher is not one who has "arrived," who has all the answers. He, also, is a learner, a searcher for new experiences and for larger truth. The liberating teacher may serve as a guide on the journey, but he, as truly as any of the other learners, is taking the journey into the richer life.

The deposits of rich race experience which are embodied in text books—particularly the Bible—in institutions, traditions, ideals, codes, and symbols will be drawn upon for the enrichment and guidance of the experience which is under way. They will be means, not ends, instruments of the curriculum but not the curriculum itself. That will be the living experience which is under way.

When the school faces this task under the conditions of

modern, complex society, it is confronted with a dilemma. It must provide experiences in Christlike living, and yet, lest these experiences be artificial and irrelevant to real life, it must identify them with the real on-going life of home and community.

In primitive society, religion permeates the entire daily living of family and community. Religious sanctions, tabus, and meanings affect and control every phase of life from the simplest routines to such great events as marriage, death, warfare, and migration. Participation of the young in the life of the family or tribe or community constitutes the only necessary education. It is both a purpose and a product of the on-going folkways. Change from one generation to the next is so nearly negligible that preparation of adult living consists in participation of the young with the mature in the economic, social, political, and religious life of the whole group.

As the organized life of the group becomes more complex with the advance of culture or civilization, specialization of function develops. Different vocations emerge. Preparation for adult living involves choosing a vocation and acquiring its necessary skills. The principal educational system for such vocational training is apprenticeship. The prospective artisan or craftsman either learns the trade of his father by working with him or is bound out to a trademaster with whom he lives and works until he himself has mastered the vocation. This is the most effective kind of education, for it makes learning a function of real living. School and life are integral to each other.

As civilization advances further, the social organism becomes increasingly complex, specialization is carried much further, and the cultural heritage becomes so vast and multiform that ordinary daily life cannot possibly deal with it all. Schools are set up as the means of transmitting this cultural heritage, and the principal concern of youth is education for the purpose of mastering this social heritage as preparation for mature living. This kind of education tends to become separated from current on-going life. It becomes academic, artificial, and devitalized. Its detachment from real life makes its influence upon the young actually inferior to that of the real life in home, playground, and community in which the young engage in their free time. Thus, paradoxically, the home and the community turn over to the school a job which seems to be too specialized for them to do directly; yet, because they constitute real life while the school seems to be unreal or irrelevant, they continue to be the real educators so far as character is concerned.

The life of the community does not embody exactly what the community wants the young to learn. The school curriculum embodies that. Because of the curriculum's unreality, however, the community continues to be the real teacher in spite of itself. The business and professional people of a community may ask the school to conduct a character education program which will teach the familiar traits of honesty, unselfishness, service, generosity, obedience, and reverence. But if these business and professional people practice in the daily life of the community standards of living of a lower type, it will be these practices and not the school's character education program which actually determine the morals of the young people.

It is for this reason that we must consider the general fellowship and life of the church as being of primary importance in Protestant nurture while the church school as such plays a supplemental role. Just as the whole community, rather than merely the school, is the real character educator of youth, so the whole church, rather than merely its school, provides the environment and incentives for learning Christlikeness. The church itself should be a school in Christlike living. When life in the whole secular community involves Christians in so much compromise, a Beloved Community, the church, in which Christlikeness prevails as the normative pattern of relationships and attitudes, is an indispensable setting for the school in Christlikeness.

Would this be Christ-centered education?

It might well be so termed since its objective, Christlikeness, is embodied in Christ. It might also be called experience-centered since the focus of operation is upon the kinds of experience which promote growth toward Christlikeness.

Means such as the following would be used to make such education Christ-centered:

1. Every available resource should be used to confront the growing person vividly and as directly as possible with the historic Jesus. This means, of course, that the gospels will be most thoroughly and frequently used as the scriptural base. Imaginative material in story, art, and drama may well be used in the interest of vividness and appeal. While it will supplement the scriptural base, it should always be consistent with the record and historically authentic. Emphasis, however, should be on the character, attitudes, and relationships of Jesus, rather than on the manners and customs of the times. Jesus should become vivid and real as a person.

2. Every means possible should be employed to develop loyalty toward Jesus and love for him.

3. God should be approached through Jesus and interpreted in terms of the character of Jesus. Even little children can learn about Jesus and through knowing him they will come to know a "Christlike God."

4. The Old Testament is best interpreted as the Bible of Jesus, giving his spiritual background and heritage. It was the Bible he read and used. He reinterpreted it for us. Our best understanding of it is through him. Only that in the Old Testament which is in harmony with his interpretation of God, of man, and of truth is valid for us today. We can enjoy its poetry the more because he enjoyed it. It is a part of our Bible because it was his.

5. The church is the continuing living body of Christ through which he carries on his ministries of teaching, healing,

serving, and loving mankind. Belonging to him makes us members of his church.

6. Jesus is the interpreter of the universe revealing that it is an expression of the character of God its Creator and Ruler. Therefore, he is master of the best and most successful way of living in such a world. Ultimately all human life and relationships must be brought into harmony with such a universe as the Kingdom of God.

As Christ becomes a personal comrade, friend, and Savior of each person, the experience of each with Christ may be expected to be unique. A personal Christ, so conceived and continuously growing with increasing insight and comprehension, will be a far greater influence in the life of each person than any merely transmitted or imposed Christ could be. Education can indeed be Christ-centered in just the degree that it succeeds in making Christ a vivid personal experience for each person. It will be truly Protestant also in the degree that this inner personal experience is realized by those who respond to its teaching.

CHAPTER 4

How Do Persons Grow?

The human organism begins life utterly dependent because most of its behavior has yet to be learned. It develops into a person through interaction with its environment. A growing person's behavior is increasingly determined by symbolized meanings rather than by "raw" stimuli. Experience develops his inherited egocentric and other-regarding drives into his controlling motives. Cultural patterns and social institutions modify human nature and determine major trends in personality, but the conscious self increasingly takes command. Character is personality under ethical appraisal. It consists of the organized systems of values, attitudes, and habits by which a person controls his interaction with his environment and so gives meaning, purpose, and consistency to his behavior. It is properly appraised in terms of developmental norms rather than absolute standards.

THE OBJECT of Protestant nurture is not merely to propagate a faith; its object is also to enable persons to develop into reality their highest potential character and worth through embracing that faith. One focus of our attention is the Christian faith: How is it reproduced in growing persons? The other focus is these growing persons: How can their encounter with the Christian faith produce the richest, fullest, most radiant personalities which their inherent potentialities make possible? The laws of their growth as persons are the laws of our procedure as teachers. Let us therefore consider how persons grow, how character develops.

What is it to be a person?

The starting point of personality is a psycho-physical (mind-body) organism which is interacting with its environment in the processes of maintaining its living existence. Mind and body act together in an inseparable way so that they constitute one unitary process or organism. The functioning of the vital organs, glands, nerve cells, muscles, and general physical structure is basic to personality growth and must be taken into account in any program of education.

The self-activity of this organism is determined or guided by preferences or tendencies growing out of its past experience as that experience is recorded in the nervous system and preserved in symbols through the memory. This past is related to the present by memory and projected into the future by symbolic imagination in such a way as to give continuity to experience. To be a person is to be aware of these experiences which have continuity and are known as one's own experiences. To be a person is to have preferences and to make choices which determine, or help to determine, the experiences one will have. A person exerts at least some measure of control over the experiences which constitute his interaction with his environment.

What most distinguishes the behavior of persons from that of lower forms of life seems to be the use of symbols or symbolized meanings in memory, in imagination, and in communication with others.[1] Through this use of symbols, arise meanings which greatly enrich and increase the significance of the environmental stimuli which enter the sense organs. Personality functions and persons communicate with each other in a world in which the symbolized meanings have greater significance than the actual physical objects which are present. The behavior of persons, then, is determined less by the actual stimuli which their sense organs report than by the meanings

[1] Walter Coutu, *Emergent Human Nature* (New York: Alfred A. Knopf, 1949), p. 89f, p. 58f.

which, out of the past experiences of the individual, have come to be attached to these stimuli. So the growth of a person consists very largely of the growth of the meanings he will have available for the interpretation of the stimuli which his sense organs report.

Psychology has generally interpreted learning as the building up of stimulus-response bonds in the nervous system. When a given stimulus results in a ready-made response, a unit of behavior has been learned. Thus, behavior is interpreted as largely a matter of "S-R bonds." It is the accumulated meanings which intervene the stimulus or situation and the response which lift behavior to the personal level. Different persons respond very differently to the same stimulus or situation because of the different meanings invoked by it. Take, for instance, the word "home." If it is pronounced or written on the blackboard, it is a simple sense stimulus on the eardrum or the retina. But this word "home" has a rich and individualized meaning to each person, based on his past experiences and the appreciations and values which have come to be associated with it. For some persons it may even have unhappy associations. The word "home," read or heard, is a sense stimulus. A person's immediate response to it is not any kind of overt behavior; behavior is ultimately manifested only as a reaction to the meanings symbolized and invoked by the word "home." These meanings, then, really become a new stimulus. The stimulus of which the person is actually aware is not the word "home" but the meanings which it symbolizes. So the only way in which the S-R bond pattern applies to this situation is to substitute for the original "sense S" a new "meaning S" which will be individualized and exclusive to each person. The actual response in behavior will be to this new "meaning S."

Personal behavior is behavior determined more by the meaning which a stimulus has for a person than by what the stimulus itself is. Every act of a person is a part of the systems of meaning which his education has built up for him, and it can be understood only in terms of those meanings. It is the function of the personality to make use of these meanings in order to enable the individual to act in ways which will be of advantage to him in adjusting himself to his environment and in making his environment serve his needs.

These systems of meaning which arise out of experience are embodied in symbols through which a person communicates or shares his meanings with his fellow men, modifies and enriches his own meanings, preserves them in memory and in literature and art, and projects them through imagination. The organism or person having these experiences with their derived meanings becomes aware of them as his "own" experiences of interpreting, acting, feeling, discriminating, and evaluating. This awareness of continuity in experience is itself symbolized into a "self." This self is aware of other selves identified with other streams of experience and systems of meaning with whom he is in communication and which constitute the most important part of his total environment as a person.

Preferences for certain types of activity or response, growing out of past satisfactions, develop value meanings which introduce purpose into behavior and a sense of the worthfulness of the self-realizing person. These values and purposes come to be organized into a hierarchy of greater and lesser values. A pattern of life takes form around them. This general mode of response and self-activity is unique to each person, being the outcome of an original organism and a stream of experience, both of which are unique. It is determined by habits and attitudes, many of which may have resulted from chance or irrational responses, which, however, have been satisfying and so are repeated.

The freedom to follow his own purposes, and the sense of achievement as his efforts enable him increasingly to master his environment or successfully to adapt himself to it, give the growing person a developing self-respect and sense of worth. This enables him to find and appreciate worth in other persons as well. He becomes aware of values and formulates or adopts purposes which are beyond and above his own individual reach. These bring him the highest self-realization in identifying himself with social or cosmic purposes or ends.

What are the basic human drives?

Christian educators are concerned about the inborn tendencies or predispositions which prompt behavior in early life because of theological doctrines regarding the dualism of human nature. The human infant is said to be created in "the image of God" and yet to be "depraved" or a "fallen creature." What light can the scientific study of personality throw upon this dilemma?

The lower forms of life inherit well-developed behavior patterns or instincts, so that much behavior, including even complicated systems of activity, is unlearned. The human infant is born with his nervous system in a "knocked down" condition. Only the simple reflexes essential to survival are already assembled. Most of his actual behavior has to be learned. The scope and possibilities of his education can be appreciated only if we distinguish between his inborn drives or tendencies toward behavior, and the actual behavior patterns which develop through his interaction with his environment. So far as the theological doctrines interpret human nature as such, they are relevant only to inborn tendencies. What are these basic inborn tendencies or drives toward behavior which characterize human nature?

It is evident that the human infant acts, as Freud said, on the "pleasure principle." He seeks only immediate and selfish satisfactions. His behavior is directed toward making his environment serve his needs. Behavior prompted by this motive would indicate that he is naturally and inherently self-centered. Even when he learns that an immediate satisfaction, if grasped, may be enjoyed at the cost of later discomfort, or may mean the sacrifice of a greater satisfaction later on, and so curbs his immediate selfish impulse, he is still acting on the basis of self-interest. Even conformity to codes imposed upon him by his social environment may really be enlightened self-interest, for this will enable him to get greater satisfactions than would nonconformity. Thus all behavior, even that which appears on the surface to be utterly unselfish or a denial of self, might seem to rest ultimately upon motives of self-interest. This tendency to direct behavior toward the subjection of the environment to the self-centered interests of the individual has been called the "trend toward autonomy." [2] It accounts for most of the behavior related to meeting the physical needs of the organism. It tends to support the dark picture of original human nature painted by traditional theology.

But the human being, even in infancy, has other hungers than the physical. Much light has been thrown upon inborn human motivation by the study of the emotional life of infants. The most ideal provisions for the physical care of babies may be accompanied by more illness and a higher mortality rate than occurs in ordinary family care which provides inferior physical conditions. Babies need mothering as much as they need food. Lack of loving attention or a feeling of being rejected may be more disastrous to the health of a baby than inadequate food or unsanitary surroundings. This is evidence of another trend or tendency in original human nature which seems to be almost the reverse of the "trend toward autonomy." It is the tendency of the individual to seek to be integrated into a super-individual group and environment.

"The integration of the individual into the social group, the assimilation of its culture, of its written and unwritten codes, are just as essential for the personality development and personality organization as any of the physiological functions. Thus it appears that personality is a larger unit than a mere individual organism, because it also includes those factors through which it functions as a participant in the super-individual units of society and culture . . . man's attitudes are to a large extent oriented toward super-individual units. . . . While the trend toward increased autonomy aims at the domi-

[2] Andras Angyal, *Foundations for a Science of Personality* (New York: The Commonwealth Fund, 1941), pp. 32f.

nation of the surroundings, the characteristic attitude toward super-individual wholes is rather the submerging or subordination of one's individuality in the service of super-individual goals. . . . For this principle we propose the term 'trend toward homonomy,' that is, a trend to be in harmony with super-individual units, the social group, nature, God, ethical world order, or whatever the person's formulation of it may be . . . the trend toward homonomy penetrates the whole realm of human life . . . without it human behavior cannot be understood." [3]

While this second trend might appear to be in conflict with the first, it is in fact, from the viewpoint of personality, an extension or culmination. In the trend toward increased autonomy the individual fits the biologically chaotic environment into his own life, and in the trend toward increased homonomy he seeks to fit himself into larger units and by such identification he actually achieves a further expansion of the individual self.

In explaining the "demand for meaning" in the "Life We Prize," Dr. Trueblood well interprets this paradox:

"The ancient truth is that the health of the self comes, not by concentrating on self, but by such dedication to something outside the self, that self is thereby forgotten . . .

"We have one of the conditions of the good life when we can function as individuals, and yet individuals who lose themselves, along with other individuals, in some organic whole. This transcends both sheer individualism, with its lonely self-centeredness, and mass-mindedness. Man reaches the fullness of self only when he finds something to live *for;* he is made that way. However simple this philosophy may seem, it is really profound. When we belong to a cause and give ourselves to it, without counting the cost, our lives achieve both social solidarity and a sense of purpose, which together give significance even to our littleness." [4]

3 *Ibid.*, pp. 170-173.

4 Elton Trueblood, *The Life We Prize* (New York: Harper and Brothers, 1951), pp. 52, 54.

Perhaps the paradox of these basic human tendencies has never been better stated than in the familiar words, "If any man would come after me, let him deny himself and take up his cross and follow me. For whoever would save his life will lose it; and whoever loses his life for my sake and the gospel's will save it." (Mark 8:34,35).

How is human motivation changed?

The inborn drives of human nature, then, seem to be of two general types. There are those which enthrone the self as the basis and end of behavior. When the educational process, operating through experience, gives these drives the ascendency, focusing attention upon the outcomes which they seek, the human ego exalts itself into the place of supreme worth, denying social responsibility and defying the will of God. But equally basic are the drives to belong, to be a part of something greater than the self alone can ever be, to find the highest self-realization by losing self. Could it be equally true that, when the educational process, operating through experience, strengthens these drives, a person grows toward God so that he finds himself in the fullest sense when he can say with St. Augustine, "Thou hast made us for Thyself, Oh God, and we are restless until we rest in Thee."

These inborn tendencies are very general and diffuse in nature. They constitute biological needs or hungers which prompt the behavior of infancy. The individual experiences both success and failure in his attempts to satisfy these hungers, and he modifies his behavior accordingly. But his changing behavior patterns often bring him new and unexpected satisfactions, which in turn become new values or desires; consequently, the individual's hungers or desires are not fixed, but are continually modified by experience. Allport [5] advances the

---

[5] Gordon W. Allport, *Personality, A Psychological Study* (New York: Henry Holt and Company, 1939), p. 191f.

principle of the "functional autonomy of motives" by which he means that inborn motives account for infant behavior, but that the motives of growing life are increasingly derived from the processes and experiences of life itself. A little child may shrink from going into the water and enter it only under strong external pressure. But he finds that he likes it and develops a strong desire to be in it as much as possible. He may stay in until he is shivering with cold and has to be dragged out to prevent actual suffering and to protect his health. A man starts making money to support his family. He succeeds beyond all expectation but can't stop and enjoy it or fulfill other obligations to his family even after he has a surplus. The driving motive of mother love is probably based more on the experiences of tenderly caring for her baby than upon any inherited "maternal instinct."

Motives are a striving for some form of completion. They are based on tensions leading on toward some self-fulfilling activity. Experience enables the generalized and diffuse inborn motives to become patterned into cravings or hungers which prompt and guide behavior in the direction of satisfaction. As these motives find patterns of expression which satisfy or succeed they are refined into axioms of behavior. In the degree that these axioms of behavior are conscious they may be formulated into moral standards. Thus character is formed.

On this principle, acquired attitudes, interests, and ideals, rather than inborn biological drives, provide increasingly the motives of growing life. Human behavior, as personality grows, is increasingly emancipated both from inherited tendencies or drives and from specific outward stimuli. It is prompted from within by motives which have been acquired as the very character of the person. Also present behavior, though continuous with the past, is freed from its domination because it is under contemporary motives, motives which have been functionally derived. Since motives are completely alterable by experience or education, the dominance of egoism or self-interest is dethroned.

There is a cumulative body of testimony to the effect that the motives or drives of personality are far more a product of the social and cultural environment than of the inborn fixed tendencies of human nature. This means that the type of personality which a given individual or a whole generation, or the people of a given race or nation actually achieves will depend less on their biological inheritance than upon the general cultural patterns into which they are inducted and the general historic situations which they confront.

Stagner, after reviewing some of the most influential current theories of motivation, including those of Freud, Adler, and Lewin, accounts for the essential data in a "social theory of dynamics" as follows: ". . . we have analyzed as typical and important aspects of motivation as related to personality, the impulses of sex, the will-to-power, acquisitiveness, and the desire for social approval. In no case is it necessary to treat these urges as completely dependent upon heredity. To a very large extent *they can be interpreted as determined by the kind of social system in which the developing individual is placed*. In a different society, he would acquire different desires and impulses. . . . This theory has important social implications because it contradicts the common view that our social system is based upon innate qualities of human nature"[6]

Since human nature seems to be so readily modified by cultural and social forces, the question is raised whether any general psychology of mankind as such is possible. A psychology based upon the characteristics and behavior of typical Americans might find evidence of an inborn aggressiveness and acquisitiveness. A psychology of traditional China would find ancestor worship seemingly an inborn tendency. The Oriental temperament is quiescent and meditative while the American is activistic and restless. Is this actually inborn temperament or cultural pattern? How long will it take the Com-

[6] Ross Stagner, *Psychology of Personality* (New York: McGraw-Hill London, 1937), pp. 275, 277.

munist regime in China to reconstruct the Chinese temperament?

Further evidence of the social determination of behavior and character is presented in the findings of an intensive study of the relationship between the behavior patterns of the 735 adolescent boys and girls of "Elmtown" and the socio-economic class to which their families belonged.[7] The families were classified in five groups from the "highest," I, to the "lowest," V. The home from which an adolescent comes very definitely conditions his behavior in relation to his school, church, job, recreation, age mates, and family. The accepted or "good" behavior in school and community is that of the upper three classes. The condemned or unacceptable behavior is that of the lowest class. So when all these children go to the same high school, those from the upper classes are well-adjusted to the acceptable behavior and fare well. Those from the lower classes are poorly adjusted and either have to reconstruct their behavior to conform or accept an inferior and stigmatized status. Thus, an actual class system operates to violate our theory of American democracy. It is not a person's inherent worth so much as his social class which gives him advantage or disadvantage in having a good reputation and in getting ahead in our class-culture society.

Sorokin, after explaining the causes or sources of altruism and egoism in human personality, reaches the following well-substantiated conclusion: "Thus we face the necessity of seeking the factors of altruism and egoism not in this or that single factor (somatic, biophysical, psychological, or mental similarities and dissimilarities), but in the total systems of persons and groups, that is, in their entire cultural and social environment and in the entire make up of their own personalities." [8]

Anthropology provides evidence of the way in which a pre-

---

[7] August B. Hollingshead, *Elmtown's Youth* (New York: John Wiley and Sons, Inc., 1949), chaps. v, vi.

[8] Pitirim A. Sorokin, *The Reconstruction of Humanity* (Boston: The Beacon Press, 1948), p. 88.

dominantly competitive or co-operative cultural pattern among primitive people is accompanied by corresponding differences in the prevalent personality characteristics. A study of co-operation and competition in thirteen different primitive cultures is reported by Margaret Mead as an interpretation of the relationship between culture and personality. Some of these primitive societies were predominantly competitive, some co-operative, and some individualistic. Others showed a tendency mediating between these patterns.

The most basic conclusion coming out of the study is: "that competitive and co-operative behavior on the part of individual members of a society is fundamentally conditioned by the total social emphasis of that society, that the goals for which individuals will work are culturally determined and are not the response of the organism to an external, culturally undefined situation, like a simple scarcity of food." [9]

So current trends of thinking among psychologists, psychiatrists, and anthropologists seem to shift much of the responsibility for the determination of personality from inborn tendencies to cultural patterns and social forces. The trend also is toward greater emphasis upon the experiences of the earliest years of life as determiners of personality. LaBarre, citing evidence compiled from studies of many tribes, particularly of the American Indians, says, "Modern anthropologists are increasingly coming around to the point of view of modern dynamic psychiatry—especially that of analytic psychiatry—that the essential conditioning of children, in other tribes as well as our own, belongs to the very earliest years of the infant, perhaps even essentially to the first few years of life. . . . To the extent that we have stereotyped ways of bringing up children, to that extent will we have stereotypes of preferred character structure in the adults of that society. . . .

"Anthropologists like Sapir, Mead, Bateson, Dollard, Benedict, Linton, and others have now piled up a mountain of evi-

[9] Margaret Mead, *Habits of Co-operation and Competition Among Primitive Peoples* (New York: McGraw-Hill, 1937), p. 511.

dence for the correctness of the psychiatric explanation of differences in character structure of 'basic personality type' among various human societies. It seems to me that this is potentially one of the greatest scientific discoveries of modern times, not only to mental hygienists, but to every citizen of the world. *The single most important thing in human cultural behavior is literally and specifically the way we bring up our children.* And the single most important thing ultimately in the politics of the world is *the kind of human being*, temperamentally, that we manufacture. . . . Through anthropological and psychiatric knowledge and control of the bringing up of our children, *we are potentially able to shape almost any kind of human personality that an increasingly integrated world requires.* Shall we have a competitive, aggressive, Comanche-like personality in our future world citizen, or shall we have an urbane, Hopi-like personality? It is not the knowledge, but the social implementation of it that is lacking. Will we want the tenseness, the explosiveness, and the compulsive competence of the Japanese; or do we want the security and the aplomb and the realism of the Okinawans? Do we want the Chinese profoundly aesthetic enjoyment of life, or the severe, driving, guilt-ridden morality of Western man?" [10]

This means that the education of the young is the most important factor in the solution of the complex problems, both individual and social, of our modern world. But it also means that the educational task cannot be assigned to an institution which operates separately from our family, business, social, and political life. To the contrary, the kind of education implied is itself a basic function of our society and culture as such, and it can only be undertaken as a phase of basic reconstruction within the adult culture into which the young are being inducted.

Sorokin's treatment of basic human motivation in connection with the problems of war, which is one aspect of the de-

[10] Weston LaBarre, "The Age Period of Cultural Fixation," *Mental Hygiene,* XXXIII, No. 2 (April, 1949), pp. 209, 210, 211, 216.

cadence of our "sensate culture," is consistent with the foregoing treatment and is significant for Christian education.
After appraising as fruitless all the political, economic, scientific, educational, and religious proposals for world peace and
a harmonious world order, he concludes that the only possible
means of achieving this end is to supplant egoism with altruism
as the dominant human motivation.

He assumes altruism and egoism as the basic human motives.
Neither is dominant in human personality as a result of inborn
tendencies or predispositions. The dominance of either is the
result of socio-cultural influences. There are three interdependent factors which determine each other and which have to
change together in effecting any significant change in any one
of them. These are the cultural, the social, and the personal.

"For our problem this inseparable trinity of cultural, social,
and personal aspects of a group means that *altruistic individuals cannot be reared in a milieu of egoistic culture and
social institutions.* Conversely, *an altruistic culture and altruistic social institutions are incompatible with egoistic members.* . . . Thus, *if we wish to eliminate wars and establish a
creative altruistic order, we must modify simultaneously our
culture, our social institutions, and the personality of our citi-
zenry in an altruistic direction.* All attempts, such as the proposed social prescriptions, that aim to change only a segment
of one of these aspects are doomed to failure. Nay, more.
They can merely accentuate friction, bloodshed, and destruc-
tion instead of producing peace, good will, and constructive
creativity. . . . Such 'bargains' do not occur in the world of
trade and commerce. Still less do they apply to the greatest
transactions of human history. If we desire to eliminate war
and to establish a harmonious world order, we must pay the
fullest price for this value: we must transform in a creatively
altruistic direction all human beings, all social institutions, and
the entire culture of mankind in all its main compartments,
including science, religion, law and ethics, the fine arts, economics, and politics. Otherwise all attempts are doomed

to be abortive and to prove harmful rather than beneficial." [11]

Extreme as this viewpoint appears, it is a logical, perhaps an inevitable, conclusion from the foregoing interpretations of human motivation and its socio-cultural determinants. The implications for Christian education and for the policies and program of the church as a whole are of the deepest significance.

How does the personality as a whole operate?

According to Angyal,[12] the general organization or structure of personality may be understood in terms of dimensions. A vertical dimension will help to show the relationship between these basic inborn trends or tendencies in human nature and the way in which they work out in channels of expression. One may begin by looking at such "drives" as the drive for action, for superiority, for acquisition, or for exploration. If they are traced downward toward their source, it will be found to be the trend toward autonomy. Or one may consider the drive to "belong to some great cause," to "join up," which causes peace loving people to respond to the war summons; the loyalty to one's family or one's alma mater; or the "love of nature." If these drives are traced downward their source is found in the homonomous tendency. The drive for security and for a "total orientation to life and the universe" would have roots in both the basic tendencies. This "depth" dimension shows that the fundamental base of motivation for all behavior is in the trends toward autonomy and toward homonomy.

If we should begin with these two basic tendencies and move upward, they would divide and subdivide, first into "axioms of behavior" which constitute the way in which the individual has organized his motives to deal with the general issues and basic values of life. Insofar as they are conscious they may

[11] Pitirim A. Sorokin, *The Reconstruction of Humanity* (Boston: Beacon Press, 1948) pp. 95, 96. Italics in original.

[12] Andras Angyal, *Foundations for a Science of Personality* (New York: The Commonwealth Fund, 1941), p. 32f.

be expressed as maxims and constitute a philosophy of life. The discrepancy between the maxims and actual behavior may represent the degree to which some axioms of behavior have not become conscious.

Proceeding upward the axioms of behavior divide and sub-divide into attitudes and their corresponding values. Attitudes are emotionalized predispositions to respond in a specific way to environmental factors. They relate the axioms of behavior to specific life situations. Attitudes are channeled through hungers or cravings into concrete behavior at the surface. As motivation rises from the basic inborn tendencies through its increasingly diverse and specific manifestations as axioms, attitudes, desires, and activities, it is more and more individualized, representing what the person has learned through his own experience. It is expressed at the surface in the overt behavior which constitutes the unique personality known to his fellows.

The growth of the personality is not limited to the higher levels however. Experience may strengthen the basic trends, giving the personality greater depth, as well as developing and strengthening motivation at the other levels.

Because behavior is dynamic, always changing and moving forward toward goals or ends, another dimension on the surface at right angles to the depth dimension will symbolize this means-ends progression and on the plane of the surface will represent the way in which the specific tendencies which have reached the surface spread out or multiply in forms and ways of expression. So that along the means-ends line of progression may be arranged side by side various activities which represent richness and variety in the behavior through which the individual pursues his purposes. This dimensional scheme, rooting in the depths of the basic inborn tendencies toward autonomy and toward homonomy, rising and dividing into individual axioms of behavior which in turn branch out into attitudes, then into desires or cravings, finally rising to the surface toward definite ends or goals, and spreading out also on the behavior surface into distinctive or individualized forms and patterns of activity: such is the inter-relatedness of motivation and behavior, and of inborn tendencies and learned ways of living.

The human organism is symbolically represented in consciousness as the conscious self or self-awareness. This conscious self does not include the total organism, but only those phases which have become symbolized as the self. Many bodily processes operate below the level of consciousness and so do not become symbolized in the conscious self or ego. Nevertheless, the self tries to extend its control over the total organism even though it is not qualified so to do. This brings a split or conflict between the conscious self and the total organism resulting in some of the personality disturbances with which psychoanalysis deals. A person may see perfectly well on the symbolic or conscious level what he ought to do. But this insight does not penetrate to the depths of the personality, as yet unsymbolized and so below the threshold of awareness, so as to produce the desired behavior. It is here that discrepancies between maxims and conduct are accounted for. This represents the struggle so dramatically described by Paul in Romans 7:13-25.

What is character?

Ordinarily we think of character as made up of certain traits or virtues. The Boy Scout Law illustrates a character code and program which assumes this view. A Boy Scout is honest, kind, loyal, courageous, reverent, etc. Many other character education programs are based on this conception of character. [13] It is easy to point out difficulties in such a view.

If a trait or virtue means a consistent pattern of behavior under all circumstances, the virtues sometimes get in each other's way. If one's employer orders him to do a dishonest act shall he be loyal and obedient or courageous and honest? Some virtues become outmoded, as when what is thrift in one

[13] Hugh Hartshorne, *Character in Human Relations* (New York: Charles Scribner's Sons, 1932), Part I.

generation becomes hoarding in the next under new conditions. "Time makes ancient good uncouth."

Also, may not such virtues characterize a life which as a whole is anything but virtuous? To be really successful in his chosen vocation a thief must be brave, patient, alert, industrious, and persistent. Unless he works alone he must be loyal, honest, trustworthy, obedient, and co-operative with respect to his partners in crime. Success for him requires the same traits which insure success in any occupation. It is the vocation that is wrong rather than the traits. So character depends on the basic purpose or direction or outcomes of a life rather than on mere traits.

Isn't character just "a bundle of habits"? Certainly habits play an important part in conduct. They make routine much of our activity, relieving consciousness for attention to what is new. Probably the growing edge of character consists largely in acquiring "good" habits. Yet even good habits may limit us and poorly adapt us to new situations. Man most distinguishes himself from lower forms of life and reaches a truly human ethical level by the habit of changing his habits. Furthermore, it is at the very point where established habits do not provide a ready-made response which is adequate, that behavior takes on its greatest ethical significance. The real test of character is a decision among alternatives which involve various values and outcomes, no one of which seems wholly good or wholly bad. Habit alone is an inadequate qualification for such complex responsibilities.

But aren't traits and habits the expression of a certain kind of "selfhood" which constitutes the real person or character? We naturally classify people into types. The appearance and manner of a new acquaintance enable us to make a quick estimate as to the general category in which he belongs. But we may be mistaken; and we know that there are many exceptions to any type classification. Many belong to a "mixed" type. Both the scientist and the Christian leader warn us that these rough classifications are very often the basis for cruel and irrational prejudice. The better we know a person the more difficult it is to fit him into a type and the more lenient we are in judging him.

Furthermore, we are all role players. We have a somewhat different "self" for each situation. A professor may swell and strut before his class, but become quite deflated in a meeting with his own professional superiors. The parishoners of many a student preacher would hardly recognize their pastor in his campus role!

> "Within my earthly temple there's a crowd,
> There's one of us that's humble; one that's proud,
> There's one that's broken hearted for his sins,
> And one who unrepentent sits and grins.
> There's one who loves his neighbor as himself,
> And one who cares for nought but fame and pelf,
> From much corroding care would I be free
> If once I could determine which is Me." [14]

So we see that these "common sense" definitions of character need to be examined. It is not clear that they furnish us a satisfactory basis for a program of character development.

Is character made up of "good behavior"?

What was probably the most thorough and painstaking scientific study ever made of character, [15] the Character Education Inquiry, resulted in seemingly discrediting most of the popular notions as to what character really is. The principal method used was to test the behavior of school children by setting up situations in which they were given opportunity to lie, cheat, steal, refuse co-operation and helpfulness, fail in self-control, or to behave in more desirable ways. The resulting behavior was classified to determine the degree of consistency

[14] Edward Sandford Martin, "Mixed," *A Little Brother of the Rich and Other Verses* (New York: Charles Scribner's Sons, 1895).

[15] Hugh Hartshorne and Mark A. May, *Studies in the Nature of Character:* Vol. I, *Studies in Deceit*, 1928; Vol. II, *Studies in Service and Self-Control*, 1929; Vol. III, *Studies in the Organization of Character*, 1930 (New York: The Macmillan Company).

in the behavior of each child, whether he always or nearly always behaved in a desirable or in an undesirable way. The purpose was to discover whether there were any generalized traits or habits of honest, co-operative, helpful, and self-controlled behavior which would predispose a child to act consistently.

The conclusions were that there are no generalized traits but that character consists of specific responses to specific situations based on experience in previous situations which have similar elements; also that there is no "transfer of training" insuring that behavior patterns learned in one situation will be reproduced in different situations. The resulting definition of character is in terms of efficient social functioning or good behavior.

The difficulty with this conclusion and the study on which it is based seems to be in the assumption that the ethical quality of an act can be judged by its outward form. On the contrary, the motive prompting an act and the meaning of both the situation and the response for the person or persons involved seem to be of basic ethical significance. Behavior is not understood as an isolated occurrence. It is the behavior of a whole person. Its ethical meaning may depend far more on its place in a whole series of acts and experiences of a given person than on how it compares with the acts of other persons involved in the same general situation. Character is something more than an infinite number of stimulus-bound specific habit responses which are predictable only in terms of elements in a situation. There must be "on the inside of a person" predispositions to some kinds of behavior rather than other kinds, which operate as organized systems of motivation, direction, and control; which respond to the outer world in a selective or discriminating way, so in part determining the actual environment; and on the basis of which observation of the past behavior of the individual will justify prediction as to his future behavior.

Character is personality under ethical appraisal. Personality itself is ethically neutral. A given personality may be said to be strong, well-integrated, dynamic, winsome, or pleasing without thereby implying ethical superiority. Any of those qualities might be found in a personality which was far below accepted moral standards in behavior. A scientist may describe personality, but it takes a philosopher or teacher or prophet to define character. But character must be defined in terms of the person as a whole. It consists of the way in which the individual has, through his own unique experience, organized the drives, the axioms of behavior, the ideals, and the hungers of his life into behavior patterns in pursuit of his goals or purposes. Character may be defined then as *the organized systems of values, attitudes, and habits by which a person controls his interaction with his environment and so gives meaning, purpose, and consistency to his behavior.*

Since character is so highly individualized, judging it is an exceedingly delicate venture. It must be judged by overt behavior, and yet no single act can reveal much of what lies back of it. Similar moral values may be sought in different ways. The value of a given act depends upon the stage of development which the individual has reached in his character growth, upon the codes or standards of his social group, and upon both his intentions and the actual practical outcomes. The more one understands the complexity of moral conduct the more ready he will be to heed the admonition, "Judge not that you be not judged."

In reporting a study of sixteen-year-olds in "Prairie City," the University of Chicago's Committee on Human Development, before presenting several "individual type" studies, observed:

"In the course of discussing these case studies it soon became clear that moral character could be understood only in relation to the over-all personality of the individual. Good character means one thing in one type of personality and something quite different in another type; character is formed differently in different personalities. For example, two girls who will be described in the following chapters, Minerva and Sally, have very nearly identical character reputations, yet they are entirely different in personality. Minerva is a sober, conscientious, rather rigid person while Sally is gay, outgoing, pliant, and kindly. Both are popular. Both are leaders. Both are thought to have very good character. But it is clear that a quite different set of factors has operated in each case to produce good character and that the two girls will behave differently in situations which test character." [16]

It is true that norms of conduct are necessary to social living. But each person should be left free to work out his mode of conformity and his reasons for conformity in accordance with his own aptitudes, motives, and experience. Also, high ethical character may sometimes be best expressed in non-conformity. True ethical conduct is the expression of the inner motive for "belonging", rather than submission to imposed authority. The uniqueness of the individual is recognized and conserved when he is given freedom to make his own adjustment to the conditions of group life. And his value to the group is dependent upon this uniqueness and his finding of his most creative position in the group.

What are the signs of character growth?

It is evident that the traditional approach to the appraisal of character on the basis of standards or norms of badness and goodness is subject to serious limitations. While such norms may have value as a general frame of reference, the behavior of living persons in the complex situations of modern society eludes such simple measures. The will of God and the righteousness of God may be absolutes, but who is Godlike enough in wisdom to know them and apply them to the behavior of his fellow men?

When we think of behavior as the interaction of the individual with his environment in which both the person and the environment are determinative factors, the concept of adjustment and maladjustment helps to appraise character. We gain better insight into the behavior of children for example by thinking of them, not as "bad" children or "good" children,

---

[16] R. J. Havighurst and H. Taba, *Adolescent Character and Personality* (New York: John Wiley Sons, Inc., 1949), p. 116.

but as poorly adjusted or well-adjusted children. This leads us to see that improvement or growth on their part consists not simply in doing something to them to make them different but in changing their interaction with their environment by adjusting the environment to them as well as them to the environment. Character is not only expressed in behavior. It is also formed by behavior. Since behavior is interaction it can in part be controlled by changing the environment and enabling the individual to satisfy his cravings by interactions which are ethically more acceptable. Character education consists, therefore, at least up to a certain point, in helping the individual to achieve a satisfactory and harmonious adjustment to life by reducing conflicts, tensions, and frustrations to a minimum.

But character is more than conformity to imposed standards of goodness or harmonious adjustment to life in its social and cosmic context. The highest levels of character are reached in rebellion against conventional goodness as not good enough, and by maladjustment to an environment which itself requires changing. This means that we must think of character in terms of continuous growth and self-transcendence. The concept of immaturity and maturity is helpful here though we must beware of assuming that character maturity is automatically a concomitant of physical, intellectual, and emotional maturity.

One of the most significant recent achievements in the study of human life is that of the developmental concept. The child grows up through certain well-defined stages of development each of which depends for its satisfactory and wholesome achievement upon the completion of the preceding stages. The Fact Finding Report to the Mid-century White House Conference on Children and Youth [17] describes the course of healthy personality development as following such successive, well-defined stages. Each stage presents the growing person with a central problem which must be solved, temporarily at least, to enable him to move on successfully into the next stage.

[17] Mid-Century White House Conference on Children and Youth, *A Healthy Personality for Every Child* (Health Publications Institute, Inc., 1951), pp. 6-25.

During the first year or fifteen months, the child should develop a "sense of trust" through satisfying interactions with his environment. For the next two years much of his energy will go into asserting his own will and independence as an individual. In this way he gains a "sense of autonomy." Having thus achieved a degree of self-direction, the child spends the fourth and fifth years developing a "sense of initiative." He may become aggressive, he begins to develop a conscience, and he explores in fantasy various possible roles for himself. The efforts of the grade-school years are largely organized around a "sense of accomplishment." The school child learns how to do things, takes pride in his own achievements, and acquires much of the "know how" for later accomplishments. Early adolescence is occupied with developing a "sense of identity." The adolescent seeks assurance regarding who he is, how he rates, what he can do, what kind of person he is to become, how he can get to be more "on his own." Later adolescence brings the "sense of intimacy" in friendship, love, and inspiration. Early adulthood normally brings "the parental sense" and full maturity the "sense of integrity," a life well organized around accepted ideals, values, and purposes. It is evident that character consists largely in the way in which the individual meets and handles his central problem in these successive stages of growth.

A similar concept, defined in greater detail, is that of the "developmental tasks" which a growing person faces in the successive stages of his growth. Dr. Havighurst definies a developmental task as one that "arises at or about a certain period in the life of the individual, successful accomplishment of which leads to his happiness and success in later tasks, while failure leads to unhappiness in the individual, disapproval by society, and difficulty in later tasks. . . . When the body is ripe, and when society requires, and the self is ready to achieve a certain task, the teachable moment has come." [18]

[18] Robert J. Havighurst, *Developmental Tasks and Education* (New York: Longmans, Green and Company, 1952), pp. 2, 5.

To illustrate, the many and varied developmental tasks set before the pre-school child during his development may be described as having the following six aims:

"1. To learn ways of physical locomotion and agility in bodily movements generally.

"2. To achieve skill in the use of the hands, in particular as a tool for learning the nature of the world, for manipulating and creating things.

"3. To learn to talk.

"4. To establish friendly relations with other children.

"5. To hold the affection and support of adults without surrendering the felt need for independence.

"6. To work out some understanding of the nature of the world and to find some set of values to live by." [19]

The source of these developmental tasks is threefold. In part they arise out of the biological maturing of the individual, as in the case of learning to walk. In part they are imposed by the cultural environment, as in the time and manner of toilet training or in forms and manner of courtship. In part they arise from the ideals and values to which the growing person has committed himself, as in choosing a vocation from motives of service and self-dedication. [20]

This viewpoint shows the fallacy and futility of setting adult standards of conduct for children and attempting through disciplinary measures and habit training to get them to conform. It is as unreasonable to expect a two-year-old, who has not yet developed any definite sense of ownership, to "share" his toys with a playmate as it is to expect him to write his name. The ethical behavior which we expect of a child or which we can "teach" him is as dependent upon his developmental stage as is the skill we can expect him to have in using tools. It is important that parents and teachers understand what may

[19] Elizabeth M. Manwell and Sophia L. Fahs, *Consider the Children, How They Grow* (Boston: The Beacon Press, 1951), pp. 17, 18.

[20] *Op. cit.* p. 4.

properly be expected of a child at each age and developmental stage in his growth so that they can work with him in the range of his own capacities and incentives toward the fulfillment of his appropriate "tasks." Many of these tasks fall within the field of definite character growth. The ethical quality of a child's behavior must be judged, not by adult or absolute standards, but by the meanings of which he is capable at his stage of development. To impose arbitrary or unreasonable demands upon him will not only bring maladjustment and insecurity upon him; it may also prevent the wholesome development of those ethical "tasks" for which he is ready and so impair his preparation for the later stages when he might reasonably and happily achieve the desired behavior patterns.

This means that character education, instead of defining its objectives in terms of traits or virtues or habits which represent mature standards, should develop graduated norms appropriate to the successive developmental stages, and thereby be prepared to work in harmony with the developing capacities and motives of growing life. Just as intelligence measurements have established the validity of a "mental age" which may vary from the chronological age of the individual, resulting in an "intelligence quotient," so accurate measures of moral growth might some day enable us to establish a "character age," judging the individual not by an absolute standard but on whether his character development is commensurate with his growth in other ways. Since ethical standards are relative to the cultural patterns, determining norms would be an exceedingly complex and delicate undertaking. But a true science of character education would seem to require attempts in that direction.

The Union College program of character education [21] at Schenectady, New York, under the direction of Dr. Ernest Ligon has pioneered in the development of graduated norms of character growth. Although many questions have been raised

---

[21] Ernest Mayfield Ligon, *Their Future Is Now* (New York: The Macmillan Company, 1939); and *A Greater Generation* (New York: The Macmillan Company, 1948).

about the way in which the character traits and attitudes involved were derived, and about the educational method generally implied, the concept of character gradients actually under experimental use is of great significance.

In the "Goals for the Religious Education of Children," [22] the Committee on the Religious Education of Children of the National Council of Churches has formulated rather concrete and explicit descriptions of outcomes expected with each grade group in religious growth. These follow in general the developmental viewpoint.

The developmental tasks at every age level from pre-school to old age, as Dr. Havighurst has outlined them, include tasks which have definite ethical or character significance. As these are validated and further refined, they will form the basis for a lifelong program of character education, setting the task and responsibility of home, school, church, and community in guiding the growth of persons toward ever fuller realization of the worthy and noble ends of human living. This developmental concept has revolutionary implications for the way in which the teachers of religion will regard their pupils, their procedures and their goals. Their objectives are embodied in a Person who not only is regarded as Savior and Lord, but who himself "increased in wisdom and in stature, and in favor with God and Man." (Luke 2:52.)

---

[22] *Goals For The Religious Education of Children* (Chicago and New York: Division of Education, National Council of Churches, 1951).

CHAPTER 5

How Do Persons Become Christlike?

Psychology regards human nature in terms of moral immaturity and inherited potential. Theology looks upon it as so corrupted as to require a divinely wrought regeneration as the condition of life with God. The mediating Christian nurture viewpoint is that any necessary work of God's grace in human nature can be effected gradually from birth through the influence of parents, teachers, and the religious community. Christlike character begins, then, in the earliest experiences in which the inborn hungers for security, for love, and for adventure are met in a social environment which embodies the love of God. A Christian faith that is firsthand and personal is achieved as one phase of the whole experience of emancipation from parental control, when the individual encounters God in a direct experience of penitence, surrender, and dedication. Even with Christlikeness as the self-chosen goal, the immaturity of the growing Christian and the evil in his cultural environment involve him in continued compromise, penitence, and rededication.

What is Christlikeness?

A typical statement of the purpose of Protestant nurture is that of Nevin C. Harner: [1] "Christian education is a reverent attempt to discover the divinely ordained process by which individuals grow toward Christlikeness and to work with that process." The goal of Christian nurture is embodied in a Per-

---

[1] Nevin C. Harner, *The Educational Work of the Church* (New York: Abingdon-Cokesbury Press, 1937), p. 20.

son. This makes it superior both in motivation and in guidance to any code of conduct or set of behavior patterns.

The process of character development is, in part at least, a process of "identification" of the growing person with persons who have prestige for him and whom he consequently imitates in behavior and attitudes. Such identification is first with the mother or with both parents. Conscience emerges from the awareness of approval or disapproval of parents which, through identification, seems to be an inner voice. This identification shifts, during the stages of growing up, to various other types of persons: teachers; club leaders; admired age-mates; glamorous heroes and heroines such as movie actors, athletes, outlaw criminals, historical and fictional heroes; and attractive and successful neighbors and friends. [2]

In many cases the identification is with an imaginary figure who combines idealized qualities and perhaps impossible exploits. For example, a sixteen-year-old in an essay on "The Person I Would Like to Be Like" wrote: "I have created an imaginary hero and attempted to fit my personality into his. I am not sure who this hero is, but part of him is what I consider myself. I imitate myself and extracts of other people". [3] Summarizing the significance of this process of character development through identification, Dr. Havighurst says: "Several of these types of identification may exist at the same time. Identification with successful age-mates occurs at all ages from about six years up to old age. Identification with parents persists as a controlling factor throughout life. Identification with 'glamorous' adults is probably the most ephemeral. Identification with attractive and successful young adults comes last in the series, and is, the writer believes, essential for the achievement by the adolescent of personal maturity." [4]

[2] Robert J. Havighurst, *Developmental Tasks and Education* (New York: Longmans, Green and Company, 1952), pp. 65, 66.

[3] Robert J. Havighurst and H. Taba, *Adolescent Character and Personality* (New York: John Wiley Sons, Inc., 1949), p. 80.

[4] Robert J. Havighurst, *Developmental Tasks and Education* (New York: Longmans, Green and Company, 1952), p. 66.

To set Christ vividly and attractively before the growing person so that he experiences this kind of identification with respect to Christ is to provide him with the most potent and ennobling influence to which he can be exposed. It enables him to say with Paul, "I no longer live, but Christ lives in me." Setting Christlikeness as our goal is taking advantage of this universal tendency of growing persons to seek identification with some one deemed worthy of loyalty and imitation.

Christlike behavior is both the way by which Christlikeness is recognized and expressed and by which this quality of personality is achieved. But Christlikeness is deeper than behavior. In the form and manner of his behavior, Jesus was a man of his times and his people. He dressed, talked, worked, and played in the manner of his contemporaries. This was a condition of the Incarnation. If, for example, instead of assuming demon possession as a cause of both physical and mental illness, Jesus had talked about germs, infection, neuroses, and hysteria, people could not have understood him. Modern scientific ideas and terms would have appeared as nonsense to his hearers. Even as it was they sometimes thought him crazy.

To be sure, Jesus' behavior was exceptional and highly unconventional. But this unusual behavior has its significance not in its form but in its meaning, in what it was an expression of, in the qualities of the personality back of it. Being Christlike does not involve trying to reproduce the manners, customs, vocabulary, and information of a first century Galilean carpenter. To be Christlike means to be a certain kind of person in terms of one's own life and times. When the significance of Jesus as the embodiment of our goal in Christian personality is seen to be not in the outward behavior of his life, but in the deeper springs of motivation, he will not be outmoded by changing conditions and customs. Forms of behavior change, but these underlying motives and values are perennial.

Referring to Angyal's "dimensional" interpretation of personality (see page 79), the uniqueness of Jesus is not as much on the behavior surface as it is in the drives, attitudes, and axioms of behavior that are in the depths of the personality far beneath the surface. The further down we search, the better we understand the behavior on the surface. For as we reach the depths of his personality we find a homonomous dynamic which enabled him to say naturally but convincingly: "I and the Father are one." (John 10:30-38.) "Here are my mother and my brothers! For whoever does the will of my Father in heaven is my brother and sister and mother." (Matt. 12:48-50) "As you did it to one of the least of these my brethren, you did it to me." (Matt. 25:40) Jesus interpreted his own behavior, including his final choice of the Cross, as a complete identification of himself with all humanity as well as with God. Only when these deeper springs of his radiant personality are plumbed do we understand the meaning of his overt surface behavior.

When we say "Having faith in Christ is basing your life on the fundamental assumptions by which he lived," we are focusing, not on the surface behavior, but on the deep driving power of his life. Unless our relationship to him releases similar power in our own life, imitating him will be sheer mockery. The heart of the curriculum in Christ-centered education, then, is exploring, experimenting with, appropriating, and embodying in the behavior of twentieth century living, the basic assumptions, axioms of value, attitudes, and driving purposes which made Jesus the Incarnation of God rather than just a Galilean peasant.

The original Incarnation involved Jesus in living as a man of his own time while he was also God's Man for all time. The Christian of today, individually, or Christians, collectively — as his Church, through which the Incarnation is continued in history — will best follow him and embody him, not by imitating Christians or churches of the first century or any other century, but by carrying his motives and purposes out in the life of their own day. In the twentieth century Christ needs Christians and churches geared to the life of our times but directed and energized by him.

We have already briefly summarized the basic assumptions

by which Jesus lived. These axioms of behavior underlie his attitudes toward God, toward men of all kinds, toward his world, toward the problems and difficulties which he confronted, and toward the future. They may be interpreted as the actual structure of Christlike character. Our aim then is to develop in persons the kind of attitudes which emerge from these assumptions. Risking your very life on the conviction that these are the best and most valid assumptions by which to live is living by the Christian faith.

Is human nature capable of Christlikeness?

Liberal Protestant Christian education has in general viewed human nature through the eyes of the psychologist. The findings of anthropology, psychiatry, and child study, as presented in the preceding chapter, support rather than disturb the viewpoint of the liberal. But Protestant nurture must orient itself, not only to what science has to say about human nature and its remaking, but also to its heritage of Christian thought and biblical teachings on the same theme. And it must be admitted that the trends in theological thinking during the last two decades have gone quite in the opposite direction from these scientific theories. Disillusionment regarding social and ethical progress has brought a new realism to bear upon the interpretation of human nature and motivation. Fresh emphasis is thrown upon the evidence in support of the traditional, dark picture of unregenerate human nature presented by theology. Are we witnessing one more battle in the age-old conflict between theology and science? Are there neglected factors in both viewpoints which may be invoked to effect a synthesis?

Psychology sees mankind as the climax of an agelong evolutionary process, finally achieving moral character and responsible social relationships out of a lowly nonmoral past. Theology sees mankind as originally created "in God's image," for fellowship with, and allegiance to, God, and with Godlike potentialities embodied in his human nature. But sin invaded man's nature and he is, as we know him, a fallen creature, this innate corruption being transmitted from generation to generation. In and of himself, therefore, mankind is spiritually bankrupt, incapable by himself of recovering his Godlike possibilities and escaping the damning grip of sin upon his life. His only hope is in a miracle of redeeming Grace by which his corrupted nature is transformed and made capable of growth in Christlikeness through a restored fellowship with God.

From the viewpoint of Protestant nurture certain limitations in the psychologist's approach and understanding must be recognized. The psychologist is primarily concerned with describing, understanding, explaining, and predicting human behavior, rather than with moral values or the worth of persons. He sets up no standards to which behavior should conform. He has no goal of personality growth other than simple adjustment to the environment. He has an indispensable contribution to make to the Christian educator in terms of insights into growth processes and ways of conditioning behavior, but the Christian faith and not the psychologist's laboratory must supply ultimate objectives and basic resources.

The psychologist's view of mankind as the climax of the evolutionary process is but a partial view of human nature. It is an essential of the Christian faith to believe that man differs from the animal kingdom not only in degree but in kind. Whatever man's biological ancestry, the most important thing about him is his spiritual ancestry. Man's kinship with God, however his nature may have become corrupted, is still the most significant quality of human life, and is the basis for the distinctive aims of Christian nurture.

Though the grip of evil upon human life may be partially explained by the persistence of animal characteristics which human nature has not as yet outgrown, the prevalence and the degree of evil which characterizes human behavior, even in our brilliant and intelligent civilization, seems to imply actual corruption of man's nature rather than mere moral immaturity. Culture may appear to be but a thin veneer over a human nature that all too easily reverts to savagery. Yet, the nature of sin seems to be not so much the persistence of animal tendencies which human nature should have outgrown, as it does a prostitution of man's divine nature which comes from his kinship with God.

Even theologians who question the inheritance biologically of a corrupted human nature still see the natural plight of man as requiring something more than intellectual and moral education. The loves and drives which dominate his behavior and attitudes seem to reside below consciousness and volition in the depths of irrational feelings. Whatever his biological inheritance, the ordinary person seems to have acquired a "second nature" which is self-centered and depraved. [5] He cannot, by his own willful effort, fulfill his responsibility to God and to his fellow men.

The epitome of sin from the Christian theologian's viewpoint consists in man's acceptance of his Godlike potentialities, not as a basis for centering his life in God and devoting his powers to worship and service under the divine will, but, rather, as a basis for setting himself up as the object of devotion and making his own selfish will the law of his life. From the theologian's viewpoint, this egocentricity can be corrected only by a radical conversion in which the usurping ego is dethroned and God takes his rightful place as judge and ruler.

Psychology, with its practitioners in psychiatry, psychotherapy, and personal counselling, seeks to relieve illnesses arising from the frustrations and tensions growing out of human erring, weakness, and immaturity by effecting adjustment within the personality and between the individual and his environment. The resources of religious faith and a satisfactory adjustment to God may or may not be drawn upon in this process. In so far as such applied psychology works within a wholly human frame of reference, its effectiveness in a great number of cases is very limited. When mankind is regarded, however, not merely as a refined animal, but as having a spiritual nature

[5] David Wesley Soper, *Major Voices in American Theology* (Philadelphia: The Westminster Press, 1953), p. 202.

which places him in cosmic relationships and which makes available resources for healing and reconstruction beyond the range of strict psychological processes, the practitioners achieve results far beyond mere human explanation. Christian faith goes beyond psychology, then, both in diagnosing and in curing the "mental illness," with its attendant diseases, which so widely afflicts mankind. [6]

Just as the psychologist's view of human nature is subject to review by the Christian educator in the light of the larger perspective of the Christian faith, so the theologian's concept of human nature should be reviewed in the light of the findings of psychology. The Christian faith itself as a fact of human experience may not be entirely understood by psychological review, but formulations of its doctrine about human nature are the results of human observation and reasoning much of which was done in prescientific terms. Those formulations may be improved in the light of psychological insights.

In fact, the traditional theological concepts seem so incongruous with what is common knowledge regarding human nature, due to popular acceptance of a generally scientific view, that these doctrines are a serious stumbling block in the religious life of many people. "Modern man and modern education are faced with the task of developing or discovering a set of values which are in harmony with modern knowledge of the nature of the world and of man. At present a large part of modern society lives in a state of moral anarchy, half-heartedly obeying traditional moral principles which people are afraid to analyze because they feel certain the old principles cannot stand the scrutiny of modern eyes. And so modern man recognizes no divine moral law, but bows to elaborate necessity, economic and political." [7]

Protestant nurture relevant to the needs of our day must be

---

[6] See Leslie D. Weatherhead, *Psychology, Religion, and Healing* (New York: Abingdon-Cokesbury Press, 1951), Sections III, IV, V.

[7] Robert J. Havighurst, *Developmental Tasks and Education* (New York: Longmans, Green and Company, 1952), pp. 67, 68.

relevant also to its climate. The Christian educator has no choice but to examine the bearing which theological concepts have upon his task. Let us look at contemporary interpretations of human nature from the theological viewpoint.

A philosophy of Christian education prepared to represent the "Evangelical" (Fundamentalist) point of view states the situation as follows:

"A Christ-centered philosophy sees man as he actually is — created by God, made in the divine image, but with that image ruined beyond human power to mend it. Yet the image, though ruined is not destroyed. God by his supernatural power is still able to make contact with fallen man; and as man turns from his sin and believes the life-giving good news about Christ, his sins are forgiven and he enters as a new creature the family of the redeemed. Thereafter, his development becomes a matter of Christian nurture." [8]

The concluding sentence implies that Christian nurture comes into play *after* the individual has become a "new creature" through a conversion experience. Presumably earlier teaching may have a part in preparing for this transformation. But the growth of the individual as a religious person awaits this process of reconciliation.

Dr. H. Shelton Smith, interpreting the processes and conditions of Christian education from the "neo-orthodox" point of view, has this to say about original human nature:

"It is the Christian faith that man in his original existence was so created in the divine image as to be in full fellowship with God, and therefore, as being without the consciousness of sin. But this faith also holds that man lost this original consciousness of the divine communion through disobedience, and thus became aware of himself as sinner. In man's disobedience the divine image becomes perverted, although not to the extent that man loses all consciousness of himself as child of God." [9]

[8] Frank E. Gabelein, *Christian Education in a Democracy* (New York: Oxford University Press, 1951), p. 30.

[9] H. Shelton Smith, *Faith and Nurture* (New York: Charles Scribner's Sons, 1941), p. 95.

There is some ambiguity about such statements as these. If this "man" who was originally Godlike and sinless is assumed to be the first human ancestor of the race in accordance with the imagery of the Genesis story of creation, then both psychology and anthropology question whether such a creature ever lived. Instead of a "fall" from original perfection, there has been a gradual rise in human history from primitive and crude beginnings to a plane of intelligent and responsible social living. The truth in the Genesis account seems not to lie in its historical literalness but in its symbolic interpretation of the origin of sin in the life of each individual. Even here it must be applied only in a general way and with caution against oversimplification.

This interpretation of human nature must be invoked with due regard for individual differences. The description applies to persons who have grown up in evil ways with their lives centered in wrong motives and evil deeds. There are obviously sufficient evil tendencies in every person to produce these results. But there are also good tendencies waiting to respond to more wholesome influences. Egocentric motives may dominate infancy as a biological necessity, but early nurture can gradually redirect these and strengthen other-regarding motives so that the age of responsibility is gained without necessarily involving the complete egocentricity and rebellion against God which the doctrine contemplates.

The assumption that each person begins life in a state of perfection, and then by some disobedient act becomes a "fallen" creature requires examination. Life may begin in innocence because the infant is incapable of knowing moral values or of making choices which have any moral significance. To pass from this state of complete amorality into the making of choices which have moral worth is scarcely a "fall." There is more moral value in a life in which most of the choices are wrong than in one which is incapable of any moral choice at all. It is obvious that each person's development to the point where he has sufficient self-awareness, personal responsibility, and freedom of action to perform moral acts, so that he is capable of either moral perfection or a "fallen" condition, has already established him in a status somewhere between the two.

The assumption that the individual is incapable of avoiding or of recovering from a condition of egocentric rebellion against God except through divine intervention and the effecting of a miraculous transformation of his original nature should be examined also in the light of individual differences and of cultural possibilities. The doctrine is tenable only if we give complete freedom to the time, the manner, and the instrumentalities in and through which God may work in accomplishing his purposes in the life of the individual. Horace Bushnell's revolutionary thesis over a hundred years ago made exactly this point: "The child is to grow up a Christian, and never know himself as being otherwise." [10] Bushnell did not directly attack the doctrine of the "fallen" condition of human nature. What he insisted upon was that any changes original human nature required to make it capable of responding to Christian nurture could be brought about by God working through Christian parents from the very beginning of life. Since the power of God's spirit can be released in the life of an infant through the influences of the Christian family, there is no reason to assume that a child must be permitted to become "ripe enough in sin to have a conscious battle with it" before becoming a Christian. Thus, Bushnell argued that the gradual growth or "once born" type of Christian experience is the most wholesome and ideal, and that the experience of being necessarily "twice born" means needless waste and demoralization of the precious years of childhood.

In accounting for the prevalance of evil in human life and the depths to which a human being can sink, orthodox theology charges original human nature with dominantly evil tendencies. There is no denying the capacity of human nature for evil doing. But many Christian educators believe that we can

[10] Horace Bushnell, *Christian Nurture* (Yale Edition; New Haven: Yale University Press, 1947), p. 4.

assume an equivalent capacity for good. Either capacity can
be affected from birth by Christian nurture. This would justify
us as parents and teachers in undertaking our responsibility for
Christian nurture from the very beginning of life. Such is the
viewpoint of the liberal Christian educator as stated by Dr.
Harrison S. Elliott:

". . . . it is a false picture of human nature to think of it
as consisting of more or less well-defined egoistic or selfish and
social or unselfish tendencies, which are curbed and restrained
or organized and directed by reason. Particularly does the
emphasis upon the strength and the evil character of the egoistic tendencies seem untrue. Such emphasis upon the pre-
dominance and power of the evil tendencies is as one-sided as
former optimistic appraisals of man as by nature good. The
fact is there are no such well-defined tendencies in man, either
evil or good. Original nature is amoral in the sense that there
is nothing in the nature with which an individual is born which
predetermines whether he will be saint or devil. Whether the
'divine' or the 'demonic' possibilities are developed depends
upon what happens to that original nature in the experiences
of life. The individual's personality is of social origin." [11]

This statement will seem to many to be based wholly on a
psychological view of human nature and to overlook the larger
frame of reference of the Christian faith. Since our point-of-
view is Christ-centered, why not find out what evidence a study
of his teachings and attitudes throw upon the understanding of
human nature? Obviously each theologian seeks support for
his views from Jesus himself. Here is the evidence presented
from the "Evangelical" point-of-view: [12]

"Far from holding the sentimental view of human nature so
frequently ascribed to him, Jesus saw men in all the darkness
and enmity to God natural to fallen humanity. Recall his picture of the heart of unregenerate man. 'For from within, out
of the heart of man, proceed evil thoughts, adulteries, fornica-

[11] Elliott, *Can Religious Education Be Christian?* (New York: The Macmillan
Company, 1941), p. 191.
[12] Gabelein, *op. cit.*, p. 29.

tions, murders, thefts, covetousness, wickedness, deceit, lasciviousness, an evil eye, blasphemy, pride, foolishness, all these evil things come from within and defile the man.' (Mark 7:21-23)."

When this passage is read in its context it is evident that Jesus was not here giving a theory of human nature, but was emphasizing his point that real defilement is not ceremonial but moral. This passage and Jesus' statement to one adult, Nicodemus (John 3:3), are the only real evidence given to support nearly two pages of argument that Jesus held the orthodox view! The doctrine bears chiefly on the condition of children before their regeneration. The mutual attraction between Jesus and children (Mark 10:13-16, Luke 18:15-17), his choice of a child as an example to adults (Matthew 18:2-6), his categorical statements about their relation to the Kingdom (Matthew 19:13-14), and to God (Matthew 18:10-14), and his own experience of growing up (Luke, chapter 2), call into question the dark picture of childhood painted by orthodoxy. His attitude toward unregenerate adults (except religious hypocrites) was tender, sympathetic, and hopeful. Jesus never condemned men as men. His manner and attitude attracted rather than repulsed "sinners." Even the parables (Luke, chapter 15) of the lost sheep, the lost coin, and the lost boy were pointed less at the evil nature of man than at the loving concern of the Father. Jesus' whole attitude toward human nature seems to lay the foundation for Christian nurture, not merely *after* regeneration in later childhood or adolescence but from the beginning of life.

What is the source of authoritarian doctrines?

Human egocentricity, selfishness, and self-sufficiency seem to account for enough evil in the world today to justify regarding this tendency in human nature as the epitome of sin. So theologians interpret the basic human predicament as, not so much the wrong relations of men to each other, as their rebellion against the will and the rule of God. Man's only adequate confession is, "Against Thee and Thee only have I sinned, O God."

This definition of the basic pattern of relationship between man and God is a natural outcome of the backgrounds out of which most of our theological formulations have come. Those who grow up under the conditioning of authoritarian homes, political systems, and churches tend to experience an authoritarian God. The origins of both Fundamentalist and neo-orthodox doctrines were in a heavily authoritarian Europe. The authoritarian parent regards any assertion of freedom or independence by his child as a revolt against parental authority, and meets such self-assertion with repression and punishment. The resulting sense of sin and guilt which the child feels is focused, not on the ethical significance of his attempted exercise of freedom, but on violation of parental authority. The conflict is really over "Who is boss?" rather than over the ethical content of the child's behavior. All "right-doing" is obeying the parent and all "wrong-doing" is defying him. To punish is to uphold parental control and vindicate the imposed rules of behavior. So the authoritarian doctrine of God, developing in the climate of authoritarian home, state, and church, interprets him as chiefly concerned with man's obedience to his authority. It interprets all human sin as ultimately a revolt against God alone.

The democratic home, in contrast to the authoritarian, sees authority as being based on the conditions of happy family life under which all family members live and help each other realize their fullest development of their capacities. Freedom and initiative on the part of children is recognized as the condition of their growth into responsible participation in family living. Misuse or abuse of freedom is not a personal assault upon parental authority but a problem which members of the family face together because they are all involved in its consequences. The mature members help the immature members to see, appreciate, and share in the consequences of wrong-doing. All exercise of freedom and the consequences thereof, whether good or bad, are handled, not with the purpose of vindicating parental authority, but of educating growing persons.

Jesus' most severe conflict was with the officials of a legalistic, juristic, religious system whose authoritarian God could be obeyed and satisfied only by arbitrary ceremonial and legalistic requirements based on authoritarian tradition. Even though a similarly authoritarian religious system may bear his name today, that does not harmonize it with his basic assumptions and interpretations. To be sure, Christian theology must deal with the problem of evil in human life, but there is a way to do it which is more consistent with Jesus' own attitude toward both man and God.

There are several practical difficulties with these authoritarian views. In a day when the values of the democratic way of life are threatened by rampant authoritarianism, the Christian faith itself may be further corrupted. The recrudescence of authoritarianism in theology will justify it in home, school, and church. The result will be, not an increased exercise of God's authority directly in the lives of children, youth, and lay church members; but, rather, the claims of authoritarian parents, teachers, and ministers that their own exercise of imposed human authority is the very will of God. This imposition of human control as the will of God subverts true Protestant faith. For American Protestantism to recover and practice its original democratic principles, then, seems to be about the only hope both for a Protestant faith and a democratic culture.

Christian educators must consider the implications of their theology for their task. As we have already seen, it is the increasingly preponderant testimony of those who study the processes of personality and character growth that the earliest years are the most important. But suppose theology says that a child is incapable of Christian nurture until he has reached the age when he understands God well enough to be in revolt against him, and then in sin and guilt, undergoes a miraculous rebirth! Does it not preclude Christian nurture altogether at its most important time? Does it not in fact make any attempts at Christian nurture in childhood sheer presumption?

On the other hand when parents, teachers, and ministers take the view of childhood presented by the psychology of personality, which incidentally seems to accord with Jesus' attitude toward children, they have every assurance that human nature as it comes from the hand of the Creator contains all the potentialities needed to justify the aim of Christlike character. They are assured that the earlier they begin seriously to work with God through the processess of Christian nurture the better chance they have for success.

The fact is: When one understands how delicately balanced and responsive a young child's motivation is; when one has knowledge of the ways in which children should be handled to insure the most desirable outcomes; when one realizes the degree of skill and artistry, patience and self-control needed to do the job of early nurture well; and when one then observes the way in which most parents actually function, he wonders that even a small proportion of the children escape complete ruination of personality in the pre-school period. That so many fine, well-adjusted, happy individuals come out of average homes is evidence that, if anything, human nature is loaded in the direction of Christlikeness rather than the reverse! At any rate the precious stuff of human nature with which we parents and teachers deal, will, with the help of God, yield results beyond what most of us have a right to expect.

Why is evil so prevalent?

Questioning the doctrine of the total depravity of human nature must not be interpreted as ignoring or belittling the prevalence and the power of evil in human life. Our generation has evidence that no imaginable wickedness seems beyond the possibility of execution by evil persons. Of course our pessimism is enhanced by the degree to which our minds and emotions are dominated by a public press whose profitable business is the purveyance of catastrophe, and the exploitation of the most depraved behavior of humanity around the world. Naturally we ask, "Why is there so much evil unless human nature is depraved?"

While Jesus seems not to have looked upon little children or even sinful adults as depraved creatures, he knew full well the diabolical grip of evil upon the human heart. He had faced its worst possibilities in his own experience, as his Temptation reveals. Jesus had no sentimental view of human nature.

Evil exists as the very condition of goodness. Only persons capable of and free to do evil have the resources for Christlikeness. Powerful tendencies toward evil are present in human nature, not because man has fallen from a state of Godlike perfection, but because he is on his way up from a lowly animal origin toward Godlikeness. He is a creature of two worlds. The tensions of his life are between his lowly origin and his high destiny. Paul called them the enmity between the flesh and the spirit.

Science supports this view, for the scientist would account for man's weaknesses and failures by his immaturity, [13] both individually and racially. He is still in the age-long toilsome climb out of his animal past into a fully human future. Much of the evil of his life is corporate. It is embodied in the cultural heritage. These vast social and institutional evils like war and race discrimination are vestiges of his less mature past. Because the growth of his technology has accelerated far beyond his moral and spiritual growth these evils have gained relatively vaster destructive power. But moral progress there is, however retarded, and the human race is destined to grow up.

Here we must observe, however, that moral progress is not inherited biologically. It is preserved and passed on only in the culture. Consequently each new born generation starts exactly where its predecessor did so far as human nature is concerned. The only advantage it can have, the only embodiment of progress to which it is capable of responding, is in the inherited culture by which it will be nurtured. The view of human nature and of personality and character growth which science gives us today however, promises very much provided

[13] H. A. Overstreet, *The Mature Mind* (New York: W. W. Norton and Co., 1949), p. 82.

(1) we do embody moral progress in our culture and (2) we make competent and universal use of education.

Psychology and psychoanalysis illumine the subjective bases of the traditional dark view of human nature. They provide an interpretation which calls for careful, intelligent Christian nurture from the earliest years. Heredity provides neither a depraved nature nor an angelic one, but almost infinite capacities for either. Original nature is not neutral, but it incorporates a multiplicity of tendencies either way. The balance among these tendencies varies from person to person, but it is normally delicate enough to give the earliest influences of nurture a determining role.

Evil prevails, not only because there are evil tendencies in human nature, but because the cultural environment which conditions behavior and character development is such as to invoke and strengthen those tendencies rather than the good ones which are also present. So that a human nature, predominantly evil in its tendencies, may be an acquired "second nature." The sources of preventable evil in human life and society are threefold.

The most readily cured evil exists because persons are weak or confused and fall below their ideals in their daily practices. Eliminating this evil is a matter of bringing these persons under such commitment to Christ that the power of God will strengthen them against temptations and providing them with a supporting fellowship in the Beloved Community of Christians. Here they may join hands with their comrades of the Way in working to achieve a total social and cultural environment which will be more conducive to the good life. This is the never ending job of Christian nurture in the life of every Christian.

A second source of evil in human life and relationships is the deliberate choice of evil alternatives by responsible persons who know they are doing wrong and who have the power to do otherwise. Probably, however, all such wrongdoers have ways of justifying their behavior so as to make evil appear to themselves as good. This kind of evil can be prevented only by converting these persons to a new way of life. This is the dramatic task of adult Christian evangelism.

The third major source of prevalent and persistent evil lies outside individuals. It consists of institutions, traditions, social structures, and customs which are embodied in the corporate life, and which are not due to the deliberate choice of living persons. This third source of evil, not recognized by traditional theology, has been clarified by psychology and the social sciences. Most of these evils are a heritage from the past. They are embodied in institutions, codes of behavior, and supposed values, inherited from the past, for which no living person is responsible, but which the present generation has found it impossible to throw off. Some of them may once have been serviceable to human welfare, and, so, good. But "time makes ancient good uncouth." There have been changes which have transformed their total effect into evil without eliminating them.[14]

For example, consider nationalism with its accompanying sentiment, patriotism. Time was when the birth of free, sovereign nations, supported by the emotion of patriotism, was probably a forward step for humanity. But in a technologically united world, sovereign nationalism, supported by patriotism and preserving itself by the war system, is the most collosal evil which ever threatened the moral progress, welfare, and very existence of humanity. Modern warfare, an inevitable accompaniment of national sovereignity and its corollary, international anarchy, potentially at least, is a combination, on a world scale, of all the evils known to man. An economic system, which may once have worked well, may be quite outmoded by technological advances, and the almost universal interdependence of humanity, and by new human needs and potential resources for meeting them. Its competitive or its monopolistic structure may be foolishly wasteful, grossly unjust in distribu-

[14] For a much fuller elaboration of this point of view see: John Bennett, *Social Salvation* (New York: Charles Scribner's Sons, 1935), chaps. I, II, to which indebtedness is hereby acknowledged.

ting welfare, and provocative of the worst rather than the best tendencies in human nature. Yet these evils persist by the deliberate choice of no living person or persons.

Individual conversions cannot destroy or effectively curb evils of the third type. Conversion confers upon the individual neither the wisdom nor the power over the behavior of the other persons involved to enable him to transform the relationships, institutions, and social behavior patterns in which these evils are embodied. And these inherited corporate evils limit or prevent the achievement of individual Christlike character because everyone is more or less implicated in them. This is the valid scientific equivalent of the doctrine of original sin. But the cure for it has to be sought beyond the transformation of the individual life. Institutions and social structures as such have to be transformed by patterns which are not individual but interpersonal or corporate.

This concept of "original sin" as residing in our inherited corporate life is more in line with Jesus' attitude toward persons and institutions than is the doctrine of a "fallen" first ancestor. Jesus would go beyond modern science and account for the conflicts, tensions, and frustrations of man by his double ancestry. Biologically and physically, as science says, he is a child of this world, of the earth, earthy. But spiritually he is a child of God with a heritage of potential Godlikeness. He can be helped out of his predicament both by a regenerative commitment to Christ and by a family and community environment which will bring out the best in him and help him to win a victory over the worst. Such conditions will help to release the power of God in his life.

How and where does Christlike character begin?

The new born babe has needs and hungers through the satisfaction of which his earliest experiences may set growth processes in the desired direction. His emotional need for security is closely parallel to his physical need for milk. "Building emotional security begins when the mother first takes the newborn infant into her arms and lets him know that he is wanted and loved. Basic is the belief that the infant's cry is not a random wail or a symptom of the baby's selfishness, but an expression of pressing physical need which should be satisfied. ... In seeking the satisfaction of his basic physical needs the infant turns to his mother, who represents to him the only expression of the outside world that he knows. He finds a friendly world if his needs are promptly satisfied. In addition to prompt satisfaction of basic physical needs, mothering expresses itself in many other ways — by giving the baby frequent changes of bodily position, holding the baby in the arms and providing close physical contact. Further, it includes the whole gamut of small acts which show consistent love of the mother for the child: the physical contacts of feeding and bathing, fondling, caressing, rocking, singing, and speaking." [15]

This need and desire for security is not wholly egocentric. It is in part an expression of the homonomous tendency to belong, to be a part of something greater than the self. Closely related is what the psychologist calls the need or craving for response from other persons. What is this but the need for love and the capacity to love? Equally strong and seemingly inconsistent with the need for security is the tendency for exploration, for seeking new experiences, the hunger for freedom and adventure. These three basic hungers, for security, for love, and for adventure, qualify the human infant from the beginning to be something more than a digestive tract. The presence and the attitudes of others matter to him.

Furthermore, the first group to which the embryo person belongs is a group whose basic pattern and motivation is not egocentricity but love. Whatever a hardhearted, competitive society may do later to strengthen his tendencies toward egocentricity and to discredit or discourage his altruism, the family is based upon the love principle, and starts him out under the influence of daily demonstrations of mutual aid and self-sacrifice.

[15] Elizabeth M. Manwell and Sophia L. Fahs, *Consider the Children, How They Grow* (Boston: The Beacon Press, 1951), pp. 6, 7.

In the family it is the joy and privilege of the strong to serve the weak. The attention one receives is determined not by his power but by his need. The basic qualification for successful family life is subordination of self-interest to group welfare.

Even though few families may function as perfect demonstrations of the love principle, in no other kind of group life is it so nearly and so frequently approximated. The human family has far more than a biological function. Even though the earliest years of life were not the most momentous and determining with respect to moral character and spiritual growth, they ought to be! For at no later period in life is the dominant social environment so favorable as in infancy when it consists almost exclusively of the family. While the biological necessities of the infant's existence might predispose him to exclusive egocentricity, his social necessities provide a powerful corrective.

So when families function in accordance with their true nature, children are literally born into a kingdom of love. They do not have to wait until they are partly grown to enter into this kingdom of love and begin to respond to it. They do not have to be brought into it from the outside. They are born into it. And what is a kingdom of love but a segment or a sample of the Kingdom of God?

These famliy relationships provide the meanings for interpreting the larger world. It was no mere whim which led Jesus to use words whose richest meanings are derived from family experiences in interpreting the Kingdom of God to his hearers. He immediately translated its political terminology into domestic terms. God is, to be sure, a King. He is sovereign. But his sovereignty is best understood in terms of parenthood. He is a father. The relationships of the Kingdom among men were also translated into family terms. Men are brothers. The power of the Kingdom is not that of military might, or of imposed authority, or of miraculous deed. It is the power which initiates the family, holds it together, and motivates all its life — the power of love. Father, brother, love — three family words, deriving their richest meaning from family experiences

— were the key words used by Jesus to share with his fellowmen the unique meanings which it was his mission to bring.

With regard to the beginnings of growth toward Christlikeness, then, two observations can be made. About as early as any personality characteristics or qualities emerge, there are other-regarding, socializing, altruistic tendencies present to modify and counteract complete egocentricity. It is not necessary to wait until middle or later childhood or early adolescence to expect the love principle to be at work. It does not have to be grafted on or superimposed upon human nature. Love is as natural as selfishness. Furthermore, the child's earliest social environment operates, not on the egocentric, but on the love principle. Consequently, when the family functions in accordance with its true nature, the satisfaction of the child's psychological hungers may operate toward altruistic motives as strongly as does the satisfaction of his physical hungers operate toward egocentricity. It is a slander upon childhood, therefore, to regard it as incapable of any but an animal-like existence or to consider it depraved.

The implications of the foregoing observations for a program of religious education are obvious. The family rather than the church is the primary agency of Christian nurture. Probably the church's greatest contribution will be in helping the family to do its task well and in providing a "Community of the Beloved" beyond the family as an extension of the kingdom of love in which life begins. The family is primary because it has the child first during the crucial early years when the inborn tendencies are receiving their first encouragement or curbing. Long before any program of church or school begins to affect the child directly, the family environment is exerting formative influences of long range significance.

Even after a child starts to school and these larger relationships such as those with his age-mates and his peer group seem to become dominant, the family still controls about eightly-five percent of the child's total time. Attitudes, values, habits, and motives which family living has already developed will determine the kind of response the child will make to the larger potential environment, and the influences it will have on his continuing development.

Furthermore, the emotional tones of family relationships and experiences, the linking together of this intimate group in common fortunes and misfortunes, common likes and dislikes, common joys and sorrows, make family experiences still the most determinative and crucial. In no other grouping are the mature and the immature bound together so intimately that they literally form and transform each other in the very processes of daily living. Christlike character begins normally in early childhood in the family. If a theory about human nature causes us to assume that it has to wait until later, we simply do not recognize the forces at work.

How is personal Christian faith acquired?

We have already interpreted Christian faith as something more than a creedal formulation or a body of beliefs. It is a commitment of the whole person. This means that the ideas or concepts which constitute the content of one's Christian beliefs are related to feelings, motives, values, and attitudes which combine to make up the personality. One's faith is his total orientation to life. Faith is not a product of either instruction or reasoning, but of the total process of living. Instruction and reasoning may help one to understand his faith better and to systematize his way of living into a philosophy of life; reasoning may help resolve inconsistencies and justify attitudes; but we live ourselves into religious thinking far more than we think ourselves into religious living.

Consider the manner in which a child acquires the basic beliefs or assumptions by which he lives. Before he has achieved the ability to do any critical thinking or make objective value-judgments, the very processes of family living have inducted him into highly important and determinative value systems, attitudes, beliefs, and prejudices. "You are teaching your child religion," is a statement which can be truthfully made to any normal parent regardless of his intentions or of his own religious beliefs and practices. For the child's first lessons in religion are attitudes, chance and thoughtless remarks, and contagious feelings to which the parents have inadvertently exposed their child. These may be either negative or positive with respect to what the parents really want their child to learn. Of course, these unconscious teachings may be reinforced by deliberate and conscious teaching. Or they may be inconsistent with it and so cause confusion and doubt. But, willy-nilly, parents are teachers.

Normally parents have great prestige. A child is likely to use his first reasoning regarding religious matters to defend against question or criticism, the "faith of his fathers" which he has already taken for granted without reasoning. Since new facts and differing opinions or viewpoints must be interpreted in terms of meanings already available, the first formal teaching of religion comes on the scene to find the stage already set with home furnishings in terms of values, attitudes, beliefs, and prejudices.

A child, for example, who is being reared in the climate of strongly Republican family tradition, may wax more emotional than his father in defending the G. O. P. against its critics, without understanding a single reason for its supposed superiority. He just knows it is the "right" party and anyone with a grain of sense belongs to it. A child from a strongly Fundamentalist home will use his reasoning powers, not to appraise or criticize or even understand the faith of his family, but only to defend it.

In describing the development of religious faith in childhood, Allport has this to say:

"The child's theology gradually begins to approximate that of his elders. And normally there is in the pre-puberty period an intense desire to identify with the in-group. Religious practices, if such occur in the family, are taken for granted; and the institutional membership of the parents is rarely questioned. The child asks, 'What are we?' and, learning that 'we' are Presbyterians, requires no further authority for the superiority of Presbyterianism. He fights, if necessary, in its defense, and may go so far as to tear Catholic hair out of Catholic heads, unless given concurrent training in tolerance." [16]

Under normal conditions, when family relationships are positive and satisfying, the earliest expression of faith of any kind, political, economic, social, or religious is apt to be something like this: the child bets his life that his dad, or his whole family is right about the basic assumptions by which they live.

This power of family life to marshall the dynamic of emotions and the routine of behavior patterns in support of religious beliefs and assumptions which may not be able to withstand the critical examination of mature reasoning, operates to support authoritarian religion. But it presents true Protestantism, with its democratic insistence upon individual responsibility and freedom, with a problem.

"In large segments of Judaism, Catholicism, and Protestantism, if the parents are 'firm believers' then religion is the subject concerning which independent, critical thought is *least* encouraged. The child is given no grounds for believing that his religious tradition is something he can gradually make his own; he is expected to swallow it, as it is spooned into him, without asking questions. Often the energies of the parents and the Church are directed toward rooting a docile, unquestioning, subservience in the child's make-up so firmly that his faith will stay with him when he confronts the doubts and temptations of the world. This authoritarian approach ignores the fact that the most effective way to deal with the doubts and temptations of later life is to begin as early as possible in nurturing those capacities for independent judgment, critical thought and spiritual discernment which enable a person to cope with unforseeable circumstances as they arise." [17]

[16] Gordon W. Allport, *The Individual and His Religion* (New York: The Macmillan Company, 1950), p. 32.

[17] David E. Roberts, *Psychotherapy and a Christian View of Man* (New York: Charles Scribner's Sons, 1950), p. 62.

The real issue faced by true Protestantism is not, "how can we get our children to embrace the faith of their parents." They already do that. Nor is it the question, "How can we get our children to embrace the faith which their parents confess." This would only result in their professing one faith and living by another, even as their parents. Neither would be really their own. The real question is, "How can we enable our children to achieve a real faith of their own?"

In one sense the achievement of a personal, firsthand religious faith is just one phase of the whole process of growing up. Religious maturity comes like maturity in other areas of living, by gradually being put on one's own. The manner by which a person achieves emancipation from the almost complete control exerted over him at birth by his parents and gains the responsible freedom of full adulthood will pretty well pattern his religious development. There are three such general patterns. Perhaps no family would follow any one of them consistently. But they indicate the major differences in the way parents regard their function or their parental responsibility.

First is the familiar authoritarian concept. Here the parents take very seriously their responsibility for rearing their children in the "right" way. Their problem is to maintain the needed control over their children. The best policy seems to be to maintain parental control as long as they can and in all the ways they can, and to put the child on his own only after ideals and habits which will keep him in line with parental ideals have been well established. Such a child will be told what is right and will be given, through rewards and punishments, incentives for doing the right.

At the beginning he is so weak and helpless and the parents are so strong and resourceful that obedience is about the only way out. He will be a model, well-behaved child during perhaps the first dozen years. If he lacks initiative and prefers the line of least resistance he may continue in dependency and subservience into adulthood, never achieving real maturity or a real selfhood. The only faith he will have will be the faith of his parents in a diluted, anemic form. Of course, something may happen to release him into selfhood and responsibility. Some transforming experience may redirect the course of his religious life into an original faith of his own. But we have indicated the normal outcome of his upbringing.

If the child in such a home has too much initiative and drive to acquiesce, he will first begin to evade control by deception. When he is strong enough he will rebel. The line between the widening area of his freedom and the shrinking area of parental control as he grows older will be a battleline, coercion met by rebellion and, then, further coercion. He will win in the end and throw off all parental control. He will also repudiate parental influence. One of his weapons in the struggle for emancipation will be the disavowal of the religious faith of his parents. He may repudiate all religion, or he may take up a different faith. In either case the influence of his parents operates in reverse. If he continues in the church it will be because influences other than the home were strong enough to counteract its negative influence. Any faith he has will be a faith of his own.

At the opposite extreme from the home in which an authoritarian faith is imposed upon children, sometimes developed by parents as a negative reaction toward such a home in which they grew up, is the home which seeks to avoid any kind of "indoctrination." Some parents evade their responsibility for religious nurture by reasoning that religion is too difficult for children to understand; also, that they want to leave their children free to decide such matters for themselves. Of course, this attitude or policy on the part of parents is itself a kind of indoctrination regarding the place or value of religion in life. If the religious capacities and needs of children could be held in a state of arrested development in such cases the policy might be reasonable even though unwise. But children cannot wait to "make up their minds" on such matters because all the time they are making up their lives, one way or another. It would be as sensible for parents to say, "We will not teach our children any table manners. We'll let them get old enough to read Emily Post for themselves, and then they can decide whether to be mannerly or not." Such children will acquire some kind of table manners or starve long before they can read a book on etiquette.

Somewhere between the authoritarian imposition of a religious faith and the futile attempt to keep the child's life a religious vacuum, is a kind of Christian nurture which promotes a vital, firsthand religious experience consistent with true Protestant principles. How does such personal faith develop? It is one phase of growing up in the stimulating and responsible freedom of a democratic home.

In such a home the parents conceive their function to be that of freeing their child into his own self-direction and responsibility as rapidly as he can take it, and in all the ways he can take it. The parents will begin very early to confront the child with opportunities for choice. He will even be free to make some mistakes which do not too seriously endanger him. He will begin early to have experiences of weighing values, choosing between the lesser, immediate value and the greater, delayed value. He will learn by experience that sin is not so much violating an arbitrary command or rule as it is the choice of a lesser good.

At first, as such a child is confronted by the necessity of making a choice, he may shrink from it and want his parents to decide for him. If, however, they continue to confront him with such responsibilities, he will be so preoccupied with the range of freedom which he already has that he will not worry about the areas of his conduct still under parental control. He will know that, as rapidly as he is willing to take responsibilities, he will be given corresponding freedom. The line between the expanding area of his freedom and self-direction and the shrinking area of parental control will be a borderland of consultation and mutual trust.

The behavior of such a child in the earlier years may seem unruly compared with that of the well-behaved child in the authoritarian home. But the parent-child relationship will be free from coercion and rebellion. Instead of a revolt against parental authority, there will be a continuing desire for parental advice, welcomed by the child because he knows he does not have to follow it. Long before the time such a child is legally free from parental control, he is on his own, honoring and valuing the ways of his parents, but having a way of life which is his own.

A part of this transformation of the way of life of his parents into a way of life of his very own is the achievement of a personal faith of his own. As the youth encounters religious (or irreligious) ideas, beliefs, assumptions, and customs which are different from those of his parents, he will be encouraged to compare them with his own and to re-evaluate his own accordingly. Such parents as he has are likely to have a growing faith and, so, eagerly share with him in the quest for larger truth. In any case, his own growing faith will be dynamic and personal. So, as we have said, in one sense the transformation of the faith of our fathers into a vital firsthand faith of our own is just one phase of wholesome maturing.

In another sense the Christian faith has its own unique sources and conditions of growth. It involves a direct and immediate relationship between the growing person and God. It includes a confrontation of the individual by his Lord and Savior, who opens the way to God and claims the surrender and self-dedication of the individual to him. This personal experience of commitment is not paralleled in any other phase of the growing life. It is an experience toward which the processes of personality growth naturally and normally lead. Under wholesome conditions of nurture it is a step within the process of maturing. But it is a definite and a momentous step. Christian nurture which is so handled as to miss or gloss over this soul searching experience is no true Protestant nurture. An objective inquiry into and study of the life of Jesus is not the same as a knowledge (experience) of him as the Christ who is our Savior and Lord. Only a decision of the whole self, a leap of faith, a revolution of the mind in which Christ becomes the central fact in reorganization of motives and values, transforms one from an observer to a participant in the drama of human-divine relationships. This revelation of Christ as Lord casts a fresh illumination upon all the facts and events of history and of daily living so that now, consciously and enthusiastically, "I no longer live, but Christ lives in me."

What happens in this commitment experience may modify both the direction and the force of the nurturing influences. It is not until this personal encounter of the individual with God in an experience of surrender and self-dedication has taken place, whether it appears to be sudden or gradual, that all the elements of a personal Christian faith have been experienced. And this experience is a decisive or controlling factor in determining the quality and power of the personal faith actually achieved.

From the human standpoint, it is our responsibility as parents and church leaders to surround growing life with all available resources, conditions, and incentives for knowing, appreciating, and loving Jesus Christ as our best way to God. Having done this, we may trust God to make himself known and personally experienced by each person in ways that may not be fully understood, but that constitute the very essence of vital Christian faith. Until this direct or immediate "superconscious" encounter with God is achieved, one's Christian faith is little more than an empty shell, however much nurture may have contributed to it. This is not to assert what is contrary to the experience of millions of Christians, namely, that this earlier or preparatory period is a period of alienation from God or of complete involvement in evil. It is rightly and normally a period of growth toward God and into fellowship with him. But it does properly culminate in such a personal commitment as has been noted. Theologically this encounter with God may be interpreted as a "second birth" or "spiritual birth."

Our attempt to synthesize the theological and the psychological interpretations of religious experience is not wholly successful. Theologians will say that we have substituted moral education for conversion and implied that the work of God within the human personality is primarily a work of ethics rather than of grace; that we have understated the "lost" or "fallen" condition of human nature as such, and have explained away the miraculous element in regeneration. Psychologists will say that we have introduced irrational and mysterious forces to explain processes which are natural and subjective.

Our only defense of what will appear as inconsistencies is that this double orientation to the traditional Christian faith and to the scientific understanding of personality is essential to a functional interpretation of Protestant nurture. The sincere and responsible Christian educator will not simplify his problem and rest his mind by a clear choice of one or the other horn of the dilemma. At the cost of being charged with inconsistency, he will still seek for his task all the illumination available from both sources, confident that this is the way to the larger truth which he does not yet comprehend.

Does Christlikeness preclude compromise?

One who has committed himself to God in surrender and self-dedication and has taken Christ as the embodiment of his ideals goes on living in a social order whose institutions and relationships are predominantly far from Christlike. Since a Christlike life consists largely in Christlike relationships, what is the Christian to do?

Of course, if his commitment and loyalty were not so tested, it would have no proven validity. Also, Christlikeness is a dynamic, growing quality of living. If there were no difficulties encountered, there would be little growth. So the tensions between the individual Christian and his social environment may be highly learningful. A Christian who takes Christ seriously finds himself involved in actions, relationships, and attitudes in his daily vocational or social life which are quite out of harmony with Christlike ideals. Shall the Christian labor union member participate in labor practices which he believes to be wrong?

Shall the Christian be a soldier and help destroy the lives of innocent people for the glory or security of his own nation? Shall the Christian acquiesce in unchristian race segregation and discrimination? Shall he be a party to restrictive real estate covenants? Shall the Christian remain quiet about political graft which he knows to exist?

There is no easy alternative for the sincere Christian who becomes sensitive to these evils. He may try to withdraw from such situations, but is there anywhere he can retreat in our present social order and be free of them? Is not withdrawing the same as deserting his duty to society and wronging his fellowmen by his own isolation and aloofness? Sometimes, as in the case of the conscientious objector who goes to prison rather than to war, he will bear his testimony in spite of its antisocial appearance. He may try to change the situations, but seldom will he have enough power to do this. He might compromise with his ideals on the ground that one has to live and no other way is open. But does he have to live? The Lord, to whom he has committed his allegiance, chose the Cross.

Probably no Christian can live and keep on living without compromise. The most sinister danger in it is his tendency to rationalize his adjustment and so allay the tension. Compromise can be character building only if one meets the following conditions: (1) Keep the tension sharp between the Christlike way and the seemingly necessary alternative. Do not rationalize it and do not let the tension relax. Be penitent for what seems almost involuntary wrong doing. Be at peace with God in spite of tension with the situation. (2) Recognize that the best possible action, though not the ideal, may sometimes be better than no action at all, or complete withdrawal; therefore, participate under protest in the second best. (3) Practice Christlikeness fully in all situations and relationships which are under one's control. (4) Work in all ways possible to change the situations which do involve compromise so that they will not. Religion must not be an escape from these situations; it must be a power to change them. Under these conditions of constructive effort, situations involving tension, conflict, and even compromise may yet yield experiences which will promote the growth of Christlike character.

Many types of situations can be constructive or destructive in the experiences which they make possible, depending on how they are used. Play, recreation, aesthetic appreciation, and the creative arts can yield rich, well-socialized, character-developing experiences. Or they can be used for pure self-indulgence with no social values or motives and with a thwarting effect on character growth. If directed toward worthy objects, friendship, affection, and loyalty to others can enlarge and enrich character. Or, if the objects are unworthy, they can be blighting and destructive. Worship can be one of the most creative and personality-enriching experiences, or it can be an escape from reality and responsibility. Even one's own failures and wrongdoing can be turned to constructive, growth-promoting experience if the attitude of penitence, surrender, and determination to do better prevails.[18]

[18] See George Albert Coe, *What Is Christian Education?* (New York: Charles Scribner's Sons, 1929), chap. VI.

CHAPTER 6

How Are Christian Education and Evangelism Related?

Religious experience in Protestant churches follows two general types, the conversion type and the gradual growth type. Much contemporary evangelism emphasizes church membership far more than any particular experience. Traditionally, Christian education and evangelism have seemed to be rivals in the church's program. This is unfortunate. They need each other, for each is weak where the other is strong. Christian education is the lifelong, comprehensive program, while evangelism is a specific focus or objective within the larger program. Such integration strengthens both. Effective evangelism includes providing for the discovery of each "lost" person for whom a given church is primarily responsible, throwing Christian fellowship and loving concern around him, preparing him for a meaningful conversion or commitment experience — so conditioning that experience as to make it life-transforming — and incorporating him as a vital participant in the life of the church.

Have Protestants over-emphasized conversion evangelism?

Protestant evangelism, as a whole has perhaps been a truer expression of basic Protestant principles than has either its educational or its ecclesiastical life. This is not to say that its evangelism has always been truly Protestant. There has been a great deal of very un-Protestant dogmatism, imposition, intolerance, and ecclesiastical authoritarianism in our evangelism. But its consistent focus has been upon an inner, personal, deeply experienced relationship to God through Jesus Christ as Savior and Lord. Emphasis has been placed upon a definite conversion experience, an event in the inner life of the individual through which a new and vital relationship with God has been established and recognized; the individual's saved or redeemed status has been confirmed; and the individual has been able to bear testimony to his sense of salvation and inner peace. All this is typically, essentially, and wholesomely Protestant. It seems also consistent with New Testament precedents.

In the Lutheran, Reformed, and Anglican groups which were originally established, or state, churches, the evangelistic pattern has been somewhat different from that in the originally independent or free churches. The state church assumes the membership of the total population just as the state assumes their citizenship. Its task is to condition their lives so that they will voluntarily grow into and commit themselves to true church membership. The independent or free church, on the other hand, is a select, self-disciplined group, setting somewhat exclusive conditions for membership, and making certain distinctive emphases in its testimony, its teaching, and its practice.

The characteristic method of evangelism in the church with a state church background is through baptism or dedication in infancy, and a confirmation of the vows, then taken vicariously for the child, when he reaches the age of responsibility and self-direction. This is assumed as the normal process. Those who fail thus to enter the church by confirmation and those whose confirmed membership is allowed to lapse are objects of adult evangelism. The characteristic evangelism of churches with an independent or free church background is an appeal to persons old enough to be personally responsible to God to commit themselves to the Christian life on the terms defined by this particular group.

Most of the older religious bodies in the United States are transplanted European denominations. Whether they were state churches or free churches in Europe, they all necessarily became free churches in America. All have undergone changes, those with state church backgrounds becoming more like the independent or free churches. The older free churches have tended to develop programs of educational evangelism resembling in viewpoint and method the confirmation pattern of the state churches. The theological bases, the motives, and the methods of adult evangelism have changed from generation to generation in the various groups. The younger religious groups which have sprung up in our free and stimulating religious climate now make evangelistic emphases very similar to those made a couple of generation ago by the older denominations. There are, then, three major types of evangelistic emphases in current American Protestantism: (1) the confirmation type practiced by churches with a European state church background, (2) the conversion or revival type of evangelism practiced by the younger religious groups, and (3) a mixture of these, tending toward the confirmation type, practiced by the older, more sophisticated and originally free churches. This variety itself is true to Protestant principles. The trend from the second or conversion type toward the third or mixed type varies from denomination to denomination and in different regions and types of community so that the picture as a whole is quite complex.

Summarizing recent studies of adolescent religious experience, particularly with respect to conversion, Allport presents the following analysis:

"Three forms of religious awakening are commonly distinguished, the first being the *definite crisis,* or conversion experience. Of a large group of contemporary college students who reported some form of religious awakening, fourteen per cent acknowledge conversion experiences. Fifteen per cent reported the second, or *emotional stimulus,* type of awakening, wherein the upheaval is slight or absent, but wherein, nonetheless, the subject is able to designate some single event which served as the effective stimulus to his religious reorientation. Taking these two types together, we have 29 per cent who report that some traumatic or semi-traumatic event underlay their religious development. The remainder of our cases, 71 per cent, report a gradual awakening, with no specifiable occasion being decisive." [1]

Is conversion necessary?

According to the view of human nature which, as we have already seen, has been most prevalent throughout Protestantism the answer is, Yes. By his original nature a human being is estranged from God and incapable of a satisfactory relationship. A miracle of spiritual regeneration must take place within the inner life of each person before he is capable of religious life and growth. Such a conversion is a prerequisite for salvation and for Christian growth and experience. This conversion preferably takes place during later childhood as an accompaniment of confirmation or the decision to be a Christian. If it is delayed until later it will involve the radical turning about from a life of sin and will have an emotional accompaniment of greater or less intensity.

When Horace Bushnell [2] challenged the assumption that children must grow up in sin and alienation from God until a conversion experience changes their nature and their status before God, he met almost universal opposition. The idea that nurture could be a preventive of, rather than a preparation for conversion, was abhorrent. Half a century later William James' *Varieties of Religious Experience* [3] questioned the validity of fixed or standardized patterns of conversion experience. It began to appear that psychological factors as well as divine or miraculous factors were operative and that there were various ways in which the whole moral and religious orientation of a life might be changed.

The Christian nurture concept under the new label "religious

---

[1] Gordon W. Allport, *The Individual and His Religion* (New York: Macmillan Company, 1950), pp. 33, 34.

[2] Horace Bushnell, *Christian Nurture* (Yale Edition; New Haven: Yale University Press, 1947), p. 8f.

[3] William James, *Varieties of Religious Experience* (New York: Longmans, Green and Company, 28th Impression, 1917).

education" became prevalent among all but the more conservative groups early in the present century, the gradual growth pattern of religious experience coming to be accepted as the ideal. It seemed desirable now to use the term religious awakening, or Christian commitment or decision rather than conversion, to describe the forward step within the Christian life by which the individual declared or confirmed his Christian status and entered formally into church membership. Even though a turning about or conversion was not involved it seemed that such an awakening or overt commitment might properly be designated as a "second birth" or "birth from above." There was probably more general agreement on what the experience itself involved than on what it should be called.

The result is that, in general, throughout Protestantism two major patterns of religious experience are recognized, the gradual growth type and the conversion type. The gradual growth pattern follows generally Bushnell's formula, that "the child is to grow up a Christian and never know himself as being otherwise." Even though in later childhood or earlier adolescence the experience of self-dedication and church membership might be called conversion by some groups, it does not carry the literal meaning of the word. The other pattern is that of growing up in ignorance of God or in alienation from him, due presumably to the absence or the failure of Christian nurture. Such a life will follow the inborn tendencies toward evil. When in adolescence or adulthood, such a person becomes aware of the error of his way, in penitence and surrender seeks God's forgiveness and help, and commits himself to walk in "newness of life," his experience is properly called a conversion.

The latter experience is of course thoroughly in harmony with the traditional doctrine of the innate sinfulness of human nature. The former, gradual growth view can be harmonized with that doctrine in either of two ways. Some would find congenial Bushnell's view that whatever changes are required in original human nature to qualify the individual for Christian experience can be and are effected by divine grace, working gradually through the efforts and influence of parents and teachers. The other view is that the decision, or self-commitment, or confirmation experience actually includes a reorientation of the life to God, which effects a miraculous change in the nature of the individual. Those who hold this view consider the term conversion appropriate to describe such reorientation. Except in cases where the term is used in this sense, then, it is the purpose of Christian nurture, not to prepare for conversion, but to render conversion unnecessary.

Much Protestant evangelism in recent years has been rendered weak and superficial by treating the conversion concept altogether too casually. Preceding the Christian nurture concept, evangelism erred in assuming that children, regardless of their family backgrounds and early religious nurture, must all undergo a standard conversion event patterned after adult religious experience. An opposite erroneous assumption is actually practiced widely today. It is that adults, regardless of their background of religious ignorance, neglect, or alienation from God, can come into church membership on the basis of a childish pattern of religious experience which involves merely a decision or a formal confession of faith without any real conversion or reorientation of the total life to God. Such unconverted church members account, in part at least, for the amazing increase in church membership totals in recent years and for the accompanying disastrous deflation in the moral and spiritual value of church membership.

Conversion is necessary except in those fortunate instances where a child has grown up a Christian and never known himself as otherwise. The importance of some such conversion experience is interpreted from the psychological viewpoint by Allport as follows:

"Where there has been some marked turn or vivid experience we usually discover consequences of a lasting, and often permanent order. This is not to say that backslidings fail to occur; on the contrary, backslidings normally follow any strenuous moral experience. The veil is drawn after all moments of rapture. But the significance of the definite crisis or emotional stimulus lies in the hunger it arouses, and in the charting of a direction of search for appeasing his hunger. Almost always the individual who has once experienced a vividly religious state of mind seeks throughout his life to recapture its inspiration." [4]

Are Christian education and evangelism rivals?

During the nineteenth century evangelism was recognized throughout most of Protestantism as the central purpose and task of the church. Christian education, conducted chiefly through the Sunday school, was recognized as the "hand maiden of evangelism." Its job was to provide Bible knowledge as a basis for intelligent and informed conversion and as a means of guiding and instructing the converted Christian to "walk in newness of life." Many of the Sunday school field secretaries and organizers were called Sunday school evangelists. The test of the effective Sunday school was the number of conversions it helped to produce.

When the modern religious education movement began to replace the older conversion viewpoint with the Christian nurture viewpoint as the normal or ideal interpretation of Christian experience, revival evangelism was still going strong. Professional educationally-minded Christian leaders, granting its appropriateness to "hardened sinners" at the adult level, insisted that childhood and youth be protected from its emotional exploitations and be reached for Christ through soundly educational methods. By 1921 Dr. George Herbert Betts in his *New Program of Religious Education* [5] contrasted evangelism and religious education in parallel columns, showing the great superiority of the educational approach to that of evangelism. Christian education and evangelism were administered de-

[4] Gordon W. Allport, *The Individual and His Religion* (New York: The Macmillan Company, 1950), p. 34.

[5] George Herbert Betts, *The New Program of Religious Education* (New York: Abingdon Press, 1921), pp. 27-32.

nominationally in most cases by separate boards. Interdenominationally religious education was organized and promoted through the International Council of Religious Education, while evangelism constituted a department of the Federal Council of Churches; and in the local church the two functions were usually identified with different agencies, programs, and personnel. They frequently appeared to be rivals for central place in the church's program.

We have already noted the Protestant conservative and authoritarian forces' reaction against these liberalizing influences of the religious educational movement. These theological forces seemed, by their dark picture of original human nature and the hopelessness of man's predicament except for divine intervention, to deny or weaken the grounds for an educational approach. They reinforced the grounds for conversion evangelism which they believed to be the only way out. They thus provided those who set the evangelistic viewpoint against the educational approach with an excellent basis for criticizing the whole religious educational movement.

Religious education as a self-conscious movement in Protestant churches suffered retardation during the depression decade, the 1930s, for economic reasons. Necessary curtailment in church budgets was effected in many cases by laying off one of the more recently employed staff members, the director or minister of religious education. This blow at the relatively new profession affected enrollment in college and seminary religious education departments where these leaders were being trained, causing the closing or curtailing of religious education provisions.

There was also disillusionment in many churches because the early promise of the movement had not been fulfilled. Probably such enthusiasts as Dr. Betts had promised too much. They had underestimated both the grip of evil on human life and the inertia of local church leadership. At any rate, the product of the religious educational program of the preceding decade came to be identified as "the young adult problem." Ministers and others concerned with evangelistic results were complaining that the newer type of religious educational program was not producing church members. Executives of evangelism began to consider conducting "missions to children" to do the needed evangelistic job in which current religious education seemed to be negligent. It began to look as though evangelism were retaliating for the criticism and arrogance of the new religious educational movement during the preceding decades.

But the 1940s began to see decided improvements in the relationships. The long range result of the proposed "missions to children" was the development, through the National Christian Teaching Mission, of the Program of Fellowship Evangelism. The program, administered jointly by agencies of evangelism and of Christian education, provides a community-wide approach in educational evangelism for all Protestant churches. It sets up in each participating local church a series of projects in which Christian education and evangelism are thoroughly integrated, each reinforcing the other.

The restudy of Christian education referred to in Chapter III also helped to establish better understanding between the two points of view. These developments seem to justify the hope that evangelism and Christian education are moving into a much fuller integration and mutual support for the exacting and difficult task facing the whole Christian movement in our contemporary world.

How are Christian education and evangelism interdependent?

Any rivalry between these functions is unfortunate because they need each other. When either is at its best, it is inseparable from the other. When separated the strength of each is also its greatest hazard. Even if we continue to have separate boards of evangelism and of religious education; even though the major field promotion of each may seem to overlook the other, in the local parish where the work is actually done, it is highly important that evangelism and Christian education be brought into a mutually supporting relationship in a unitary process. There are several ways in which each needs the other.

Christian education is rich in the content of its curriculum, dealing comprehensively with the Christian's spiritual heritage, with Christian beliefs, and with the responsibilities and privileges of the Christian life. Its great weakness has been in the motivation or the dynamic which would put this knowledge and understanding into vital operation. It has been strong on the "what" of Christian faith but weak on the "why." Its weakness is illustrated by the Ozark farmer who needed desperately to improve his crop, but refused to enroll in an agricultural extension course because, as he said, "I ain't a farmin' now near as well as I know how to."

Evangelism, on the other hand, has been strong in its motivation, but too frequently the power it has generated has not been harnessed to intelligent, stable Christian living. The content of Christian discipleship has often been interpreted in very narrow terms, and converts have been left with partial, limited, ill-proportioned interpretations of the discipleship to which they have committed themselves. What is needed is a program for the making of Christians which will harness the high-powered dynamic of evangelism to the rich and steadying content of Christian education.

In other words, Christian education has been strong in its intellectual appeal while evangelism has usually made its major appeal to the emotions. An intellectualistic program easily becomes academic and devitalized, its ideas never being kindled into ideals. Until Christian education deals as effectively with the feelings as, for example, the motion picture, it has a secondary place of influence in growing life. Evangelism has dealt with the emotions. In fact, extreme forms of evangelism have exploited the emotions to produce a caricature of genuine religious experience. Emotions are unstable. An experience which has been excessively emotional will seem unreal and illusory when the emotion subsides. It is only by a balanced experience in which emotions are stabilized and given expression in appropriate, intelligently guided forms of behavior that a wholesome and constructive religious growth takes place. It is evident then that it takes a combination of intellectual and emotional experience to produce a vital, dynamic, well-balanced Christian personality. Evangelism and Christian education need each other, and when they are separated each is partial and ineffective.

Again the emphasis of Christian education is on gradual and continuous growth, whereas that of evangelism is on a crisis experience or a dramatic turning point in life. Neither of these emphases presents a true and balanced interpretation of wholesome religious experience. Even granting that the religious life as a whole is properly interpreted in terms of growth or of learning, the place of crisis experience must still be recognized as normal and deeply significant.

In fact, whether it is knowledge, skill, or attitudes which are being learned, the process is not represented by a gradual and continuous inclined plane. Learning always proceeds more like a stairway with its sudden "risers" and its level "treads." Suppose one is trying to solve a difficult mathematical problem, to understand a mechanical operation, or to make a problematical decision. One may puzzle along quite a while with seemingly little progress. Then, suddenly, a fortunate hunch or quick insight will clarify the whole situation and one can put the new insight to work while his mind can move on to other problems. Or suppose one is learning to play tennis and is trying to master a certain serve. Suddenly, perhaps almost by accident, he gets it just right. He has the "feel" of it now. But in order to perfect that serve and get it so that it comes right, not just occasionally by accident, but regularly, whenever he wants to use it, he must practice it long and persistently. During this period of practice he will probably lose more games than if he were to fall back on easier, more familiar serves. If he really intends to be a good player, however, he must move on to the mastery of this more difficult but more effective serve. Though during the time he is mastering it his "game" may actually seem to suffer, when he has it mastered, his game can move on to a new level beyond any previous one. Finally, suppose one is trying to develop the attitude of reverence in a group of young people who do not have a very adequate background of worship experience. This is perhaps a discouraging process. It seems too hard for them to become quiet and attentive and to enter into the spirit of the occasion. But at last everything goes just right. Their feelings are gripped. They get a taste of "the beauty of holiness." They now have a new appreciation of what worship is. But it will take patience and practice for them to make this a regular experience; to enter into it so expectantly and so naturally that they will regret any impairment of the conditions. After they have achieved these preliminary goals they will be ready to move on to higher levels of worship experience.

These are all illustrations of normal learning in the realms of knowledge, skill, and attitude. But they follow the stairway rather than the ramp pattern. The "treads" or "plateaus of learning," as they are called, represent the period during which new insights, skills, or values and attitudes are being practiced into the regular habit structures or behavior patterns. During this practice period no new gains seem to be made. They are periods of discouragement when only persistent loyalty to a long range goal will keep one on the job. But they are just as fruitful and just as necessary as the sudden "risers" which thrill one with his rapid progress. The only significance of the "riser" experience is derived from the practice or "tread" experience, for it is the latter which really effects the necessary changes in the psychophysical organism involved in any real learning.

Learning the religious life follows this same stair step pattern of all learning. Evangelism gives much attention to the "risers" but does not provide adequately for the patient practice of the "treads." Christian education does a good job on the "long haul" of the practicing and confirming experiences but is apt to overlook or handle poorly the crisis or "riser" experience which seems not to fit into routine. Again, an adequate, comprehensive handling of the religious life as a whole calls for a combination of Christian education and evangelism, each matching the other's weakness with its own strength.

The same principle applies to the question of decisions. Evangelism fixes its attention on one supreme decision, the all-out commitment to Christ as Savior and Lord. It easily overlooks the fact that this often comes as the climax of many lesser but contributory decisions, and that it but lays the basis for many more decisions which must be confronted successfully if the ever-widening relationships and responsibilities of a maturing life are to be Christianized. Christian education is aware of the many decisions involved in day by day Christian living. But preoccupation with these may obscure the great life-transforming, all-out decision for Christ to which they are tributary and toward which they converge. When Christian education and evangelism combine, adequate attention will be given both to the decisions which guide and qualify daily life and to the Decision which gives life its dominant direction, its quality of dedication, its sense of mission.

Evangelism sharpens the contrast between the life of one who is a "new creature in Christ Jesus" and the life of the worldling with his selfish concerns and his secular interests. The categories of "saved" and "lost" leave no vagueness as to the significance of one's relationship to God. Christian education, on the other hand, with its emphases upon continuous and gradual growth into Christlikeness, is vague about such categories as "saved" and "lost," dealing much more with relativities than with absolutes. There is validity in both viewpoints but danger in exclusive attention to either. Certainly there should be a clear definition of what it means to be a Christian and what it takes to make one. As we have already noted, a major handicap of contemporary Christianity is its vagueness and ambiguity on this point. This grows, in part, out of the relativity of the educational viewpoint. On the other hand, exclusive stress on fixed categories of "saved" and "lost" overlooks the necessity of Christian growth, of a continuous becoming, as the condition of spiritual health and religious vitality. Each viewpoint is a corrective to the other. Only a synthesis of evangelism and Christian education deals accurately and realistically with the nature of the Christian life and the status of the Christian.

Perhaps another way of indicating the need of this synthesis is to observe that Christian education gives much attention to the broad and complex relationships involved in living as a Christian whereas evangelism concentrates upon the Christian's transformed status before God. Obviously these relationships are interdependent. "He who does not love his brother whom he has seen, cannot love God whom he has not seen." (I John 4:20). But, also, "By this all men will know that you are my disciples, if you have love for one another". (John 13:35). The Christian life has both its vertical and its horizontal dimension. It takes a synthesis of evangelism and Christian education to give due recognition to both dimensions.

The evangelist has always been very conscious of his dependence upon the operation of divine forces within human lives for any success in realizing his purpose. His work is but the human side of a human-divine partnership in which the greater share of the task is God's. This consciousness of dealing with resources and powers which are more than human invests his function with a momentous significance, touched with mystery, which gives evangelism a prophetic role. The evangelist stands in awe of his own task. He speaks for God. Although the Christian educator has equal reasons for being aware of this human-divine partnership, his work may seem to be more fully within the sphere of human effort. The methods of teaching and guidance are not unique to Christian education. The teacher tries to understand his pupils through psychology and his task by the laws of learning. He tries to penetrate any mysteries that surround the learning process. Much of what he is doing seems quite comparable to what goes on in any school, whether secular or religious. It is easy to infer that teaching is somehow of a lower order than evangelism.

Here again evangelism and Christian education need each

other. The evangelist is necessarily a good practical psychologist in that he must know how to appeal to and influence people
so as to get a desired response. But, insofar as the methods and
resources which he uses are understood by psychologists, he
should know and follow sound psychological procedures and
not surround them with a mysterious sanctity which interprets
the results of suggestion as a miraculous act of God. God has
his indispensable part in evangelism without imputing to him
what is actually human technique. As much as the teacher, the
evangelist needs, and should appropriate and use with sincerity,
the insights and techniques of psychology and pedagogy. And
the teacher, as much as the evangelist, is God's fellow laborer.
The Christian teacher is one through whom Christ teaches. His
task is the climax of all other teaching.

Are evangelism and Christian education the same thing?

From the foregoing, it might appear that we have eliminated
any real difference between these two functions when each is at
its best. Isn't the whole program evangelism? Isn't it equally
education? Probably both Christian education and evangelism
can be charged with "imperialism" in the sense that enthusiasts
for each are inclined to make it co-extensive with the church's
total program. Everything the church does is evangelistic in
its ultimate purpose and basic nature. But everything is also
educational in that it seeks to effect desirable changes in persons. If we were to redefine these two terms so as to make
them mean the same thing and use them interchangeably, we
would then probably have to find new terms for some meanings
which are not quite identical even if they are related.

Since Christian education properly begins with the earliest
years and continues throughout life, and since it is concerned
with all the experiences through which individuals and groups
grow and undergo desirable changes, it is a very inclusive term.
Of course, one could select the specific study features of the
church's program and label these "education" while putting
everything else under other terms. But this would draw quite

artificial distinctions, isolate study from its indispensable concomitants in action and feelings, and overlook the necessity of a wide range of experiences out of which meanings must arise as knowledge if study is to be effective. The more vital and meaningful education becomes, the more it is related to life as a whole and so requires a broad and inclusive definition. We may say, then, that Christian education includes all those provisions which are made through church and home for persons to have those experiences which are essential to their commitment to, and their growth in, the Christian life, and to their participation in achieving a more Christian social order.

This broad program includes many objectives. Not all these objectives can be in focus at any one time. In fact, for any objective to be achieved there must be times when it receives central attention as though it were the most important of all the objectives. The organization of a total program requires that these objectives, one after the other, shall be in focus while other matters are for the time being held in abeyance. The effectiveness of the program will depend in large measure upon the timeliness of the focus upon the various objectives. There is a time just before marriage when premarital counselling is the most important thing the educational program can provide. There is a time when the newly acquired ability to read and the broadening experiences of school life will determine what should be done in the primary grades. There is a time when Christian motives in the choice of a vocation should come to focus. Likewise there are "seasons of the soul" for evangelism. The whole program has basic evangelistic significance. It is all indirect evangelism. But there come times when we teach for a verdict. The evangelistic objective, which has been present but latent all along, now comes to focus. The Great Decision is in order. We stress evangelism as though nothing else mattered. Christian education has now become evangelism in the conscious, direct sense. When the decision has been made, the specific evangelistic objective has been reached. Now other objectives come to focus.

Evangelism therefore consists of those means and methods used in seeking the lost, bringing them within reach of the church's evangelizing message and program, and effecting their commitment to Jesus Christ as their Savior and Lord. It falls within the scope of an educational program broadly conceived, and consists in a sharp evangelistic focus within that program. It continues with respect to each person, either continuously or intermittently, until the desired outcome has been achieved. It is desirable to keep the good word "evangelism" to designate this specific objective and process within the larger program of the church. It is important to recognize also that the total program from its beginning should contribute toward the desired evangelistic outcome and that the conservation and cultivation of the results of the specific evangelistic process are also the responsibility of the program as a whole. If we were to extend evangelism to include all these indirect preparatory processes and the whole spiritual cultivation process following the commitment, we would need to find a new word for the direct and definite process of winning decisions for Christ. If there are many other ways in which evangelism is being done, we may, in our preoccupation with its vague and generalized forms, actually miss this central thrust of the process.

How will this synthesis affect the program?

With this inclusive interpretation, Christian education cannot be a fragment or even a department of the church's program assigned to a semi-independent specialized agency. It must be integral to the church's total life and mission. This will call for appropriate and responsible administration, support, and participation on the part of the church itself and its whole constituency.

The minister's job, responsibility, and qualifications will need to be reinterpreted in a great majority of the churches, especially where he is the only professionally trained leader. He is equally responsible for Christian education and evangelism, and much of their careful integration should come through his leadership.

A synthesis of evangelism and Christian education should sharpen the concern of the whole educational program and personnel for the unchurched. When evangelism is operated separately from Christian education, the only concern of the church for the unchurched persons for whom it is responsible is apt to be limited to the evangelistic committee or department. Obviously, the church's greatest resources for throwing Christian fellowship around unchurched persons as an indispensable step in winning them is in the fellowship, study, and service groups, most of which are educational. An evangelistic concern on the part of all these groups is indispensable to effective evangelism.

One of the weaknesses of past Christian education has been its failure to develop an effective sense of churchmanship. Large numbers of the present unchurched population have former Sunday school experiences and records. But they never became assimilated into the life of the church as such. A much sharper focus upon evangelism and its concrete outcomes in the educational program would help to develop this church consciousness.

If the relationship we have proposed between evangelism and Christian education can be developed into practical operation, the evangelistic focus in Christian education will probably be sharpened. This will help correct many of the previously noted limitations in the educational program.

Will this synthesis conserve our Protestant heritage?

Nothing could increase the appropriateness and effectiveness of the church's program for its Protestant task better than to bring the evangelistic and the educational processes into the kind of synthesis here proposed. The personal, inner, experienced character of the Protestant faith calls for focusing evangelism upon the personal relationship with God and the personally committed life. The responsibility of the individual for his own priestly interpretation of his experience with God and for determination of the content of his own faith call for a broad, creative type of Christian teaching which frees him from intellectual dependence on others. The kind of teaching which consists in the sharing of experience rather than the imposition of dogma honors the testimony of each individual and assumes that it is based upon the kind of experienced relationship with God for which evangelism seeks.

What are the essentials of sound evangelism?

Since we are giving major attention in this book to the essentials of a sound educational program for Protestants, and since we have interpreted evangelism as an integral part of such a program, it seems appropriate to outline here the essentials of a sound evangelism.

Those who are the objects of evangelism fall into two major groups: (1) persons who grow up within the Christian nurture of family and church so that they are never really "lost," either in the literal or in the spiritual sense; (2) persons who have grown up in alienation from God or who have become alienated and so are lost both in the sense of being beyond the reach of the evangelizing influence of the church and in the sense of being estranged from, or in rebellion against, God.

Most of the provisions for the evangelization of the former group are so integral to the total life and program of home and church that they can hardly be identified as evangelism. Many of the graded lesson courses will have laid important backgrounds in knowledge and attitudes. Emphases such as were interpreted in earlier chapters as constituting Christ-centered education would make every teacher an evangelist with respect to long range goals in working with children. Care should be taken to see that in this sense there is an evangelistic motive throughout our teaching.

When the normal time for an expected personal commitment approaches, special preparation is needed. This is both a review or focusing of the preceding learning experiences and a means of making the commitment experience itself as rich and meaningful as possible. This special preparation is frequently provided in a pastor's class for prospective communicants or church members. There is value in preserving continuity with the church school experience by having the regular teachers of the persons involved share in the class work. The plan should enable the minister to have personal acquaintance with each of these prospective church members and deal with any individual needs or problems. This may be the time to consider with some of these young people questions of vocational choice and voluntary Christian service possibilities. Some of the issues involved have been stated elsewhere in terms which may be appropriately quoted:

"Certain dangers should be guarded against in this whole preparatory process. On the one hand the program can be made so much a part of the regular Sunday school work and so much a routine matter that it really does not mean a decision on the part of each person. He merely gives consent and goes along with a system which seems to leave no convenient place for choice. There are psychological or spiritual seasons of the soul. Persons mature at different rates. Girls ordinarily mature a couple of years earlier than boys. To handle such a program on a strict age or school-grade basis is certain to miss the most appropriate or crucial point with some of those involved. When decision or confirmation comes along as inevitably as graduation from grade school or high school, it is likely to mean just that for the young person — the end or conclusion of his Christian education. Instead, it should be a forward-looking, life-commitment experience, not just a graduation ceremony. In order to make sure that it will have the fuller meaning, there ought to be a point at which the young person as an individual is definitely confronted with the opportunity freely to make the decision as to whether he will or will not at this time make this full commitment to Christ and the Christian life.

"Another danger is that the time will come when the individual is ready for the decision, but because it does not seem to fit into this routinized process, he will not find any satisfactory means of expressing his commitment. The desire may subside and not recur at the right time and, consequently, the individual may fail to carry out a purpose which at one time was ready for expression. Children from effective Christian homes who have taken full advantage of the Sunday school and church programs from early childhood may wish to take this step a year or more earlier than their companions. Pastors and teachers should be alert to such needs and be ready to meet them. It is questionable whether any person ought to be held back from a forward step which he wishes to take in the Christian life simply because it does not fit into our system or schedule.

"The problem, then, is so to organize this process of pre-decision preparation that it will be easy and natural for each person to make his decision for Christ at an appropriate time, and yet keep the way open for a free, uncoerced decision either way. When the class is about to start or this program is introduced in an existing class, each pupil, and also his parents, should be interviewed to make it clear that its purpose is not to bring pressure to bear upon the pupils to make a decision for Christ but only to give careful consideration to what is involved, each person being left entirely free to decide for himself what his stand shall be. Those whose decision is negative are simply regarded as not ready, and thus the objects of further cultivation and solicitude." [6]

Except for this specific preparation for the self-commitment experience, the pervasive evangelistic motive and spirit of the whole church program will provide sound evangelism for those who fully participate in that program. Evangelism for those who are unchurched involves several successive provisions which we will now outline in terms of the Fellowship Evangelism Program of the National Christian Teaching Mission. [7]

[6] Harry C. Munro, *Fellowship Evangelism Through Church Groups* (St. Louis: Bethany Press, 1951), pp. 121-123.
[7] *Ibid.*

The Lost: Whatever doctrinal term may be preferred as a designation for the unchurched, the term "lost" is a literal description of their condition. Like the lost sheep (Luke 15:3-7) each of these persons must be located or discovered by a concerned person before he can be rescued. The first consideration, then, is the recognition that there are, within reach of a given church, certain persons who are not Christians and to whose lives Christ needs access. The first question is, "For which of these lost persons does this church have responsibility?" If we say, "For all of them," we ignore the responsibility of other churches and the fact that each of these persons is probably more likely to be reached and attracted by some one of the churches than by any of the others. It would be more realistic and provide a better basis for a fruitful approach if this church were to say, "Our primary responsibility is for those who are more likely to be attracted and won by our church than by any of the others."

This policy is usually embodied in a "prospect list." But every church in the community may make up its own prospect list, and there may yet remain unknown and unsought many who are lost more hopelessly than most of those on prospect lists. Furthermore, the same person or family may be on more than one prospect list resulting in what are apparently competitive approaches. What is needed is a plan by which every man, woman, and child in the entire community will be on the "responsibility list" of some church so as to avoid both overlooking and overlapping.

Discovery: The best plan for making up responsibility lists without either overlooking or overlapping is through a complete house to house religious census, taken by the churches co-operatively. This is done by assigning to each church a census area commensurate with its membership. The census is made simultaneously, usually on one Sunday afternoon, and the results all assembled and sorted on a central sorting table. From this table every church receives its "preferences" and its share of the "no preference" cards. The church can then make up its responsibility list, knowing that if it does not reach those on it, probably no other church will.

There is much religious census-taking done by individual churches or denominations. If this works for one denomination, it will work for others, and, sooner or later, there will be a succession of partial, spasmodic census-taking projects overrunning the same community. They soon become such a nuisance that householders refuse co-operation and no one can take a satisfactory census. The co-operative, interdenominational census, on the other hand, when it is thorough, when it distributes responsibility lists fairly to all religious groups in the community, and when it is an integral part of a larger program insuring immediate and careful use of its resulting data by all the churches, is a sound and indispensable step in effective evangelism. The churches in every community should make provisions for using this method co-operatively before it is discredited through its fragmentary and spasmodic use by particular groups.

Once a "lost" person has been discovered and placed on the responsibility list of a given church he is no longer lost in the literal sense. Someone concerned, through whom Christ can reach the hitherto literally "lost" person, knows where and who he is, and something of the background on the basis of which to approach him. For a church, from time to time, thus to compile its complete and accurate responsibility list is to take the first step toward an effective evangelistic outreach.

Fellowship: The simplest and most readily available human means of opening the life of the "discovered" person is to surround him with the cordial and concerned fellowship of a Christian group. The church's richest resources of fellowship are in its group life. The study, service, and fellowship groups of the church are, or should be, small enough to provide an intensive or intimate fellowship not available in the corporate church. Also, they provide a variety of age and interest groupings which make a maximum appeal to the stranger. The second step in effective evangelism, then, is to harness the available fellowship of these groups to the job of surrounding every unchurched person with a group of the age and interest best calculated to attract him. This is done by allocating the total responsibility list to these groups for intensive cultivation. Such fellowship cultivation not only brings them within reach of the church's evangelizing influence; it is a beginning of the process of assimilation into the life and work of the church so necessary to the vital church membership later sought.

Each group carries a twofold evangelistic responsibility: (1) to throw its fellowship around the unchurched person and enable him to feel at home in the group; (2) to move him along through this fellowship into the larger life of the church.

Preparation: As the group succeeds, this person naturally begins to think of his own personal relationship to Christ and of the possibility of church membership. He now needs what the routine work of the group or of the whole church may not provide. He needs specific preparation for the commitment or conversion experience. He needs an understanding of his own condition and limitations; of what is involved in the confession of Christian faith; of the responsibilities and resources of Christian discipleship; of the steps he should take in becoming a Christian. He may have personal difficulties, tensions, or problems which need the help to be provided through confidential personal counselling. He needs help and guidance in finding his way to God and in opening his life to the regenerating resources and power of God.

This kind of preparation was usually well provided in the traditional revival meeting. It may be cared for in a pastor's confirmation or church membership class for adults, supplemented by personal counselling. It is not usually an integral part of the ordinary visitation evangelism campaign, and it may easily be overlooked in the continuous evangelism in which the gospel invitation is given at regular services. Sometimes it is assumed that this need will be met by the church program after conversion. But the commitment experience itself cannot be enriched and deepened by interpretations which come after the event. Provisions should be made for the experience itself to have all the profound meaning and transforming power which the individual's spiritual capacity makes possible. Postponing these enriching interpretations until after the event is like asking the convert to sign a blank check.

Conversion: Among the prospective members of any church will be persons with different backgrounds and different degrees of readiness for church membership. Some will be coming in by letter of transfer from another church; some by simple affirmation of their recent past church membership and Christian experience. Christian courtesy would seem to require their reception without further ado.

Those, on the other hand, who come to make their first profession of the Christian faith and life, or to reaffirm their Christian commitment after a period during which it has lapsed, should be received only with the assurance that an inner spiritual experience is the basis of this outward act.

It is important in maintaining a truly Protestant experience and procedure that we keep a proper sequence and relationship between the inner spiritual experience of personal relationship with God through commitment to Christ as Savior and Lord, and the act of joining the church. In the Protestant sense and in the New Testament sense those who constitute the true Church of Christ are identified, not by their relationship to a particular institution, but by their relationship to Christ himself. Much of our current evangelism is conducted as though one first becomes a member of the church, this particular church, and thereby he comes into relationship with Christ. This may be consistent with the Roman Catholic concept of the Church and of salvation. It is contrary to true Protestant principles.

The membership growth of the earliest Christian group is described as follows: "And the Lord added to their number day by day those who were being saved." (Acts 2:47b) This implies that the first or primary relationship of the new Christian is to Christ. He becomes identified with, committed to, saved through Christ. This identification with Christ makes him automatically a cell in the Body of Christ, his Church. Church membership is a derivative or a corollary of a personal identification with Christ. This identification with Christ makes a person a means through which Christ is embodied, his purpose is carried forward, and his work is done.

Thus a person really does not "join the church" any more than he "joins the family." He is born into both. If he is born into a Christian family so that he is enabled to "grow up a Christian, and never know himself as being otherwise," he might be described as "once born," since his spiritual birth actually seems to date from his physical birth as a gradual unfolding of potentialities. But if he has been denied this kind of nurture so that his religious development is delayed or misdirected, a second or spiritual birth will describe his reconciliation with God through union with Christ. In either case, any vital, real membership in the church is dependent upon an actually accomplished relationship with Christ.

Many of our church membership drives which are called evangelism overlook this spiritual nature of church membership. Persons are urged to join the church on the assumption that somehow this will bring them into right relationships with Christ. The evangelistic policy that says, "The first thing is to get them into the church so that the church's program can help them find Christ" ignores this prerequisite to real church membership. To be sure, many people do join the church and then actually find Christ afterward. But a much larger number merely join the church assuming that is all there is to it, and, unfortunately, in all too many cases that is all there is to it. When statistical goals cause evangelism to press from discovery directly to church membership, by-passing fellowship cultivation, preparation, and conversion or genuine spiritual commitment, such goals and procedures become spiritually hazardous to all concerned.

Churchmanship: Where proper provisions have been made for fellowship cultivation and preparation, the new church member has already been assimilated into some of the church's life and responsibilities. It remains now for him to find his place of effective participation and service. Presumably there is a rich and varied program of activities and experiences through which his spiritual growth will be promoted. A conference with the minister should lay this program before him with the suggestion that a part of the opportunities are considered as "required," that is, as being indispensable for everyone. Beyond these essentials is a variety of "electives" within which he may find a major interest and develop some degree of specialization in his church life and service. There should be some simple means by which he could be made aware of the progress he is making; perhaps having periodic conferences with the minister regarding his growth and future plans would serve this purpose. Further consideration will be given the development of churchmanship in Chapter 7 on "How Does the Church Teach?"

CHAPTER 7

How Does the Church Teach?

The church teaches more by what it is than by what it does or says. Protestant freedom with its inevitable diversities produced denominationalism, the "free enterprise" system in religion. Authoritarian exaltation of each sect as a "church" eclipsed the true Reformation. But Protestantism today has turned self-critical and in the ecumenical movement and council pattern is seeking a more effective expression of its essential unity in Christ. Each ecumenically minded church thus qualifies itself to help fulfill the Reformation. Such a church moves toward its full effectiveness in five ways: by becoming a love-based community — a "colony of heaven"; by leading growing persons into creative churchmanship; by becoming a school in Christian living; by dealing constructively with its denominationalism; and by using its inner tensions creatively as a means of growth both for individuals and the group.

What is the church?

When we refer to a church's teaching program we think of classes, conferences, study groups, and sermons. Important as these formal educational processes are, their effectiveness in promoting true Protestant nurture depends upon what the church itself is and the kind of spiritual climate with which it surrounds these learning-teaching activities. Any church teaches more by what it *does* than by what it *says*. It teaches more by what it *is* than by what it *does*. It is the mission of a church not merely to talk about Christ but to embody him. The real Church is no mere human society organized to promote a man-made program. The real Church is a new kind of society originating in those who responded to God's redemptive Word in Christ, and embodying the living Christ in history as a continuation of the Incarnation. It is through the true Church that the living Christ is provided with hands and feet, ears and voice by which he goes about his present day ministry. The Incarnation continues in history in the degree that the churches actually embody the living Christ. A church properly functioning is a community of the beloved, a fellowship of the Holy Spirit, a fellowship of such spiritual quality that it embodies and expresses the Holy Spirit.

Which church is ours?

What do we mean by "church"? There are two principal senses in which the term may be used. The Assembly which met in Amsterdam in 1948 to consummate the formation of the World Council of Churches had as its theme, "Man's Disorder and God's Design." Applying this theme to the churches themselves, we have a twofold concept of the church: the Church of God's Design and the churches of man's disorder. In using the term "church" it is important that we have clearly in mind which church we mean.

The Church of God's Design is the divinely ordained means by which God's purpose in Christ was projected into human history through Christ's followers. As the living present body of Christ, continuing the Incarnation from generation to generation, the Church is unlike any human institution. It is divine in origin, in purpose, and in destiny. It is invincible and invulnerable. Did not Christ himself say in response to Peter's confession, "On this rock I will build my church and the powers of death shall not prevail against it." So regarded, no wonder the Church inspires our utmost confidence and enlists our deepest devotion and loyalty!

But which of the several churches in your town constitutes

this Church? As we look abroad upon the multiplicity and variety of ecclesiastical institutions which men have organized, and which divide their loyalties and dissipate their religious devotion, we look in vain for the Church of God's Design among these many human churches of man's disorder — unless, indeed, we are spiritually arrogant enough to assume that this particular church which we call "ours" is the one which really matches God's Design. Here is precisely our danger. Here is the unforgiven sin of Protestantism, the complete violation of the basic and valid principle of Protestantism. We erect this human church of ours into an absolute, the one true Church of God's Design, while we regard all these other churches as human churches of man's disorder. The true Church of Christ was present in the Protestant Reformation movement. But it was neither the Lutheran Church, nor the Reformed Church, nor the Anglican Church, nor any of the Independent or free churches. It was the Reformation Movement itself. When it crystallized into these several human organizations and they were then erected for their respective constituencies into absolutes, the Church of Christ was dismembered and the Reformation itself was lost among the churches. As a result, in the face of the multitude of unchristianized individuals and the mounting moral and social problems of the typical American community, to say nothing of impending world catastrophe, Protestantism presents a fragmentary, discordant, impotent embodiment of Christ. If Christ is trying to live and work and fulfill his purposes in such a community by using as his earthly body all his followers in that community, he is cruelly hampered and frustrated by the relationships existing among these various fragments of his body. This elevation of human churches to the place of the Church of God's Design makes their teaching sound far more like Babel than the voice of Christ.

In spite of this basic denial of our true Protestant principle, many glorious things can be said about the churches of our day. They are growing faster than ever. If the rate of church membership growth in America continues to exceed that of population increase during the last half of this century, as it has during the first half, the century will close with no one left outside some church! The organization of new churches and the erection of new church buildings testify to the institutional health and vigor of the churches of our day. The enlargement and improvement of provisions for Christian education are evidence of the seriousness with which most churches take their educational responsibility.

But nothing within the life of the present day churches is more significant than their growing dissatisfaction with their disunity and the failure of their dissociated parts actually to embody Christ in the community and the social order. The ecumenical movement within the life of the churches represents this self-criticism and this aspiration actually to achieve the true Church of Christ. One expression of this unifying trend is the merging of denominations which have much in common in tradition, form, and policy. In a broader sense the Faith and Order and Life and Work movements, culminating in the World Council of Churches, have been courageously exploring the ground common to the great majority of Christians and the means by which this actual unity can find better expression. The council movement, which is bringing the churches into practical fellowship and co-operation in common undertakings at every level from local community through city, state, national, and worldwide agencies, embodies this broader ecumenical trend. Clearly the church as a whole is moving out of its period of greatest disunity into a more adequate expression of its common faith.

But accompanying this outward ecumenical movement is an internal reformation beginning to take form within our existing denominations and churches. This is recognized as a movement within contemporary theological thinking: "Within nearly every existing Christian communion there is a growing challenge to complacency with the existing forms and traditions. Each communion is actually only a fragment of what the full Body of Christ should be. The question being asked from within the churches is, 'How can the Universal Church of Christ be more adequately expressed in our particular tradition?' The internal reformation of the Church takes as its presupposition what the present Archbishop of Canterbury has said, 'No age of the Church, no school of theologians, no single Church, has ever comprehended the "wholeness" of the Christian faith without any falsity of emphasis or insight.' This opens the way for a radical self-criticism on the part of every existing church." [1] So, many of our Protestant churches are seeking within their diversities a new unity which will enable them to give the living Christ fresh and effective embodiment in the life of their communities.

Most of our Protestant churches have already made the major doctrinal concession involved in this new unity by recognizing as fellow Christians the members of other denominations and by receiving them into membership on the basis of such recognition. When a local congregation qualifies spiritually and joins with its neighboring churches corporately to embody Christ in the community; when it humbly recognizes that its apprehension of the whole truth of God is limited and that therefore it needs to seek further for wholeness of truth; and when it is inclusive in its fellowship, lest it exclude some follower of Christ whom he accepts, a local church makes itself a true part of the Church Universal.

What is the true Church of Christ?

The true Church of Christ in any locality would be comprised, then, of all his committed followers or disciples through whom he is able to live and work and accomplish his purpose. This would probably include some of every church membership roll but would not be identical with any such roll or with all of them put together. To conceive thus the true Church of Christ and to act accordingly is a step in the direction of the Church of God's Design.

---

[1] Daniel Day Williams, *What Present-day Theologians Are Thinking* (New York: Harper and Brothers, 1953), pp. 124, 125.

We shall consider the church in all its forms and branches realistically and fruitfully when we see that one task of Christian education is to transform these churches of man's disorder into the Church of God's Design. Education must not seek to impose upon succeeding generations the church that *is*. It must seek to liberate the young from this inherited human institutionalism into the church of tomorrow, which will be one good generation nearer the Church of God's Design. This is the most vital way in which the church grows; it grows out of the churches of man's disorder toward the Church of God's Design.

What must the church do to be saved?

Like an unsaved person, the human church must seek salvation by meeting the terms on which salvation can be achieved. There must be penitence, surrender of all pride and self-sufficiency, reliance upon the mercy and grace of God through Jesus Christ to receive and to transform, and devout commitment to walk in newness of life. The church must be willing to lose its life in order to find it.

We must begin with the church we know best and have most chance to work through, our own church and denomination. We may admit that this will not go far toward transforming all the churches of man's disorder into the Church of God's Design. Yet it can be a beginning. There is nowhere else to start, and the time may be running out. How can our Protestant mission of reproducing the personal, vital, dynamic religious experience of the early church best be fulfilled in our own church? How must our church's program be changed to undertake the church's own spiritual reconstruction from within? How can we qualify our church to make its teaching effective by backing what it says with what it actually is?

There are at least five ways in which our task may be approached. These supplement and support each other. (1) The church may become a supporting fellowship or community in Christlike living. (2) We may lead growing persons into an experience of creative churchmanship. (3) We may organize and conduct the church as a creative disciplehood, a school in Christian living. (4) We may deal constructively and creatively with our denominationalism. (5) The church may grow through its own inner tensions.

Can the church become a supporting fellowship in Christian living?

We have seen that the habits and attitudes which constitute character grow out of the interactions of the growing person with his environment. The quality and outcomes of these interactions are determined both by what the person already is, and by the opportunities and incentives provided by the environment. The Christian family, based as it is upon the love principle, and functioning in accordance with its true nature, environs the young child with needed opportunities and incentives in the direction of Christlike living. To be sure, the family exists in an environment which exerts tremendous secularizing pressures upon it. Only as it keeps itself a haven of love-controlled living can it fullfill its true function. When it does, the earliest years of life for its children provide the kind of Christian nurture which enables them to get at least a fair start toward Christlike character.

One of the greatest services of the church is to constitute itself a "family of families," providing mutual support, specific guidance, and a sense of collective security in a secular environment, for families which are seeking to fulfill their function in Christian nurture. This will require the church to be a distinctively Christian community within the larger secular community, providing for these families a supporting fellowship and community relationships which will supplant some of the secularizing influences otherwise dominant. No other educational objective or provision surpasses in importance what the church may do to help its families accomplish their function effectively.

But the church has a direct responsibility to the children of these families which requires it to constitute itself as a community of Christian living, a real "colony of heaven." The child who has been environed and nurtured in a Christian family may find that his relationships in the larger world beyond the sheltered family circle seem to deny what the family has assumed and affirmed. Public school experience, fortunately, may not be too incongruous with this family background. And, yet, the school is all too much dominated by the competitive spirit of our secular society. The strong and able do not help the less fortunate, but compete with them for grades, recognition, and scholarships. The playground is dominated by competitive games. Athletics dominate the campus and partake too often of the worst features of our competitive society.

And when children come up against the way of life embodied in the movies, in commercial advertising, in industrial and business relationships, and in the civic, political, and recreational life of the community at large, they will find that "real life" largely rejects the government of God. If nowhere outside the family circle they can find the love principle at work in community living, they may easily conclude that the family has not given them any realistic interpretation of life and the world. If it is the lone family against the world as the interpreter of life to youth, the resources and pressures of the world will prove too powerful in many cases. One of the greatest services which the church can render to youth and family life is badly needed at this point. The church should provide for growing persons a social environment involving wholesome community living beyond the family circle, but still based upon the love principle. This will provide some continuity between the life of the family and life in the world at large, validating the way of life learned in the family and proving that the love principle is operative in the larger life of the world, in at least this one community constituted by the church.

This provides the church not only a reason but a mandate to expand its activities and relationships beyond the essentials of ecclesiastical operation into the rich and varied experiences of community living. Much of the social, recreational, and cultural experience of its constituency should be provided as a part of this distinctively Christian community living. This is both because these experiences ought to be part of the church program in order to give it sufficient range to constitute a real community, and because turning these functions over to secular social, educational, and commercial agencies would make them on the whole a liability rather than an asset in furthering the church's purpose. The church is the only community agency which serves equally all members of the family and seeks to provide continuous guidance and enrichment for growing and continuing life from cradle to grave. It is therefore competent to provide a "community within the community" dedicated to the moral and spiritual welfare of all persons.

The church does not provide a program of recreation or dramatics or hobbies merely as a bait to attract persons within its reach so that it can then exert a religious influence upon them. When such activities are used purely as bait, those who respond are likely to be at least as smart as fish; they will probably swallow the bait and spit out the hook. Also the "bait" motive is apt to lead to the placing of these activities on such a secular level that they may exert nothing but a negative influence upon the realization of the church's legitimate purpose. The church incorporates such activities into its regular program because they are a part of the wholesome community life in which the church wishes to engage its constituency, and because, when they are an integral part of this life and fellowship, they, in and of themselves, have intrinsic religious values. They multiply the character-forming, interpersonal and person-group relationships which fall within the love-based community.

A rich program of community living under the auspices and guidance of the church helps to preserve continuity of experience for those who are growing up through the various changes and adjustments which are involved in the services provided by secular groups. For example, if young people, during their high school years, find practically all their social and recreational life in the rich program of "extra-curricular activities" which the usual high school provides, they may fare very well while in school. But upon graduation the school drops them. If they do not go on to college and continue these activities there, they are left in a social vacuum. They must replace the lost fellowships of high school from the larger community. Its resources available to them may be anything but wholesome and desirable. If, on the other hand, they have found much of their social life and fellowship in a church group, they are not stranded on leaving high school but will probably now enrich and extend their relationships and activities in the church program. The religious community will have tided them over one of the adjustment periods.

The attention of the church's leadership is focused upon its various program elements of worship, study, service, and evangelism, and the results gained are apt to be evaluated in terms of these program elements. It is altogether possible, however, that the community relationships involved in conducting these program activities have as much potential character forming influence as any of the specific activities. Just as boys and girls learn their ideals and habits of honesty, altruism, success, and public service more from the prevalent practices of successful persons in their community than from courses in character education in the school, so the general life and spirit of the church in its community life may be teaching more than these conscious program elements. Whatever specific purposes the various activities of the program may have, if the life of the church as a whole provides its participants with a rich and genuine experience of living in a community dominated by love, this will probably be the church's greatest contribution. If it does not provide that, the values of its various program elements are thereby seriously limited. This has implications of the greatest importance regarding the organic life of the church. For its own organizational life and relationships to be thoroughly consistent in actual practice with the love principle which it professes and teaches is perhaps its best promulgation of that

principle. To violate that principle in its organizational practices is to deny the very faith it professes. This sets an exacting
standard for the church as an institution.

How do we teach creative churchmanship?

The first requirement is to remove any existing barriers between the "church" and its "educational program." Means frequently employed toward this end are use of the term "church
school" to replace Sunday school; establishment of an educational committee as a committee of the church, or an educational division as one of several parallel functional divisions in
the church's operational structure; or employing a director or
minister of education. Each of these measures may help. But
what we need basically as a means of providing an adequate
experience of churchmanship on the part of growing persons
is twofold. We need to develop throughout our church constituency a more adequate conception of what constitutes the
church; and we need general recognition of the comprehensive
and pervasive character of Christian education.

The typical Protestant church conceives itself as a Sunday
morning congregation, a board of officers, and an official membership roll, all revolving around the minister. Because most
of the experiences needed in living and learning to live the
Christian life cannot be provided efficiently through this
"church," a multiplicity of fellowship, service, and a study
groups spring up around these experiences, functions, and
specialized needs. These are usually considered "auxiliaries."
They have all degrees of identification with, or separateness
from, the "church." Usually some of them are so separate that
they tend to expand their functions so as to become little self-
sufficient churches which divide loyalties and offer a spurious
or partial churchmanship experience.

What is needed is re-education of the entire church constituency, beginning with the minister, toward the conception
that this total organizational provision for Christian experience
constitutes the church. Although corporate worship is probably

the most "churchly" thing which takes place among a congregation, it constitutes only one of the church's functions. When
other functions are usually identified with organizations which
are not the church, barriers are erected, perhaps all unconsciously, between these functions and the worship experience,
and between those aware of primary identification with these
"auxiliaries" and the "church" itself. Every person needs experiences such as the corporate worship of the congregation
which identify him with the church as a whole. He needs also
specialized experiences of study, service, and fellowship which
are best provided through the church's group life. The church's
program and its conception of itself should facilitate both types
of experience as supplementary to each other and mutually
supporting. The minister's attitudes, relationships, and accepted
responsibilities are a symbol of and an influence toward either
the divisive, narrow concept of churchmanship, or toward the
unifying, comprehensive concept. One church introduced valuable connotations into its terminology by labeling its various
program activities as "The Church at Worship," "The Church
at Study," "The Church at Work," and "The Church at Play."

The young should be considered, and should consider themselves, as genuine participants in the church and not merely
as candidates. The reception of a young person in later childhood or early adolescense into the church as a "member" implies
an anomalous relationship earlier. Suppose, for instance, he has
grown up in the life and fellowship of the church doing everything which was expected of him at each level of his growing
Christian experience. Why should he now "join" this church,
in which he has from infancy felt at home, any more than he
should "join" his own family when he decides he likes it? The
ceremony should be handled rather as a recognition of a relationship which has been true all along and to which both the
individual and the church now bear public testimony. This is
not to deny the importance and value of a decision and even
a crisis experience as the occasion of this public testimony. It
is simply to clarify the child's earlier relationship to the church

and to indicate that the step he now takes is one within Christian experience and within the church rather than one from the outside.

From the earliest years children should, to the limit of their capacity, have a sense of participation in the church itself. Establishing something called a "junior church," which is an imitation of the real church, probably accentuates rather than removes the barrier to true churchmanship for most young persons. Even a children's sermon in the regular church service is in danger of patronizing the young and setting them apart instead of providing an experience of identification with, and participation in, the corporate fellowship. Both the program itself as a whole and the conditioning of the young for participation in it need careful planning to provide essential experience.

When the church is a real family of families, as early as the junior years, fourth to sixth grades, children should look regularly to the corporate worship services of the church as their principal worship experience. Departmental worship should aim at preparing them for and helping them to enter with appreciation and meaning into these corporate worship experiences. To this end some modification may be needed in these services. To delay the practice of participation in this corporate worship until the adolescent years is to leave it until a period during which it is much more difficult to establish such a practice.

Of course children differ in their attitudes toward such church participation. The question should be raised regarding each junior child: Should he now be expected to attend the regular church service? The answer will be clear by asking three other questions: (1) How does he himself feel about it? Does he want to attend? If he does not, then his desires should be changed either by creating more readiness on his part through indirect influences, or through making the service more appealing to him. (2) What does he do when he does attend? Does he really participate in at least some of the program, or does he merely cover up his boredom by irrelevant activities? (3)

What better alternative is there? If the program cannot be made attractive to him, can some other activity be used to help prepare him for happier participation? The laws of learning preclude the use of either coercion or artificial motives, such as rewards, to accomplish church attendance.

The feeling of belonging to and having responsibility for the church from the earliest years enables children to regard the church realistically, seeing both its values and fine qualities and its weaknesses and inadequacies. Church loyalty does not require an idealistic or perfectionist conception of the church. This would lead only to disillusionment later anyway. To make children and especially young people feel that their church is not something perfected and inviolate, but that it is in the making, subject to improvements and achievements in which they can have a part, is to develop in them a vital and responsible sense of proprietorship. They are shareholders in something whose value they themselves are helping to create. The staunchest loyalty develops around something we are helping to create or working to improve, something in which we ourselves have a stake, rather than something handed to us ready made and complete. The program of the church should, therefore, engage all its constituents, young and old, in critical self-appraisal and efforts toward improvement. The young are often better qualified for this function than the old.

Some portions of the church's program should be graded to age-group capacities and understanding. But it is equally important that other program elements engage those of all ages, as does the family, in common shared experiences and responsibilities. These church-wide projects are essential to churchmanship. For example, to have the offerings of all age groups made to the church itself is far better than to have them handled as though they were in payment for educational materials used by the children. The educational expenses should be in the church budget. Offerings should relate the giver directly to the total church program and outreach. Certain missionary and service projects of the church should engage all age groups.

Plans for a new building or other improvement, beautification of grounds, the launching of an outpost Sunday school, experiences of inter-racial fellowship, celebrations and festivals, Family Week and family camps, church open house: such are church-wide unifying experiences for all members of the church family.

Democratic administration of the whole church is essential experience in churchmanship. A totalitarian or a bureaucratic church administration denies to the rank and file membership, especially the young, the experiences of responsible planning and true community membership. Any Protestant church which practices authoritarian administration has "denied the faith." It may seem to be more efficient institutionally, but it precludes essential experiences for true Protestant churchmanship. Even churches which have inherited nondemocratic forms of polity can, through planning conferences, advisory councils or cabinets, and free and open group discussion, achieve many of the values of democratic experience in churchmanship. Only in this way can mature, responsible churchmen be developed. So, administration itself is an essential part of the church's educational provisions.

How can we make the church a creative disciplehood?

The first followers of Jesus were a fellowship of learners. They were called disciples. In a very basic sense the church itself is a disciplehood — a school. Everything which it does has learning significance for the participants. Even conducting a funeral can be turned to educational uses. The concept of the church as a school, then, has important implications.

The whole church teaches. The general atmosphere provided by the church setting; the backing given the teachers by church, parents, and community; the seriousness with which the teaching program is regarded; the spirit of co-operativeness, harmony, good-will, and mutual appreciation prevalent in the church fellowship, or the lack of it: all either reinforce or tend to discount the explicit teaching work done in the classes. The whole church is a school. Joining the church may well be likened to matriculation in a school. It is the beginning of a growth experience or of a new stage in growth. The church program as a whole is a curriculum of experiences providing for that growth. Some of these experiences or "courses" are essential for everyone. They are the basic "required courses." Others are "electives" in that they provide a rich variety of choices according to one's interests, needs, and aptitudes. On matriculation a conference with the "dean" or minister should result in a carefully planned program and schedule of activities providing for balanced growth. There should be progression from level to level of achievement. Regular conferences with the dean should provide a check on progress being made and corrective measures, if needed. The only graduation would be into places of leadership and merited responsibility. Learning would never cease. Every member of the church, young and old, would be engaged in it. Such a conception of the church is nearer to the original disciplehood surrounding Jesus, and nearer the spirit of the early church, than is our typical Protestant church with the backward-looking, stagnant spiritual experience of most of its members.

To regard the church as in some respects a school is not to set the ordinary secular school up as a model. The church's school has great advantages over the ordinary school. It has in its membership the very finest people of the whole community. One of its greatest contributions is to enable its immature growing members to have friendly and intimate fellowship with its more mature members. Fortunately, its great resources of potential leadership make it possible for its groups to be small and intimate enough for personal acquaintance of the immature with the mature. The usual small class of six to a dozen closely associated with a teacher, and, preferably, also an associate teacher, is a far better unit for learning religion that the larger, more formal classes like those of the public school. If there seems to be inadequate leadership for these many classes and groups, it is not because the potential leadership material is not available. It is because there is not an adequate policy and program of discovery, enlistment, preparation, and motivation of these leaders. A church at its best will capitalize upon its greatest human resource — a resource far beyond that inherent in the membership of any other agency — its potential resource of radiant Christian personalities. It is the function of the church as a school to provide for the richest possible sharing of life between its mature and its immature members. The ordinary church school or Sunday school provides the machinery for this. When the whole church conceives of itself as a school in Christian living whose basic method is such sharing, true spiritual growth is inevitable.

How can we deal constructively with our denominationalism?

The inevitable corollary of our Protestant religious freedom is religious diversity. This diversity expresses itself in our multiplicity and variety of denominations. In a religiously heterogeneous population they seem to be inevitable. Denominationalism has both assets and liabilities.

Among the assets are: complete freedom of the individual conscience in matters of religious belief and practice; a much richer total religious experience due to the freeing of the human spirit to explore and to experiment; the discovery and the testing out of new truth and fresh types of religious experience; a considerable choice on the part of each person as to the type of church in which he will find fellowship, worship, and work — with the opportunity to shift from one type to another if he desires; the emphasis, by particular groups, of important religious truths and types of experience which might otherwise have been neglected or lost.

Protestantism represents the system of free enterprise in religion. Different groups have had a stimulating influence on each other. Each group has been put on its own to make good on the basis of its own special emphasis and has had to survive on its merits. Even though, at its worst, this has been destructively and wastefully competitive, at its best, it has produced wholesome motivation to devotion, loyalty, and service. Christians have been led to "provoke one another to good works." The originality, versatility, and creativity of American Protestantism has given it a vigor and vitality which is seldom found in established or authoritarian churches. Any plan to correct the abuses and inefficiency of this system of free enterprise in religion must provide for the preservation of these many assets in one way or another. They are characteristically Protestant and American.

But the system as it has operated has been costly and inefficient. Much of the spiritual energy produced has been wasted in friction, overlapping, and competition, leaving upon community life very little effective impact of religion itself. The unchurched population has often been confused or repulsed by the variety of seemingly competitive appeals. Funds and personnel have been expended to keep weak denominational units alive in communities otherwise adequately churched, while other communities have been practically churchless. Many communities which need one or two good churches with competent, resident ministers have half a dozen struggling churches with part-time, nonresident ministers who provide highly incompetent service. Lack of any statesmanlike planning or policies of adjustment has left great numbers of city churches stranded in the wake of shifting populations, or continuing to serve widely scattered congregations with no relationship whatever to the community in which the church is located. Protestantism has almost retreated from any effective religious ministry both to the downtown portions of cities and to the open country.

Denominationalism has made religion the most divisive and disruptive force in hundreds of communities, rather than the constructive, unifying, community building force which it should be. It has necessitated the secularizing of public education and the separation of religion from other great areas of living. Most issues out of which denominations originated are no longer relevant to current living; the real issues which now divide Christians do not correspond to our denominational structure but threaten intra-denominational integrity or are avoided and neglected in our church programs as being too dangerously controversial.

Much attention is given to the distinctive denominational heritage but almost none to the spiritual heritage of the community as such. Dogmatism, intolerance, and lack of inter-church fellowship have walled neighboring Christian groups off from one another and prevented the very sharing of testimony and comparing of experience which constitutes the creative asset of religious freedom. As our denominationalism has characteristically operated it has prevented or violated or wasted the finest potential values of our Protestant principles and heritage.

Two principal changes in our free enterprise system of religion will correct the worst weaknesses, preserve the assets, and actually insure a larger measure of freedom to the individual and the local church. The first of these is the surrender on the part of denominations of their assumption of absolute sovereignty. Just as our international relationships have reached the place where sheer human survival requires the surrender of enough national sovereignty so that a stable world order can be established, so our inter-denominational situation requires the kind of common planning and strategy that can come only on the basis of some limitation of denominational sovereignty.

This is not a limitation on religious freedom. Religious beliefs and practices are not involved, but only the relation of religious institutions to each other. Furthermore, religious freedom is most important to the individual, next most important to the local church group, and of questionable importance to an ecclesiastical system, which as often endangers as safeguards true religious freedom. If these ecclesiastical systems, which have no basis anyway in true Protestant principles, would modify their policies so as to make possible the operation of true councils of churches on each geographical level, all the assets of our Protestant freedom would be preserved and most of the liabilities liquidated.

The second change is closely related. It is to recognize the twofold relationship of the typical local church. Such a church is normally part of a *religious communion.* From this relationship it receives its distinctive spiritual heritage and testimony; it receives guidance and resource materials, its ministerial supply, and more or less guidance and counsel; it also participates through accredited agencies in world-wide missionary and benevolent activities. This relationship provides the individual and the church with a supporting fellowship for distinctive religious experience and testimony and enables them to go deeper and achieve greater stability than they could if they were surrounded only by a more heterogeneous religious fellowship. This relationship is well established in our Protestant church life. It is important and should be preserved.

But such a church is something more than a denominational outpost in the community. If it is to function locally so as to do its share in providing an efficient embodiment of Christ in the community, it must also be a part of a *religious community.* It is inevitably related to neighboring churches of other denominations through which Christ also seeks to work. This religious community may have a rich religious heritage to which each person is as much entitled as to his denominational heritage. These neighboring churches inevitably share a common task of evangelizing and Christianizing their community. They work under a common set of conditions including common allies and common enemies of their work, unlike those of churches even of the same denominations in other communities.

The local church's relationship to its *religious communion* identifies it with widely scattered churches which have a common distinctive religious heritage and a common background. Its relationship to its *religious community* identifies it with churches of a rich and varied heritage and background, but which are geographical neighbors, and share a common community heritage, a common task in that community, and a common set of conditions under which to do their work. In moving toward the Church of God's Design which would give Christ fresh and effective embodiment locally, the community relationship is, if anything, of greater importance than the communal relationship. Obviously, our churches and their whole constituencies need re-education to lift this community interchurch relationship to a place of importance fully equal to the communal interchurch relationship.

These geographical relationships would express themselves in truly effective councils of churches. Denominational agencies and officials would have to grant local churches enough freedom from denominational domination, to enable and encourage them to function effectively through such councils as genuine religious communities. This would be an extension rather than a limitation of true religious freedom. There is no reason why the co-operative churches of a whole city or country should not have as good a right as the scattered churches of a denomination to plan common programs of service, evangelism, fellowship, worship, education, and social action. In fact, the only designation of New Testament churches is by geographical areas rather than by denominations.

A major task of a liberating type of Christian education is the education and re-education of the church's constituency to these conceptions of the church. This will come primarily not through instruction but through experiences: experiences of local interchurch fellowship, planning, and program building, on a community-wide basis; experiences in reconstructing the church's own policies and attitudes and relationships; experiences in creative, forward looking churchmanship. These will constitute important elements in the curriculum.

How can the church grow through its inner tensions?

Our Protestant freedom with its resulting diversities leads inevitably to tensions within the total Christian fellowship. These can be divisive, destructive, and even paralyzing, as they have so often been, if they are not handled in such a way as to promote enrichment, cross-fertilization, and growth. Used constructively and educationally, these differences and their accompanying tensions can transform our Protestant denominationalism into the democratic, spiritually free, richly diverse Church of Christ. Such is the process of transforming these churches of man's disorder into the Church of God's Design.

But the strongest tensions among Christian groups today often exist within denominations and local churches. For, wherever there is genuine freedom, resulting diversities will produce tension. An institution which is alive has growing edges. Not all persons respond alike to similar situations. Some persons grow more rapidly than others in their insights, interests, and purposes. If there is an atmosphere of freedom, some persons in any group will be "progressive." They value experimenting with the new more than treasuring the old. Others will be "conservative." To protect tested and established values seems to them better than to risk them for untried ways. Unfortunate indeed is the church which does not have as its growing edge a group or a number of individuals, pulling the whole church forward toward new insights, larger commitments, and more venturesome undertakings. It is fortunate also that such proposals must meet the critical scrutiny of those who safeguard older values. The resulting tension *can* be destructive controversy, but it *should* be wholesome "growing pains."

The healthy institution, like the mentally healthy person, grows through solving problems, making choices among conflicting alternatives, effecting a synthesis of the best out of its past with the best that is new. The church which evades or avoids all matters on which opinions or feelings are divided is already half dead. It is like a person so sheltered from problems of adjustment that he never learns to think. For all real thinking is problem solving. These tensions, which represent the church's growing edge, constitute the most creative and significant part of its educational curriculum in churchmanship. When there is complete unanimity on every issue faced by a church, either it is evading all real issues or it is under totalitarian control. In either case, it is no true Protestant church.

What the church needs for handling tensions is a technique which insures complete democratic freedom, fair treatment of all opinions, a means of moving forward on the basis of majority judgment, but with minority viewpoints and their free expression carefully safeguarded. The bonds of Christian fellowship and mutual respect and confidence must be so carefully nurtured and strengthened that they can survive the frankest consideration of differences.

When a local church has the courage to foster the creative and pioneering experience which inevitably creates tensions; when it has mastered the educational and spiritual techniques of handling them; when it can resolve them on the ever higher level of synthesis; it will have developed its own provisions for healthy institutional growth. It will have demonstrated also how all Protestantism could move forward toward the Church of God's Design.

CHAPTER 8

What Is The Curriculum?

The Christian curriculum consists of those experiences essential to growth in Christlikeness. These cannot be imposed but must arise out of learner purpose. The environing Christian family and church help to arouse such purposes. The curriculum revolves around two poles: learner experience and the content of the Christian faith. The study program consists of units organized around each of these poles. The denominational source of most study materials limits their value. True Protestant nurture requires a broader orientation. Worship must be effectively related both to the religious heritage and the contemporary experience of the worshippers. Service, including experiences of responsible leadership, benevolence, missions, social action, and stewardship, is essential curriculum. Christian fellowship is the medium which gives spiritual quality to the curriculum. The entire church program, including preaching, is curriculum and should be systematically and democratically planned.

The Christian curriculum consists of those experiences of the growing person which arise from conditions so selected and organized as to lead him, at each successive stage of his development, into the most Christlike relationships with God and with his fellowmen of which he is capable. The curriculum itself is experience. But it is not just any kind of experience. Its quality and content are determined by the Christian faith. But the Christian faith cannot be imposed upon the growing person. He must achieve it through the necessary experiences.

Curriculum construction, or program building, then operates within the field of power between two poles — the current experience of the learner and the meaning and content of the Christian faith. Neither pole can be the exclusive determiner of procedure; neither can be overlooked.

To outline the kinds of experience essential to the Christian curriculum is one way of stating the objectives, for means and ends merge. The necessary experiences will involve the growing person in: (1) becoming acquainted with and accepting Jesus Christ as the revealer and interpreter of God; (2) finding in the life of the family and the church the embodiment of the love of God in human relationships; (3) finding security and peace in the forgiveness of God for his failures and wrongdoing, and power in the grace of God for walking in newness of life; (4) entrusting his future to the goodness and the power of God; (5) understanding and appropriating his spiritual heritage as embodied in the Bible and in Christian institutions, doctrines, and customs; (6) responding to the call of God to find his place of service in the work of the world; (7) actively discharging his responsibility for working with his fellow men to achieve a social order which increasingly fulfills the will of God; (8) seeking by witness and example to win others to Christian discipleship; and (9) sharing in the Christian world mission.

These experiences which are essential to the Christian curriculum can no more be imposed upon growing persons than its goals. Attempts to impose them will be abortive, resulting in experiences of quite a different quality. Therefore, the primary concern of the teacher or the teaching institution is to arouse within the learners the desire to have such experiences. Only in the degree that learner purposes coincide with teacher purpose can satisfactory experiences of learning be insured. Recognition of learner purpose as the essential core of the learning process is known as the "project principle." Any activity which carries out a learner purpose is a project. Regardless of the amount or the form of the activity, if it is carried out because the teacher wants it done and the learner sees no good way of avoiding it, there is no project. How can this project principle be followed in the Christian curriculum when its goals are derived from the Christian faith rather than from the natural impulses and tendencies of growing persons?

One way is for teachers and leaders to enter as deeply and as sympathetically as possible into the interests and purposes already present in the lives of the learners. Jesus went fishing with his disciples before he got them to go "fishing for men" with him. This develops a common ground of understanding upon the basis of which a larger sharing of purposes is possible. But even more basic is the functioning of the family and the church as embodiments in their group life of these goals and experiences. A primary driving force in human nature is the desire to "belong," to "rate." The child accepts and "internalizes" family practices as the way of identifying himself with the family. He does and likes what the gang requires as the condition of rating. If growing persons find themselves surrounded by an attractive and desirable religious community which is lovingly engaged in exemplifying Christlike living, they will appropriate these goals for themselves as the condition of acceptance and satisfactory participation in such a community. Learner purposes leading into the essential experiences of the Christian curriculum emerge out of the stimulating environment of family and community life which embody such purposes. The teaching program is not carried on "in a corner." But, granted this supporting environment, the curriculum is not left to chance. It is a carefully selected and organized sequence of provisions for essential experiences.

The organizing center of such a curriculum will alternate between (1) the emergent experiences and needs of the individual and his group as they face specific situations involving Christian choice and action, and (2) the sources for the enrichment and guidance of these experiences to be found in the Christian faith as recorded through race experience and as embodied in the living church. Whether the organizing center of a particular unit of the curriculum be contemporary learner experience or some major meaning or resource of the Christian faith, the curriculum itself, the "running course," still consists of learner experience. The essential meanings of the Christian faith for the individual can be acquired only through his own experiences. It is the function of the family and the church to provide such a rich and relevant environment that these two types of experience will tend to flow together. The nearer the basic Christian doctrines are embodied in daily living in family, church, and community, the more the two poles converge.

When the curriculum is so conceived the distinction between curriculum and method disappears. Method is simply the means or procedures used to enable a learning group to have the experiences essential to the desired outcomes. The curriculum will be organized as largely as possible around projects, and the method required will be determined by the nature of the project under way. Lesson courses or curriculum units will be more in the nature of procedure guides than of bodies of content. Of course, content will be involved, but the guidance provided will be in terms of the procedures needed in making this content contribute toward an experience of learning on the part of the learners. The curriculum itself is both content and method. Let us see what this means in the following illustrative situation:

Here is a class of high school girls in a Chicago church. They were chiefly interested in cosmetics, boys, and evading parental restrictions. Two or three of them had definite dramatic ambitions. Certainly their Sunday school lessons and the usual procedure did not interest them. Their teacher arranged a party for them in her home at which the principal feature was a cosmetics specialist and demonstrator, of good taste, a real artist, gladly supplied by a noted department store at no cost. She brought along a complete supply of all kinds of cosmetics and spent the afternoon interpreting to the girls the restrained and artistic use of cosmetics, and encouraging them to avoid the extremes to which girls using their first cosmetics so often go. She taught a truly significant lesson in womanliness and real charm, and certainly the girls profited by it and enjoyed it. They were now ready to follow their teacher anywhere.

Later, she picked up their dramatic interest, reading portions of Job and enabling them to sense something of its dramatic grandeur. The girls decided to work out their own dramatization of the whole story. When they had perfected it they gave a party for their own mothers and presented their version of Job. This led to its being given before a much larger group. The girls had discovered that the Bible can be a fascinating book and, some of them at least, had sensed some of the deeper meanings of this early approach to the agelong problem of evil and suffering.

Ideally, of course, the whole curriculum should be made up of such purposeful and creative experiences as these. But the limitations within which the ordinary church school program proceeds render impractical such a curriculum of free, emergent experiences. It is an ideal toward which to strive. Much of our work must follow a far more routine procedure because of limitations of qualified leadership, of time, and of facilities, and because of our necessary dependence upon guidance and source materials which would be unusable if they were rich and diverse enough to embody such a curriculum of emergent experience. Recognizing that the curriculum in its broadest and most creative form would consist of such units tied together in some sort of sequence and so skillfully motivated as to cover in a balanced way the whole range of desirable experience, we must define the practical curriculum which can operate in the typical church in much narrower terms.

Where do lesson courses come in?

We have already noted that curriculum and program are identical, since a program is a systematic provision for persons and groups to have the kinds of experience which will produce the desired changes in them. A part of this program is determined locally from week to week, as, for example, the preaching and the programs of midweek services.

But the resource and guidance materials for most of the study program are usually secured from some recognized publishing agency, in most cases denominational. These published materials are properly called curricular materials to indicate that they are merely the tools and resources of the true curriculum which is a program of actual experiences. These materials are of several types and are based upon different curriculum concepts.

The Uniform Lessons are both the most widely used and the least experience-centered of such courses. They are planned and used generally on the doubtful assumption that familiarity with fragments of Biblical material will result in desired Christian experiences. In order that the same Biblical material may be used for groups of all ages, these lessons deal chiefly with the narrative or story material of the Bible; older persons who depend on Uniform Lessons are left in comparative ignorance of what for them would be the most valuable of all Biblical material.

Uniform Lessons have usually dealt with fragments of Scripture, failing to develop true historical perspective or insight. They run in cycles which do not provide for progression or real growth in understanding. There has been improvement in all these respects, and the great advantage of the Uniform Lessons has been that they provide a "vertical" basis for unity in the program of all ages in home and church. In the editorial development of the outlines into lesson helps, in the actual teaching of the lessons, and in the outlines themselves in more recent cycles, there has been recognition that the Biblical material must be brought into functional relationship with experience. Much attention has been given to the "application" of the lesson to life. The result is that "life" is dealt with, but only in a fragmentary, superficial, and verbal manner so that seldom is any thorough approach made to any of the great trunkline experiences of Christian living. But this concern about the "application" often eclipses genuine Bible study; consequently, neither subject matter nor experience receives effective treatment.

Group-graded or departmental-graded lessons provide courses for each of the yearly grades through high school. These lessons are much more closely related to the experiences of the respective age-groups. In general, they are organized around the major bodies of religious knowledge such as the Life of Christ, heroes of the Old Testament, early Christian leaders, missions, and church history. A disadvantage of such materials has been their failure to provide for any "vertical" unity, or any common themes which helped to unify the experiences of the whole family or the whole church constituency of all ages.

Recent trends in denominational curriculum development show two significant improvements. The first is that common "vertical" themes such as the "life of Christ" or "the church" are set up for a whole year, or a shorter period, and then the materials for each age-group, no less thoroughly graded, are related to this theme. Without sacrificing the graded principle, this plan supports the equally important principle of unity. The second improvement is that the curriculum is planned for joint use of home and church. Equal care is given to material for the parents and for use in the family and to related material for the teachers and for use in the church. These improvements also make it much easier to relate to each other that part of the program based on curricular materials or lesson courses and those parts of the program which are developed locally, such as preaching, mid-week meetings, and service projects.

Other common types of "handed down" curricular materials are young people's society topics, and themes and study materials for missionary societies. In addition, for young people and adults, are many elective courses from which local groups can develop their own study program. When electives are based on interest or felt need they are likely to be closer to experience than the "handed down" type. But they are also likely to be less well balanced in emphasis and more fragmentary.

A major limitation on the quality and adequacy of the study materials now in use throughout the Protestant churches is their denominational source. The prevalent system of denominationally produced curricular materials is based upon two false assumptions: (1) that the curricular needs of the constituency of each denomination are peculiar, and therefore can be met only by materials produced for that particular constituency; and (2) that the curricular needs of the constituency of each denomination are so nearly the same — east, west, north, or south; rural or urban; small church or large; industrial, suburban, or campus — that one nationally uniform system of materials will meet all needs.

The first of these assumptions has not prevented a great deal of co-operative production of materials. Much of the basic structure in terms of lesson outlines is produced interdenominationally. There has been considerable syndication of the actual materials, the same publication coming out under the imprint of several denominational publishers and so being made "satisfactory" to the constituency of each. This has effected some economies. But, except in such isolated instances, the denominational system remains intact. In fact, the last two decades have seen a trend away from the use of common outlines and syndication, and toward the development "from scratch" of denominational systems of materials. This is providing some extremely valuable experimentation. It is making the present a period of creativity in study materials. It does not, however, carry us toward any real solution to the need for better and more adequate curricular materials for Protestantism as a whole.

If it is the purpose of Christian education in each denomination to provide its constituency with the richest resources and incentives for entering into their full Christian and Protestant heritage, then the needs of one denomination are generally so nearly like those of the others that by far the greater proportion of the needed material could be common to all. To the extent that the leaders or agencies of each denomination feel that their own constituents require material or emphases peculiar to themselves, special needs could be met in a small portion of the materials. Such portions would be distributed only among the churches of that denomination for which the special material was prepared. However, a better expression of true Protestantism would be to include in the materials for all, the rich variety of these peculiarities, as our testimony to each other. Thus, those in each denomination would be introduced to their own particular heritage and testimony, but they would have the enriching experience of being exposed also to the peculiarities of many others. There could be an actual face to face sharing of these testimonies by neighboring church groups at the community level. The great common ground on the basis of which a real religious community is possible would be revealed, as would be the enriching contributions which are available from our various traditions.

The only valid argument against such a comprehensive and fair incorporation in our study materials of our total Protestant heritage, is the charge that it might weaken denominational loyalties. Surely, though, the main objective of our study program is not merely to preserve our denominational separateness and the prejudices upon which it is based; or to prevent the exposure of our growing generation to alternative Christian interpretations and experiences. Would not a Christian faith resulting from a fair consideration of our total Protestant heritage be more virile than one resulting from exclusive exposure to one particular interpretation? It is easy to see which of these policies is more like that of the medieval authoritarian church and which is more an expression of true original Protestant principles. The general policy based upon this assumption that each Protestant denomination must have curricular materials peculiar to it alone is one basic weakness in Protestant Christian education. It is interesting to hear a denominational publisher himself violate this assumption when he proudly reports how wide the circulation of his own materials is in other denominations! There are denominational differences. It seems probable, however, that they could be dealt with more educationally and more constructively by co-operatively produced materials with denominational adaptations than by the present prevalent denominational systems.

But the greatest weakness, educationally, is in the second assumption — that the constituency of each denomination is so homogeneous that its curricular needs can be met by one denominational system of study materials. It is economically possible for the very largest denominations to provide some variety in their lesson systems, allowing some selection on the part of the users; but medium sized denominations cannot produce any considerable variety; and the smaller denominations often have to be satisfied with imprint editions of materials made available by one of the larger denominations, and perhaps slightly "adapted" to their needs. Local churches do, however, exert much greater freedom of choice than the denominational system contemplates, for in nearly all denominations, there is a large circulation of the materials published by "independent" publishers. The selling strength of these materials rests in their expert adaptation, not to any one denomination, but to a particular, well-defined type of constituency within many denominations. This illustrates the fact that the study course needs within the heterogeneous constituency of a nationwide denomination are too varied to be met by any simple denominational system.

But the means to the solution of this problem is not the independent commercial publisher. The denominational publishing house has rendered an inestimable and indispensable educational service to the Protestant churches. It will and should continue to do so. Practically every substantial improvement in the study course systems of Protestant denominations have involved these publishers in financial risks and losses. The kinds of materials desired by the educational leaders of the denominations could never have been produced as a sheerly commercial venture. The forward moving educational program has been supported by appropriate materials only because back of the educational boards have been educationally-minded rather than commercially-minded publishers. These publishers have already formed a Co-operative Publishers' Association and are preparing for the next forward step toward a better study program for Protestantism. Let us see what it should be like.

What is needed is the co-operative development and publication of a great variety of curricular units for every age group and every type of constituency. These should be produced in a variety of forms. For the most part they should be undated. The custom of dating the study course materials is extremely wasteful, costing our churches a considerable proportion of what they put into these materials and rendering them practically worthless except for the one time they are used. These rich and varied resources of study materials should then be handled by the denominational publishers with the help of carefully prepared "lesson course guides." These guides would help the educational committee or teaching staff of each local church to formulate their own teaching aims, goals, or emphases in line with their particular situation or needs. The guides would enable them to select from the rich resources available the program materials which would be most effective in carrying out their purposes. This would make it possible for a given church or all the neighboring churches of a community to plan a program directly related to their needs, to their resources of leadership, and to the general work of the church or community.

To begin with, many churches would still prefer to have someone else do this planning for them, and simply hand down to them "the lesson for the day". Each publisher could compile out of the rich resources available such a handed down system for those who wanted it and they would be as well off as they are now. But, for the growing number of churches wishing to develop their study program as an integral part of a total church program, the curriculum guides offer a far better system, showing them how to set up their program and furnishing them with rich and varied resources. Denominational materials could be introduced where needed, but their place in the total would accurately symbolize the significance of what is peculiar to the denomination in comparison with what it has in the common Protestant and Christian heritage. This would set the church's study program in the direction of an ecumenical Protestantism rather than squarely athwart its pathway, as in the present situation with denominationally earmarked materials.

A good start in this direction has already been made by the Co-operative Publishers' Association in the production of texts for leadership education, for the vacation church school, and for the week day church school. Similarly, the Missionary Education Movement (now a part of the National Council of Churches), under the imprint of the Friendship Press, has produced annual series of missionary education texts and reading books. These have been planned and produced interdenominationally. They have followed annual "vertical" themes or emphases, have been graded to the use of various age groups, and have provided an enriching and unifying basis for an all-Protestant program of missionary education. To apply this principle all along the line would make available much richer sources of material at lower cost. Such might have been the outcome of the proposed "International Curriculum" cited in Chapter III.

These curriculum developments for the vacation church school and the weekday church school and missionary education have as a whole been more experience-centered than has been true of much widely used Sunday school material. The vacation church school has available larger blocks of time in much closer sequence. This has encouraged a more varied and freer program. The week day church school, usually under professional leadership, and influenced by its close relationship with the public school, has developed much indigenous curriculum. Some of this has been excellent from the viewpoint of an experience curriculum.

With the dependence of its lay, largely untrained leadership upon these handed down curricular materials, how can the actual on-going program in the local church become more an experience curriculum, thereby producing much better results in learning to live the Christian life?

For one thing, the most learningful experiences are sometimes sought, not by confronting actual situations, but by reading about them or hearing stories, or the testimony of those who have participated in them. Interest in missions and participation in missionary support come from reading missionary stories, seeing pictures, hearing the testimony of missionaries on furlough. Very few of the millions who share in the missionary enterprise ever actually see the mission field situation. Yet they have a real missionary experience vicariously. Studying the messages of the Old Testament prophets may open the eyes of present day churchmen to social injustices of which they were unaware. Kagawa cites the reading of Drummond's *The Greatest Thing in the World* and reading about the work of Frederick Denison Maurice and Arnold Toynbee for the depressed laboring classes of England, as turning his attention to the slums of Kobe and Osaka where he went to live and to share in and relieve their misery.[1] A lesson on gratitude for the many workers who serve us and provide for our comfort, welfare, and safety — such as the postman, the milkman, the policeman — may for the first time open the eyes of children to really see these workers. Sometimes experience proceeds from knowledge to actual situations rather than vice versa. Where it seems difficult to begin with real life situations, it may often be possible to begin with information and end with confronting actual situations.

Is there a place for content courses?

A complete Christian curriculum would be comprised of two major types of courses or learning programs. First would be programs whose organizing center consists of the principal experiences in Christian living. These would begin with or be based upon the situations, problems, responsibilities, and relationships involved in daily living. Their purpose would be to bring this living, or samples of it, under the influence, enrichment, and control of Christian leadership and group life and lift it to a religious level.

[1] Wade Crawford Barclay, *The Church and A Christian Society* (New York: Abingdon Cokesbury, 1939), pp. 249, 250.

To guide in bringing these experiences to a Christian level it is necessary to give systematic study to the sources of Christian evaluation and motivation. Consequently, the program must provide for systematic and intelligent Bible study to equip the growing Christian with this background of evaluation and judgment. Such Bible study should not be a mere proof text method of supporting our opinions and prejudices. It should be an open-minded search for the original meaning of Biblical material. It must follow certain canons of literary study if it is to be sincere and fruitful. Three such rules apply: (1) There must be a sincere effort always to give the words of an author, as nearly as possible, the very meaning which he originally intended. This requires a considerable knowledge of the author, the background out of which he wrote, his reasons for writing, and the situation which he was addressing. (2) Each passage must be interpreted in the light of its context and of the general meaning and character of the whole book of which it is a part. (3) Each passage should be read and interpreted for the kind of literature it is: poetry as poetry, drama as drama, history as history, folklore as folklore.

To deal with Biblical material in this honest and objective way requires serious and thorough courses in Biblical introduction. It calls for a broad approach to whole books or groups of books, an understanding of the special interests, purposes, and contributions of various writers, and some insight into the historic backgrounds of the various periods during which Scriptures were being composed. Such courses would be heavier in content than most of the familiar types of Bible study. They would move away from literal interpretation of fragments out of a "flat" Bible into a real historical approach to understanding the Bible as a body of sacred literature.

There will be content courses involved in an adequate approach to the other areas of experience as well: studies in the content of Christian belief; in the nature of children; in family relationships; in church history; in understanding the labor movement, the liquor problem, and international relations; and in knowing about the church's missionary and benevolent enter-prises. Sometimes a project in personal religious living, in family life, or in Christian social action will call for such a content course to provide needed enrichment and guidance. Sometimes this type of content course will suggest timely and important projects. The organizing center of curriculum procedure, then, may alternate between life situation or on-going experiences and bodies of information and interpretation which enrich and guide such experiences. When content courses are thus directly related to on-going experience, they are functional rather than purely academic. The whole curriculum is either directly or indirectly experience-centered.

This alternation between the content and the life situation or "experience" approach is illustrated in the general organization of the co-operatively published materials. The Standard Leadership curriculum "general courses" include Religion in Personal and Social Life, the Bible, the Church, Psychology and Methods for Church Leaders, and Missionary Education. Then follow courses for workers in each of the departmental age groups, and in Leadership Development and Administration. The Co-operative Week-day Church School Series are organized into four areas of study: the Bible, Christian Living, God's World, and the Church. A given school may follow one of these areas or make an elective combination of them. Similarly the Co-operative Vacation Church School texts present the areas: God and His World, Jesus, Our Bible Heritage, Church, Personal Relationships (Christian character), and Wider Relationships.

Are sermons curriculum?

While theoretically the Bible and Bible study are central in the Protestant church program, actually in the great majority of churches it is the sermon which is central. Is the sermon to be regarded as an integral part of the curriculum for those toward whom it is directed, or is it a special function not subject to the ordinary laws or conditions of teaching and learning? There are sharply divergent opinions on this. Some hold that preaching is in a class by itself. The early church differentiated it from teaching by using the term *kerygma* for preaching and *didache* for teaching. Preaching takes place in a special context and setting, the corporate worship service. It enjoys an unparalleled prestige and place of authority in Christian tradition and custom. It is consequently greeted with a unique expectancy by the worshippers. In a peculiar sense the preacher is the mouthpiece of God's direct message. He proclaims the divine events of the gospel, the acts of God requiring human response. Preaching may be regarded, then, as the special means through which the Holy Spirit guides the hearers into all truth. This might justify its position as the center of attention and its irrelevance to most of that which is considered curriculum. It would be difficult to explain the preponderant investments made in its preaching program by the typical Protestant church except upon such assumptions as these.

But if they are no more than mere assumptions, shouldn't they be examined? Many preachers teach adult classes. Is there an essentially different quality, authenticity, and authority in their words in the two situations? Laymen sometimes preach. Do they truly preach, or do they merely teach from behind a pulpit? Is the Holy Spirit limited to one form of discourse? Do the outcomes of either teaching or preaching depend upon the response of the hearers? Are those responses determined by a different set of psychological laws or factors even though hearers might sit in the very same pews to be taught by a man of God one hour and to be preached to by the same man the next hour? In fact, aren't false assumptions regarding the efficacy of sermons preventing many a church from developing a real program of adult Bible study and Christian learning? By preaching alone, how many ministers have effected in the lives of their hearers the changes toward which the preaching was aimed? The assumptions underlying much authoritarian preaching actually makes the preacher responsible for results which are seldom evident in the lives of his hearers.

Isn't this irrational prestige accorded sermons the stronghold of the very un-Protestant authoritarianism which so hampers the true Protestant principle?

Whichever view one takes, certainly the preaching program would be even more effective if it followed the principles of sound curriculm development, were integrated with the other elements in the learning program, and took into account the psychological laws of learning.

The program of preaching should be based more upon a careful and objective survey of the interests, needs, deficiencies, and capacities or aptitudes of the learners than upon the particular interests or experiences of the curriculum maker or preacher. Educationally-minded preachers like to engage some of their lay constituents with them in planning the preaching program, or at least its immediate objectives and emphases. Check lists, questionnaires, opinion scales, exploratory discussions, and interviews are means of discovering the needs and deficiencies which should be considered. The preaching program should be an integral part of the total program which includes the work of many of the church groups. Sermons which are not only isolated from each other but from other activities and experiences which the learners are having, may have far less effect than their sheer merit as sermons deserves. The isolated experience of listening to a sermon, however good it may be, is seldom enough to effect needed change. It should be a part of a larger and more varied whole. Even to support it with a worship theme is not enough.

In planning the preaching program as curriculum, its relationship to larger bodies of content should be considered. It should often be accompanied by related Bible study or reading materials, or suggested observation, experiment, or interview. Anything to get the sermon reflected upon or related to other experiences will increase its educational value. If the preaching program could be integral to the discussion, thinking, and study of some of the study groups, the effectiveness of both would be strengthened. If the sermon could raise questions or set problems for discussion groups, it would become educationally effective. In fact, a sermon which is worth listening to at all deserves much more than mere listening.

The preaching program should be so planned that those who participate in it regularly really arrive somewhere in terms of systematic understanding, knowledge, and use of the Bible, Christian doctrine, techniques of personal religious living, Christian interpretation of social issues and problems, and the program of Christianity for the redemption of mankind. The irregularity of church attendance may seem to require the minister to make every program self-contained. This, however, sacrifices the on-going educational and spiritual needs of the regular attendants to the current interests of the irregular. Perhaps if the preaching program assumed a more regular attendance and a more continuous experience, it might actually achieve this more thorough process.

By far the greatest hope for real adult education in our churches rests with the minister. If his preaching program could be made the center of a comprehensive educational curriculum for his people, the vital growth of the church in the ways we have already suggested would be assured. Until the preacher accepts the basic responsibility for effecting the needed changes in his adult constituency, and uses educational means of harnessing his preaching program to this task, there is not a great deal of hope for an adult education renaissance in the church. But a reconstructed preaching program, integral to the total curriculum of experiences needed, would have a good chance to accomplish the required transformation.

What is the place of worship?

Worship can and should be the very heart of the experience curriculum. When experience reaches the truly religious level it partakes of the essence of worship. It is the inclusion of the worship experience which makes Christian education most distinctive from education in general. The most churchly function of the church, that which most distinguishes it from other group life, is its function of worship. The identification of the individual with the beloved community is probably best symbolized in the corporate worship program. But we face some real problems in attempting to make the worship life of the church integral to its educational program.

The materials and procedures of worship have seemingly undergone much less reconstruction than other elements of the curriculum in order to bring them into line with the experience-centered point of view.[2] We can best understand this relative stability in worship materials and procedures if we have a thorough understanding of the true nature of worship. The essence of the worship experience is, of course, a realization of God's presence and a feeling of being in communion with him. In addition to providing the conditions for this experience with God, the corporate worship service is properly designed, not only to develop a sense of identification on the part of the individual with the beloved community, but also with the whole "communion of the saints," the church universal and the church through the ages. To this end, its content includes symbolic materials in art, literature, liturgy, and ceremony which come out of the past and may seem to be very slightly related to the current on-going experience of the worshippers. The Bible itself comes out of the ancient world from a people who were different from us. It is usually read in a language which is strange and archaic. The hymns reflect theological concepts and religious experiences and sentiments which are unreal and even out of harmony with much of our actual teaching and preaching. The prayers may seem to assume actions of God and concepts of life and the universe which are inconsistent with our common sense or scientific views and with our inner experience, and so seem unreal. We do not really mean what the prayers say. As a result the worship experience seems to involve a definite break with present vital and on-going experience, and to constitute something of an escape into an unreal and mysterious world.

[2] Harrison S. Elliott, *Can Religious Education Be Christian?* (New York: The Macmillan Company, 1941), pp. 288, 289.

The general conception of God implied throughout the public worship service emphasizes his transcendence far more than his immanence. He is separate from natural processes; his relationship to human affairs is maintained more through special providences than the normal processes of living; his will is arbitrary rather than embodied in the reality of the universe: these are the general assumptions underlying much public worship. The sermon, which usually constitutes the dominant element in the corporate worship service, is frequently, in its tone and function, authoritarian, dogmatic, or merely hortatory; such a sermon does not provide the guidance and the setting for a genuinely worshipful meditation and problem-solving experience. It is not integral to an experience-centered curriculum.

In developing the study features of the educational program in the direction of an experience curriculum, quite a different approach to worship is involved. For if the study program is to reach a truly religious or God-conscious level it must lead into worship experiences and be continuous with them. When it does, the meaning and content of such worship experiences will be quite unlike the ordinary public worship service. The beginning point will be the problems, needs, and enterprises of current living. Materials and procedures out of the past will be drawn upon for purposes of guidance and enrichment, but the test of their usefulness will be their reality and their relevance to present experience. Consequently they will be carefully selected and evaluated on the basis of their meaning and value for today. Worship will be correlated with study, not by approaching materials which have similar content from two very different points of view, but by pursuing the study experience into the very presence of God, there to see our problems, needs, enterprises, and resources as they look when God looks at them with us and releases through us his own resources for responsible and consecrated living.

The general emphasis in such an experience is upon the immanence of God, upon his presence in and action through the natural processes of his universe. Although our human dependence upon him is recognized, emphasis is placed upon our meeting the conditions which will release his power and accomplish his will, rather than upon petitioning him to take over and solve our problems for us. Such worship will be more a reverent and earnest search to discover the will of God than listening to an authoritarian proclamation of it. It will involve quiet and relaxed meditation upon one's needs, problems, and responsibilities, in which one does his own best thinking for himself, instead of merely accepting the results of the thinking of someone else. It will empower one to meet the demands of courageous living by the immediate experience of God's presence and of consequent spiritual resources, rather than merely stimulate one through exhortation.

It is clear that unless the study program leads into experience upon this worship level it will lack both the insights and the dynamic of religious experience. But it is equally clear that much of our public worship does not provide this kind of experience. If we cannot find a way to bridge the gap between the kind of worship which is integral to an experience study curriculum, and the kind which prevails as corporate worship, we face several serious problems. How can we provide for children the kind of corporate worship experience which will be real and meaningful to them, and at the same time develop in them the experience of churchmanship by identification with the corporate church? How can we prevent one kind of worship's competing with or creating dissatisfaction with the other? How can we make use of the rich resources of traditional worship materials and techniques in such a way as to edify and guide current experience rather than seeming to retreat from or ignore it?

The solution is probably not to adopt either one or the other of the approaches as the right one or the exclusive one. Both have values. Extreme emphasis upon either the transcendence or immanence of God neglects important truths and needed values. Though our worship experience should be consistent with our scientific knowledge about the universe, and our use of prayer should be in accordance with both sound psychology and sound theology, the worship experience itself may well carry one beyond the realm of sense experience and of scientific concepts into the realm of spiritual Reality apprehendable only through what Sorokin calls the "superconscious." This does not rule out the search for God through sense experience and reasoning processes. It recognizes that there is a realm of human experience with God, sometimes called mysticism, to which there is enough testimony to require the recognition of its validity. Worship is not understood or experienced in its fullness except as this realm of experience with God is taken into account. Our total approach to worship in program building should make use of the values of both these conceptions of worship, and should seek to combine their values and eliminate their weaknesses.

The total worship life of the church for all age groups and in all phases of the program should be regarded as a major curriculum enterprise. It should be approached, not in fragments, but as a whole. It should be undertaken, not in isolation from the study, fellowship, service, and other elements of the program, but as integral and indispensable to them. The public worship, including the preaching, is neither an isolated element nor the central determining factor in the total program. It is one element in a whole program in which all elements should be considered interdependent. If the total program is to be mutually supporting and consistent throughout, no part of it will be determined except in proper relationship with the whole. This calls for a general planning committee or series of committees with provisions for co-ordination, so that all who are responsible for program development can work as a part of the whole.

Out of this planning it is to be expected that such revisions and adjustments will be made in the various worship and study programs, that the worship experiences which are continuous with study, will also lead naturally into participation with interest and profit in the corporate worship of the church.

One type of worship may be informal, the other formal, but the theological and psychological assumptions and foundations will be the same. Both will be vibrant with present day meaning. The rich resources of the past will be drawn upon, not for their own sakes or merely to put on a colorful and stately program, but for their functional value in enriching and guiding current experience. The variety of experience, which is the basic assumption of our Protestant heritage, will call for varieties of opportunity for worship. Yet the unifying effect of the corporate worship experience will be carefully sought.

What are essential service experiences?

If Christlikeness is learned through typically Christlike experiences, certainly service will have a large place in such a curriculum. In our simple fourfold outline of the program, service includes several types of experience which cannot here be more than briefly outlined. These are: (1) service or leadership in the church's own programs; (2) Christian leadership in community activities and agencies outside the church; (3) helpfulness to those in need — usually called "benevolences"; (4) participation in the Christian mission throughout the world; (5) engagement in Christian social action to help bring about a more Christlike social order; (6) a total stewardship philosophy and practice. The great majority of persons are dependent upon the church to arrange for them or provide them with the opportunities for most of these types of service activity.

1. When the church's own program lacks an abundance of well-qualified and motivated leadership, it is evidence that the curriculum as a whole or the method followed in the program is defective. There may be a lack of emphasis upon such service as an essential experience for growing Christians. But the program should be so conducted as to reveal and develop the latent leadership ability which is present in any normal group of persons. That is one of the difficulties with the traditional transmissive and authoritarian program. It is leader-centered

rather than learner-centered, so that most of the activity and responsibility is assumed by the leader. This leaves the members of the learning group passive and receptive, and gives them no opportunity to develop leadership skill through their own experience. Such a leader makes and keeps the group dependent upon him rather than qualifying them to take the initiative and undertake responsibilities which will develop some of them naturally and inevitably into able leaders. The first by-product of a creative and experience-centered program is competent leadership to carry that program on even though the original leadership be withdrawn.

When people who have the latent ability to qualify for effective service in the church's program decline to do so, they give evidence that the whole spiritual life of the church is at a low level. Eagerness to serve and willingness to put forth serious effort to qualify are inevitable outcomes of a deep spiritual life. The leadership problem cannot be solved by pleas or exhortations or appeals to duty. It will disappear before a program which centers the learning process in the active participation of every person in the group in some responsible share in the program. Whatever program activity goes on in the parish, one of its purposes should always be to develop future leadership for that activity through an apprenticeship participation.

2. The church which absorbs in its own program all the leadership ability and motivation which it is able to produce, cuts itself off from its most effective means of influencing the community at large. Not only should the regular program of the church produce automatically all the leadership which that program needs; it should also produce a surplus of well-qualified and motivated Christian leadership for many of the organizations and programs in the community outside the church. These other community organizations, such as school boards, PTA's, clubs, lodges, municipal agencies, recreational groups, and service agencies, constitute much of the life of the community. Most of their leadership is voluntary. That

leadership exerts a profound influence upon the moral and spiritual climate of the community. If the churches absorb in the running of their own programs all the able leadership which they produce, then these other dominant influences of the community will be manned for the most part by non-Christian leaders. The churches can hardly expect their whole-hearted support for the ideals of personal and social living for which the churches should stand. The churches, therefore, by default in this matter of leadership, will have permitted much of the community life to fall under leadership which does not share the ideals of the churches. It would be hard to imagine a more shortsighted or abortive policy.

On the other hand, when the church program so centers in responsible and worthwhile Christian activities that a surplus of able leadership is produced, and when the churches consequently are able to dedicate or commission some of the best of this leadership to find their places of service in secular community agencies, the churches have inevitably projected their ideals and influences into the life of the whole community. This in turn creates the kind of moral and spiritual climate which makes easier and more fruitful the actual program of the church itself. The curriculum of service enlistment and training, then, should provide for this double range of competent Christian service.

3. What could be more Christian than loving ministries of helpfulness to those who are unfortunate or under-privileged? Such experiences are a part of the curriculum of Christlikeness. But of all parts of the program of Christlike experiences, this is one of the most difficult to administer. Three dangers must be avoided. First, needed help should be rendered in a way to avoid making the recipient continuously dependent upon it, or in any way subservient to those who render the help. Rather the recipient should be encouraged and enabled to become self-reliant and independent. Second, the relationship should be one of Christian love, which means mutual respect. Regard for the personal worth and self-respect of a

person or a family receiving help is the only Christlike attitude in rendering service. Third, such relief measures must never be undertaken in a spirit of virtuous superiority, or as a substitute for the kind of Christian social action needed to reconstruct society in order to remove the preventable causes of human distress and misfortune. The difference in economic status which makes one person the giver and the other the receiver of benevolence is all too often due to the fact that one is the beneficiary and the other the victim, directly or indirectly, of conditions regarding which every Christian should be humble and penitent.

Thus, in modern, complex society the Christlike motive and concern to help those in distress may find expressions quite different in form from the ministries of Jesus. Motives, originating largely in his example, have resulted in the establishing of social service agencies whose professional staffs, through scientifically valid methods, administer relief in ways designed to avoid the above dangers. Much of the social service opportunity which the church will incorporate in its curriculum of Christlike living will consist in support of voluntary agencies of social service through the church or the community chest. Cases of need coming to the attention of Christians will often be best handled by referral to such agencies. When the church does bring its members into direct relationship with those in need, it will be to add the Christlike "plus" of personal fellowship, respect, and love to the efficient service rendered by professionally manned agencies.

Those responsible for planning and developing the church's program of Christlike activities through which its members grow and embody Christ, face one of their most difficult problems in this realm of social service. They must avoid the dangers we have noted above. They must provide opportunities for growing Christians to express the personal fellowship, concern, and love of Christ toward the unfortunate and underprivileged. Otherwise, how can they meet Christ's own test of the Last Judgment, "As you did it to one of the least of these my brethren, you did it to me"? (Matthew 25:40) Yet they must avoid engaging untrained, voluntary lay workers in promiscuous service activities which will hinder or confuse the systematic programs of the social service agencies. This calls for a carefully and prayerfully wrought policy which will guide all the groups and program activities of the churches as a whole. This policy should relate the church intelligently and constructively to the social service agencies of its community, but it should not depersonalize the service motive to the extent of limiting it to financial contributions to professional agencies. Also, the whole social service program should be integral to the study, worship, and fellowship elements in the program. Each of these types of experience require service motives and experiences of loving helpfulness to Christ as he is embodied in the human suffering and need visible to all whose eyes are dedicated to him.

4. Christ's concern for world evangelization, embodied in the Great Commission (Matthew 28:18-20), becomes the concern of everyone who would be Christlike. Missions is not an "elective" in the Christian curriculum, even though some Christians and some churches have acted as though it were. The fact that missionary administration, with the securing of the needed funds, has usually been the responsibility of one agency, whereas Christian education has been that of another, has all too frequently separated missionary education from Christian education as a whole. Just as the separation of evangelism from Christian education weakens and impairs both, so the Christian mission throughout the world and the local church program of Christian education are indispensable to each other. The better curricular materials are increasingly taking this into account.

The missionary phase of Christian education is designed to do more than disseminate missionary information or increase missionary offerings. Its aim is to grow missionary persons. This involves growing Christians in the most vivid and realistic relationships possible with those people around the world on behalf of whom they have missionary concern and responsibility. Fortunately many means of doing this effectively are available in the modern program. Pictures, slides, films, curios, exhibits, dramatics, correspondence, interchange of gifts or pictures or scrapbooks, visits of missionaries on furlough, visits of Christian nationals, and reports from world travelers are all means of enriching the missionary program. In many cases the most effective participation is in specific projects of mission work with which the local group can have more or less continuous contact. The interpretation of missions as world fellowship helps to prevent the attitudes of superiority and patronage which impair the Christian spirit of missions as well as of social service. Those responsible for planning the total church program should emphasize the integral place of missions within the program rather than the distinctiveness of this type of Christlike experience.

5. Our understanding of the processes and determining forces through which persons become Christlike emphasizes the influence of cultural patterns and social relationships. The aim of developing Christlike persons is futile without the corresponding aim of engaging them in more Christlike relationships through improved institutional and social life. To seek or receive or enter into the Kingdom of God means to engage in efforts to make God's will authoritative in all of life. A Christian who seeks or receives or enters into relations which violate Christlike living is not seeking the Kingdom of God. There are two reasons why a curriculum of Christlike experiences must include opportunities and responsibilities for Christian social action designed to make the will of God authoritative in the social order.

First, Christlikeness involves one in bearing testimony against institutions and relationships which violate human welfare and so thwart the purposes and will of God. To find appropriate and effective ways of embodying this testimony in action ls essential experience in becoming more Christlike. A growing Christian cannot wholly withdraw from the evil of this world.

His embodiment of Christ and his growth in Christlikeness consist in part in his resistance against that evil and his efforts to overcome it in both his own life and the lives of others. Consequently, engaging growing Christians in deliberate and determined action to accomplish these "unfinished tasks of the Kingdom of God," as Dr. Coe calls them,[3] is close to the heart of any curriculum of Christlike experiences. Christians must be led to come to grips effectively with the entrenched evils in our cultural, institutional, and social patterns, in which they are inevitably more or less implicated, for the salvation of their own souls. To condone or acquiesce, or do anything but resist, is to forsake Christ.

Christians need opportunity to unite their efforts with others through the church in effective social action because only by such corporate action have they any hope of effecting the needed changes. The churches during this century have been phenomenally successful in enlisting members. (The growth has been at a rate more than double that of population growth!) But this success has been offset by their tragic failure to curb the mounting evils in our economic, political, and international relationships which defy and thwart the will of God and prevent individual Christians from Christlike social relationships. Our present world-wide predicament is the consummation of the preoccupation of churches and church members with personal piety to the neglect of social responsibility. Christian social action is not an "elective" or an afterthought in the curriculum of Christlike experiences. It comes close to being the very heart of it.

As we have previously observed, the experiences of resistance to entrenched evil and of seeking the government of God in which Christians need to engage in order to develop their own Christlike qualities, coincide with those enterprises of Christian social action which they need to undertake corporately in order

[3] George A. Coe, *What is Christian Education?* (New York: Charles Scribner's Sons, 1929), p. 162 ff.

to achieve a social order in which Christlike living is possible. The church's study, worship, service, and fellowship program, therefore, is not something separate from its responsibility to engage its members in effective social action. A program of social action is indispensable to the completeness and the effectiveness of everything else which the church attempts to do. The casual or negative way in which responsibility for social action is regarded in the program policies and plans of the majority of churches accounts in large measure for the futility and frustration with which any realistic Christian must regard our mounting church membership statistics. This is perhaps the greatest unsolved problem of contemporary churchmanship.

6. Underlying all these aspects of the service element in a curriculum of Christlike experiences, is one's basic attitude toward his own abilities and talents, his vocation, his income, and his property. A corollary of the original Protestant principles of universal priesthood and direct personal responsibility to God was the abolition of the distinction between the sacred and the secular. One's abilities are called "talents" to emphasize the trusteeship principle of the Parable of the Talents. The term "vocation" means literally a "calling" of God. A true Protestant Christian cannot enter a "secular" occupation. He is called of God whether to the ministry, the mission field, the factory, or the farm. This means that income and property resulting from occupation are also God's, the recipient being only a trustee. If this basic stewardship principle is central in the curriculum of experiences provided by the church, the foregoing aspects of the service program will all be essential expressions of it. They will arise naturally and will enlist the needed support both in personnel and finance as indispensable curriculum experiences. Stewardship is not a special feature, or a peculiar notion of some Christians, or a device to keep the church out of debt. It is an essentially Christlike attitude, central to Christlike living.

Is fellowship part of the curriculum?

We have already noted the importance of the church congregation's being the "beloved community" in which growing persons have opportunity for relationships and group life beyond the family and in a community where the love principle prevails. It is obvious that fellowship is the principal medium of this community influence. This sets a high standard for all the fellowship life of the church and all its groups. The church's fellowship is not merely a means of attracting persons within reach of a religious program. It is itself a means of growing in Christlikeness. No part of the total curriculum deserves more careful planning and leadership. Just because much of the social and fellowship life of the secular community may be negative in its bearing upon Christlike experience, the church's fellowship, while equally attractive and joyous, must be positive and rich in Christlike qualities.

In the past the church's disapproval of the negative influences of much of the social and recreational life of the community has been expressed in placing some forms of amusement or recreation under the ban. Sometimes this has been quite irrational, as, for example, when a church prohibits its young people from participating in well-chaperoned high school dances, but actually encourages them to frequent a commercial, unchaperoned skating rink with a far lower moral tone than the high school.[4] Most of our more liberal churches have seen such inconsistency and have lifted the ban on "worldly amusements." All this has done is to abolish one of the rapidly diminishing distinctions between Christians and non-Christians. The church's proper concern is not so much with the form which the recreation or group fellowship takes as the essential quality of the relationships involved. This concern is best expressed by providing under the church's auspices, and under the influence of its finest leadership, opportunities for fellow-

[4] A. B. Hollingshead, *Elmtown's Youth* (New York: John Wiley and Sons, Inc., 1949), p. 263.

ship and play which will maintain a Christian quality of relationships.

The church is concerned not merely with supplying its constituency with "harmless amusements"; its deeper concern is to use the life of fellowship and play essential to the joyousness and friendliness of the beloved community as a major means by which the life of that community promotes growth in Christlikeness. So the groups engaging in such play and fellowship activities must be sufficiently Christian to make possible the maintenance of the required quality in their activities and relationships. Criteria of Christian play and relationships should be developed and applied. However, a smug clique of self-righteous persons, carefully avoiding contamination from outsiders, would be anything but Christlike. For one of the responsibilities of the Christian fellowship group is to select, one by one, persons who are not Christian, and throw their loving and concerned fellowship out around them as the first step toward winning them for Christ.

It is obvious that the fellowship life of the beloved community must be carefully planned and supervised so that it will both maintain the necessary quality of relationships, and will try to lift to that level, through Christian fellowship, persons who are not yet committed to Christ and his way. There is of course significant fellowship involved in all the study, worship, and service activities. The fellowship program functions, then, in two ways. It is the community medium through which all the experiences of study, worship, and service are carried out. It is the "carrier" of the whole program. Also, it is the provision for play, recreation, and enriching social intercourse in which much of the life of the beloved community consists.

What are the marks of good program building?

The church exists, not for its own sake, but to provide a program of experiences for its members through which they may grow as Christians and work together to embody Christ's purpose and release his power in their community and in the world. The program is the means through which this is done. At the center of the church's life and activity should be a representative committee or board whose job it is to plan this program as a whole both on a long-range basis and from week to week and year to year. This program-determining body needs some simple principles according to which it works so as to insure a satisfactory result. Here are some guiding policies or principles which may help.

The Committee should state in the words of its own members the *purpose* of the church's program so that it will actually serve as a guide to program building. This purpose should include long range goals and more immediate objectives. Every program activity should be justified by the way in which it helps accomplish these purposes.

The program should be *indigenous*, or "home grown." The church receives program suggestions and resource materials from many agencies. Some of these are indispensable sources for the use of the church; others are merely attempts to use the church for the promotion of some cause or interest which may or may not be essential to the purpose of its program. The minister's desk is often a bottleneck where this wealth of potential program material accumulates. If the church is to be truly Protestant, an advisory lay committee should help screen this material and, on the basis of an intelligent policy, select what is needed and incorporate it into the proper program channels.

The program needs *unity*, but not uniformity. The different program elements should be well adapted to various age-groups and interest-groups, yet there should be enough unity of theme so that every group has a sense of participation in a church-wide program. It is important to avoid the divisiveness and confusion of many unrelated activities, and to keep every program element continuously related to the central purposes of the church.

The program should have *variety and emphasis*. It is impossible to work at all phases of the church's purpose all the time. The building of a program is the process of breaking up into manageable units the broad purpose and the rich resources of possible experience. One good way to achieve both unity and emphasis is to follow a "church year" which from season to season lifts up appropriate emphases as organizing centers for the whole program. The liturgical churches have traditionally followed such a calendar of emphases and festivals which are designed to relate all of life to the great doctrines and events of the Christian faith. The principle has much value and can probably be worked out with even greater relevance to present day living.

The program should have *balance and comprehensiveness*. It is impossible to keep all the proper aims or purposes of the church in focus at the same time, and this leads to the danger that some important needs or responsibilities may be overlooked altogether. Also, there is the danger that greater attention may be given to some interests than their significance warrants. Ministers naturally have their own preferences for some program elements and will unconsciously neglect others. The program planning group, then, has the responsibility to see that a full, well-rounded program is developed, that nothing essential is neglected, and that the experiences are so organized and made available that every person has opportunity for a full, symmetrical growth personally, and for participation in the essential responsibilities and relationships of the Kingdom of God.

CHAPTER 9

What Is The American Way in Education?

Our problem is to discover how we may follow the principle of the separation of church and state based upon our Protestant demand for religious freedom, while still preserving the essentially religious character of our heritage and culture. God's place in education is not as an "elective" tacked on in Sunday School, but as the unifying basis of all truth and the goal of all learning. The parochial school, weekday religious education, family religion, moral and spiritual values in public education, and religion as such in the public school curriculum are all proposals toward a solution. No one national plan seems feasible. Local autonomy to experiment both in public and religious education, close co-operation between church and school, and a fuller development of the Protestant principle of creative freedom will show the way.

What is our problem?

No nation has ever placed greater confidence in or made larger investments in its educational system than has the United States of America. Yet, a combination of circumstances prevents our schools from yielding the full results we hope for, and confronts us with a highly complex educational problem which appears increasingly difficult of solution. The problem is finding how to enable our American educational system to preserve the essentially religious character of our heritage and culture, while also preserving the American principles of religious freedom and the separation of church and state.

Our founding fathers realized that political democracy with universal suffrage calls for universal education, and that such education is the responsibility of the state. Because one dominant motive which had brought the founders of this nation to these shores was the quest for religious freedom, they were determined that the new nation should provide a haven of religious freedom for all peoples. This had two significant meanings for the religious life of America: first, religion would be an essential and pervasive force in all our life and culture; second, religion would be expressed in a rich variety of forms and institutions, many of which were importations from the old world. Religious freedom with equal opportunity for every variety of religious belief and practice, precluded any established or state recognized church, and, consequently, required the complete separation of church and state institutionally and administratively.

This meant that public education, provided as it was by the state, must be neutral in its attitude toward the various religious beliefs, practices, and institutions of our people. There was no implication that the state or its institutions and leaders should be neutral or negative toward religion as such. In many ways the essential place of religious values and practices in our American life and culture has always been assumed. God is recognized and man's responsibility to him implied, in such basic American documents as the Declaration of Independence and the Constitution of the United States and those of the several states. "In God we trust" is stamped upon our coins. Sessions of governmental bodies are opened with prayer. Property held and used by religious bodies is exempt from taxation. Chaplains are provided in the armed forces and in government institutions.

Our public schools have in many ways recognized that we value religion as an essential part of our life and culture. Devotional exercises are conducted in many schools. Religious holidays are observed. The great majority of our public school teachers are religious persons, many of them working actively in local churches. Their influence on the whole is of positive religious value.

The American people are avowedly a religious people and their culture and traditions have an essentially religious quality and content. While neutrality toward our religious diversities required the exclusion of specific religious teachings from the public school curriculum, it was never contemplated that public education should thus be rendered "godless" or should indoctrinate growing persons with a completely secular view of life and the universe.

In the earlier years when the public school curriculum was limited to the "three R's," leaving vast areas of life untouched, the exclusion of the "fourth R," religion, was not so serious. But as the public school curriculum expanded to include nearly every interest of life—vocational, social, cultural, and recreational—public education became about as broad as life itself. The exclusion of religion from such a broadened curriculum seemed to imply that it was unimportant or negligible. This constitutes a most effective negation of religion. In the degree that public education is the dominant influence in the life of a growing generation, it becomes, inadvertently, education in irreligion or in secularism, that philosophy of life which leaves God out, or relegates religion to a compartment of life unrelated to the principle activities of living. As Dr. Buttrick has so well said: "In our fear of indoctrination we have practiced worse indoctrination: *by our silences in secular education we have indoctrinated children to believe that God does not exist and that Jesus Christ does not matter.* In protecting the scruples of agnostics we have trampled roughshod over the convictions of believers." [1]

Other influences in our American life have strengthened the drift toward secularism. The adjustment of religious concepts and beliefs to the increasingly prevalent scientific point of view has been difficult. As a result many people have sur-

[1] George Arthur Buttrick, *Christ and Man's Dilemma* (New York: Abingdon Cokesbury Press, 1946), pp. 135, 136.

rendered religion itself along with outmoded beliefs, in favor of a purely materialistic view of life which they think more scientific. Our preoccupation with the achievements and material benefits of technology has obscured spiritual facts and values. Involvements in two world wars and the hysterical preparation for a third one within half a century, have the effect of enthroning force, violence, and materialism, and of repudiating ethical and spiritual values. It would be difficult enough to curb the rising tide of secularism and preserve the spiritual values of our heritage even if public education were dedicated to that end. With its major influence inadvertently exerted on the side of secularism, the outlook for our American culture is grave indeed.

Obviously, the founders of our nation and of our public school system never contemplated such an outcome. Our problem now is finding the means to enable our educational system to fulfill its function in a religiously heterogeneous democracy, while preserving both religious freedom and the spiritual values and resources in our traditions and our culture. And our deepest concern for maintaining these spiritual values as the essential character and motivation of our American culture, is not for the sake of these values or the institutions such as the churches which embody them. Rather, it is that our culture and our whole social order is sick nigh unto death for the want of these values and motives. History's scrap pile is high with the wreckage of former brilliant civilizations which collapsed when their spiritual rootage decayed. Our own modern culture has been characterized as a "cut flower civilization." Our moral and spiritual retardation, which constitutes our most dangerous hazard, will be accentuated rather than decreased unless we can find a way to incorporate the motivation and the guidance of religion in our educational system as a whole.

What is God's place in education?

The place of religion in education is twofold. The first, and most obvious, place is as subject matter in the curriculum.

Courses in religion may parallel other courses such as those in history, literature, science, and philosophy. The justification for including it in this category is that religion is as much a part of our basic cultural heritage, and is as universal an interest as any of these other curriculum subjects. The difficulty in our American system of state schools is that religion in America exists as a variety of denominational organizations, forms, and beliefs, toward no one of which the state or its schools may show preference. There are differences of opinion among the patrons of our schools regarding these other curriculum subjects. Yet these differences are not usually sufficiently organized and emotionalized to cause the school trouble in dealing with them. Unlike sectarian organized religious opinions, particular opinions or peculiar beliefs in regard to these other subjects have not been erected into absolutes and made synonymous with the will of God. The public school can deal with differences among its patrons as long as these are recognized by all concerned as mere human opinions. But when particular opinions are regarded as "revealed truth" and strong ecclesiastical institutions discipline and motivate their constituents to defend such "truth" against opposed "human error," the community school had better "keep its hands off." In one sense, this means that religion is a far more important curriculum subject than any of these others because people do care so very much about it that they will not trust the public school with it. In spite of this, there are proposals, which we must later consider, for bringing religion into the curriculum in a really effective way.

But our whole western heritage and cultural background compel us to recognize for religion an even more fundamental place in education. Religion is not merely one among many parallel curriculum subjects. It is the very foundation for the whole meaning and purpose and direction of education. The most serious defect in our American educational system, from the viewpoint of our cultural heritage, is not that religion has so largely dropped out of the curriculum. It is that our American education is adrift upon an open sea without any authoritative chart or compass to give it direction and destination.[2]

To be sure, our educational pilots are busily at work finding "moral and spiritual values" in the secular curriculum. Some are even concocting a new religion of democracy and science.[3] But this new religion is not the religion of the churches or of the people, nor is it likely to furnish the direction and the dynamic by which education can close the gap between our technological power and our moral and spiritual competence. This tendency of the public schools to develop their own anthropocentric religious faith confronts the churches with a major challenge. It is assailed by all religious educators whether Fundamentalist, neo-orthodox, or liberal.

After citing various proposals by public educators that democracy be taught virtually as a religion, Dr. Gabelein says: ". . . With naive faith in its wonder working power, we have committed our youth to public education as the essential means for perpetuating democracy. And now we find that those who profess greatest ardor for democracy are betraying it through a pagan ideology that claims democracy as ultimate, rejects transcendental authority by leveling truth to human experience, and seeks to retain the 'spiritual values' of so-called mythical religion after dissipating the myth! . . . *The democratic principle of freedom of conscience and of worship, which forbids the teaching of any particular religious doctrine of Ultimate Reality in public education, applies with like force against the teaching of the anti-religious doctrine of secularism which denies Ultimate Reality.*"[4]

Professor F. Ernest Johnson, representing a liberal Protestant viewpoint, agrees in the following words: "A frank advocacy of

[2] For example see Bernard Iddings Bell, *Crisis in American Education: A Challenge to American Complacency* (New York: Whittlesey House, McGraw-Hill Book Company, Inc., 1949).

[3] H. M. Kallen, "Democracy's True Religion," *Saturday Review of Literature,* New York, July 28, 1951.

[4] Frank E. Gabelein, *Christian Education in a Democracy* (New York: Oxford University Press, 1951), p. 89.

naturalism as a religious philosophy would be assailed violently as an infringement of the Constitution. . . . But let it be clearly recognized that the most basic issue today concerning the relation of religion to public education is the claim of secularist educators to the right to introduce a frankly anti-theistic philosophy." [5]

One need not agree with all the assumptions underlying Dr. H. Shelton Smith's indictment of the experimentalist philosophy of education and democracy which dominates progressive secular education, to appreciate and endorse his closing challenge:

"The question is not, as many have supposed, Shall the public school teach a religion? For, according to our survey, religion of a kind is already in the state school. It is that sort which we have called anthropocentric religion, and which Dewey in 1908 implied in the phrase, 'the positive creed of life implicit in democracy and science.' Whether or not the experimentalist educator may ever have formulated his creed in terms of commonly recognized ideology is beside the point. The main point is that he considers progressive education to be essentially religious. It is this assumption that either explicitly or implicitly motivates his fundamental opposition to other forms of religion, and especially those forms associated with the organized faiths, Catholic, Jewish, and Protestant. Thus the paramount question is this: What kind of religion shall the public school teach — the religion of the churches or the religion of humanistic experimentalism? Sooner or later this must become the focal point of a crucial battle. On its outcome largely hangs the fate of democratic culture in America." [6]

It might appear that the schools were being attacked by the churches no matter which way they turn. They are criticized for indoctrinating their students with secularism, but when they turn as far toward religion as they can go without encroaching

---

[5] F. Ernest Johnson, "Religion and the Schools: What Can We Hope For?" *Religious Education*, Chicago, The Religious Education Association, July-August, 1948.

[6] H. Shelton Smith, *Faith and Nurture* (New York: Charles Scribner's Sons, 1941), p. 202.

upon the theological domain of the churches, they are criticized for teaching a spurious religion. Obviously the churches must find a more constructive way of dealing with this dilemma. Our problem of spiritual retardation will not be solved by an anthropocentric public school religion, nor will it be solved by a church religion which is in conflict with the spirit of democracy and of science which pervades public education.

The religion which can do this must be both scientific and democratic in its viewpoint and spirit, but the grounds of Reality and Truth on which it will rest will take into account a "Given" not created by man, a Reality which man does not control but to which he subjects and adjusts himself.

Our true cultural heritage takes its basic character from the assumption that Truth is one and it constitutes the nature of our universe. The various branches of human knowledge which make up the cultural heritage embodied in the curriculum are only fragments of truth. These fragments have their meaning and their validity, not in their separateness, but in their relation to the Whole. When education becomes but a compilation of some of these fragments, and they are never seen in their relation to, or dependence upon, the Whole, it becomes exactly what we have in our American secularized educational system. It deals with the total periphery of life but never gets to the center, the meaning and worth and purpose of it all. For just as God belongs at the center of life, he belongs at the center of education.[7]

This assumption underlay the origin of American education, for it was started by the churches and its motivation was religious. The principal effect of this was not merely to make religious truth a part of the curriculum. The real significance was that every subject in the curriculum was approached and interpreted from the viewpoint of religious meaning and values. It is this conception of education which underlay the founding of all the earlier institutions of higher learning in America, and

[7] See Henry P. Van Dusen, *God in Education* (New York: Charles Scribner's Sons, 1951), chap. III.

which still justifies the church-related college. It constitutes the most convincing argument in favor of parochial schools. Because the diverse religious interpretations and practices of the churches were themselves obviously fragments of truth about the Truth, rather than the Truth itself, the founding fathers deemed it necessary to avoid a preferential attitude toward any of the particular religions in the state schools, so the teaching of religion as a curriculum subject was excluded. Secularization of the whole philosophy and orientation of public education, which has been a later development, was neither contemplated nor necessarily involved.

There are many evidences of the futility of such education which, not only leaves God out of the curriculum, but also leaves him out of the basic assumptions underlying everything that is in the curriculum. The resulting weaknesses have seldom been better analyzed than by Dr. Charles Malik, Lebanon's Representative to the United Nations, and also to the United States, in presenting "The Challenge of Communism" to the Chicago Council of Foreign Relations:

"The balance of spirit is in a sense the most important task, for a man, no matter how weak or poor or ignorant, will be exceedingly strong and rich and wise if only he has an idea for which he can die and therefore for which he can live. Communism provides such an idea. The Communists have a purpose in life beyond their immediate cares and worries.

"The non-Communist world does not have such a sense of mission. There is, therefore, so far, an unequal spiritual struggle between it and the Communist world. So long as this is the case, peaceful co-existence must remain a pious hope. For there will always be an uneasy tension in the minds of men afflicted with the widespread malady of purposelessness. They will always feel they are unjustly cheated of something: the unifying and liberating sense of purpose.

"The source of this agonizing injustice is that the Western world, as it seems to me, does not believe strongly enough in the importance and power of ideas. It trusts far more in gadgets and in the manipulation of the emotions than in the truth and potency of ideas. In many instances, Western man is too much wrapped up in himself, in his own self-pity, his own self-worry and petty, little problems. He does not sufficiently rest in joy on the marvelous vision of objective and independent truth, throbbing with life and meaning and salvation.

"The ideal of taking a college degree, getting married and settled, rearing a family, having a dependable job, making lots of money and having a solid and ever expanding bank account — this ideal conceived purely in these terms is not good enough. It is, if I may say so, a very timid ideal. It is not dangerous enough; it does not answer to man's deepest hunger for truth and community, where going out of one's self is a joy, and where it is more blessed to give than to receive.

'Confronted with this ideal alone, Asia — if I must be frank with you — is not impressed. In fact, despite all her darkness and misery, Asia can still do better. And an Asian who knows something of the highest values which have characterized the Western positive tradition at its best can turn to the West and say, 'You can do much better also.'

"If the thirsty souls of honest seeking men throughout the world are going to be satisfied, a mighty living true faith must be discovered or created to balance the militant faith of Communism. Pure nationalism will always be handicapped by reason of its particularism, whereas the need in this physically unified world is for something just as universal as Communism but infinitely more profound and true. He does not know the infinite positive hidden riches of the non-Communist world in Asia, in Europe and in America, who does not believe that such a faith can be released in it." [8]

It is clear that the solution to our problem must deal with both aspects of it — the place of religion as a subject in the curriculum and the place of God in the total philosophy and orientation of education.

[8] Charles Malik, *The Challenge of Communism* (Chicago: The Chicago Council on Foreign Relations, 1951), pp. 10, 11.

Does the Sunday school provide the answer?

About the time when public education in America was being secularized, the Sunday school movement was spreading across the nation. It was promoted by enthusiastic lay leadership. It was more a community than a denominational movement, being organized for promotion and supervision by communities, districts, counties, and states, and bringing into fellowship and mutual aid lay workers of all denominations at these various geographical levels. During the nineteenth century it looked as though this enthusiastic community movement of the people might parallel our public school system with a system of Sunday schools which would reach all the people and would incorporate the religious element in the total educational experience of each generation. It is easy to understand the enthusiasm for this seeming, happy solution to our American educational problem. Why has it not fulfilled these earlier hopes?

In the beginning the educational standards of the Sunday school and the public school were not far apart. But the public school with its employed teachers under responsible supervision, gradually growing into a profession with continuously mounting standards; with its democratic rootage and support firmly established in the community so that it became a symbol of community concern and integrity; with its expanding schedule and continuously richer program; with its support by compulsory attendance so that it reached virtually all the people: the public school soon out distanced the Sunday school, leaving it stranded as an obsolete, not to say discredited, educational agency.

When the Sunday school came to be recognized by denominational agencies, not only as a responsibility, but as a most effective means of denominational promotion, it lost its community character. The widespread non-denominational system of Sunday school unions and associations at the various geographical levels largely disintegrated when the support and loyalty which they had built up were redirected into denominational channels. Although denominational supervision sought to raise the educational standards by promoting teacher training and better curricular materials, the morale of the movement suffered. The divisiveness and wastefulness of the denominational system impaired the community outreach of the Sunday school and rendered effective co-operation with public education difficult. The higher educational standards created through denominational supervision have actually had discouragingly little effect upon the quality of work under way in the great majority of Sunday schools. In spite of forty years of vigorous denominational effort to replace Uniform Lessons with a graded curriculum, in the majority of schools Uniform Lessons persist, or graded lessons are rendered ineffective through an obsolete methodology.

It has become evident that the Sunday school program has tended to isolate religion from the general educational experience of growing persons, rather than to integrate religion with that experience or to effect a religious interpretation of it. Consequently, even if the educational standards of the Sunday school could be brought up to a favorable comparison with public school standards, the dual system of education would be far from satisfactory. A closer identification of religion with life as a whole is needed if religion is to be vital.

Whatever the reasons, it is clear that the Sunday school movement, either in its earlier community phase or its later denominational phase, has not solved our American educational problem. Less than half our people are reached at all by the Sunday school, and only a small proportion of those enrolled are receiving religious education of a quality comparable with public school education in the same community. The Sunday school unquestionably has an important role to play in any adequate American plan of education. But it will be only part of a more comprehensive plan. To play that part, it must undergo important improvements, some of which have already been implied and others of which will be suggested in the next chapter.

Is weekday religious education the way out?

Weekday religious education, as we shall use the term, means classes in religion taught under church auspices during the public school day on periods of time "released" by the public school schedule for this purpose. Children are enrolled in these classes and excused from public school duties accordingly, on the written request of their parents. The time is usually limited to one or two sixty-minute periods each week. These periods are sometimes "staggered" so that different grades are released successive periods, enabling one teacher to teach a number of groups in sequence. More generally, however, all children are released the same hour, necessitating a teaching staff and other facilities for handling them all at once. Public school rooms have in many cases been used on the basis of a nominal rental, though this practice is now generally regarded as illegal. The schools or classes have sometimes been entirely denominational, in some cases partly denominational and partly interdenominational, and in other cases wholly interdenominational. This same principle has taken the form of Bible study for high school credit, as in North Dakota, or of teachers of religion provided by the churches, who operate much as a special teacher of art or music does in the public school system.

This plan has obvious advantages. It brings religion into close and favorable relationship with the public school curriculum, helping to unify the learner's religious experience with his other experience. It brings religious teaching within the serious educational framework of the school. It usually makes possible the employment of better qualified leadership than does the Sunday school. In actual practice it usually reaches many children who receive no other religious teaching. Since it involves the cooperation of the school with the church, it helps to relieve the stigma of complete secularization from the school.

The first released-time plan was used in Gary, Indiana, in 1914. Its spread has been somewhat spasmodic and precarious due to such difficulties as: securing adequate and sustained financial support; securing the sustained backing of the churches; providing satisfactory housing and facilities; providing leadership and program comparable with those of the public school. The movement has been retarded recently by the decision of the Supreme Court of the United States in the "Champaign Case," March 1948. This decision seems to have declared illegal the use of public school buildings for such classes, use of public school administration or facilities for promotion, administration, or supervision of such classes, and any serious or inconvenient adjustment in the public school program or schedule. It did not affect the released-time principle as such. The facts that several prevalent practices were declared illegal, that the decision itself is ambiguous, and that the limitations enforced by the decision impaired some of the advantages of the plan as generally followed, have raised questions as to whether such a plan can be counted upon as a major contribution to the solution of our problem. However, there is a widespread conviction that this decision does not truly represent either a valid interpretation of the United States Constitution or the desires and attitudes of the majority of American people.

While the Supreme Court's decision applies to the released-time plan of weekday religious education, and constitutes a limitation upon this plan for incorporating religion into the weekday curriculum, the trend in state schools of higher education seems to be decidedly in the other direction. Practices which go much farther toward making religion an integral part of the state school's program than the one outlawed at Champaign, are in practice in numerous state schools. While in a majority of these institutions the courses in religion are in the regular academic curriculum and so are not offered or controlled by any particular religious denomination, in a number of cases the courses are offered by church controlled institutions off campus, but are fully accredited. These latter cases certainly represent co-operation resembling that of the week day religious education plan. It is to be hoped that the general dissatisfaction with the Court's decision may finally result in a more favorable interpretation. In the meantime, this plan for bringing religious teaching into the closest and most favorable relationship with the state school curriculum should be promoted and used as one step toward the solution of our American educational problem.

Does the parochial school offer the solution?

From the beginning, the Roman Catholic Church and some of the Protestant sects have questioned the validity of the whole public school principle. They have taken the sound position that religion is both a special subject matter in the total educational curriculum and also a point of view and a method of approach in dealing with all other subject matter. It is, therefore, impossible to divide education into secular education and religious education. Since religion permeates all life it must be a part of all education. Secular education would be education in irreligion. If the community is religiously heterogeneous, so that religious freedom requires the separation of church and state, then, so the argument goes, education becomes the function of the church, which can make it religious throughout, rather than of the state, which will necessarily make it secular throughout. Consequently, the only sound educational system is provided by parochial schools. If education is to be supported by the state on the basis of a school tax, the argument continues, this support should be avaliable for parochial schools which meet established educational standards, as well as for state schools which exclude religion.

Our generation has had dramatic and tragic evidence of the dangers in an educational system which the state comes completely to control. Education, under such a system, becomes the most powerful instrument of the political dictator and his totalitarian statecraft. Religion and religious institutions have proven the one force able to challenge totalitarian statism. In the measure that a trend toward statism constitutes a threat to our American democracy, a vital and effective place in education must be maintained by private schools and church schools.

The church still maintains a place of influence in American education at the college level. The argument on behalf of the church-related college is substantially the argument for the parochial school. Religion belongs *in* education, not apart from it or merely alongside of it. When education is monopolized by the state, there is a real danger that statism under the guise of patriotism will become exalted as a religious sentiment, and that religious motivation will come to be prostituted to the uses of political regimentation and totalitarianism. The preservation of our free American institutions and of democracy itself may depend more on maintaining an educational system which in some measure is free from state control than on maintaining a state educational system. At least the existence of church colleges and other types of church-related education alongside a state system of schools seems essentially American and democratic.

From the viewpoint of a sound educational philosophy and of the effective integration of religion in education, as well as from the standpoint of "a free church in a free state," the position of those who advocate parochial schools is unassailable. But it has serious practical weaknesses. The state must look to education to produce a citizenship qualified for effective participation in community life and in a democratic political order. Dare the state trust the church to produce in parochial schools the democratic citizens it needs? Is it any more reasonable for the state to trust the church to safeguard its interests in church schools, than for the church to trust the state to safeguard its interests in state schools? The very conditions requiring separation of church and state preclude either church or state from conducting a total educational program satisfactory to the other. Furthermore, a parochial educational system would be inefficient, costly, and wasteful. Many religious groups thus made responsible for education, would be incompetent to provide it. Can religious freedom be granted only to those groups who are able to meet certain educational standards? If sectarian divisiveness were to permeate our educational system, what chance would there be to assimilate our heterogeneous population into any satisfactory community life and common American mind? Could democracy even survive without the powerful democratizing effect of our great public school system, secular though it may be?

If parochial schools were to be held chiefly responsible for our American educational program, it would be necessary in the public interest to establish some kind of educational standards. After all, we require an educational *system*, not just a multiplicity of unrelated and sporadic educational units under entirely autonomous and technically irresponsible ecclesiastical institutions. But when the state or some public accrediting agency sets up educational standards mandatory for church schools, has not the principle of religious liberty been infringed? Is the state not in such instances, legislating for the church?

The parochial school system obviously is not the solution to our American problem, even though the challenge of its philosophy of education and religion must be faced by any other solution proposed. Even the Roman Catholic Church itself has, during the last generation, become much more realistic in its recognition of the large proportion of Roman Catholic children who, willy nilly, are being educated in our public schools. It has become much more favorable to some plan such as weekday religious education on released-time, by which religious education provided by churches can be brought into the closest possible relationship to the public school program. Some such plan as this, rather than the extension of the parochial school system, promises the best solution.

Should religion be taught in the public schools?

Among both church leaders and public school leaders there has been a recently growing interest in the possibility of reintroducing into the program of the public school some regular and systematic provision for religious teaching. Some believe that there is a "common core" of spiritual values or religious truth which could be so defined and taught that it would be satisfactory to all the various religious bodies. Since such teaching would not be sectarian but could represent common agreement, it would properly be incorporated in the regular school curriculum.[9]

Some of the stubborn questions which this proposal must confront are: When everything to which any religious group would object has been taken out of this "common core", is anything left which is sufficiently explicit and concrete to be recognized as truly religious? Granted that a unanimously approved common core curriculum could be devised, who could teach it to the satisfaction of all? The teacher's own personality, practices, viewpoints, and religious affiliations and background are probably more important determinants of the actual results than are the curricular materials. Teachers of religion should, of course, be church members. But to what extent will the members of one church permit their children to be taught religion by members of another church? Will the churches ever surrender to the public school the right to teach religion? Even if they did would this not violate the principle of separation of church and state? Would not conflicts and confusion develop in the religious life and beliefs of children who received part of their religious teaching in a public school and part of it in a church with some sectarian emphases and prejudices?

Another proposal for incorporating the religious element into our public school curriculum suggests the use of religious resources for the enrichment of regular public school studies. This would leave courses in religion to the regular church programs, but would make careful provision for the appreciative and constructive incorporation of religious elements wherever relevant in the program. Biblical literature, instead of being discriminated against by exclusion, would take its proper place as a source and dominant influence in much other literature.

---

[9] See, for example, Clyde Lemont Hay, *The Blind Spot in American Education* (New York: The Macmillan Company, 1950).

History would deal with religion and religious institutions. Social studies would recognize the churches as among the universal and formative influences in social and community life. Religious sanctions would be recognized in ethics.

A somewhat different point of view regarding the possibility of teaching religion in the public schools seeks, not a core of common agreement, but, rather, an objective scientific approach to differences. Many subjects on which there are differences of opinion among both the patrons and the teachers of our public schools are, nevertheless, being handled successfully in the public school curriculum. In fact, a creative and open-minded approach, rather than a transmissive or authoritarian approach, to almost any subject in the curriculum, will involve various opinions and viewpoints. This is the very meaning of a free liberal education. Biology, economics, civics, art, literature, and philosophy all have their conflicting schools of thought. True liberal education consists in a consideration and appraisal of all the principal viewpoints or theories, with the freedom to arrive at one's own convictions in the light of all relevant data and values involved. Why should religion not be approached in the same open-minded way in a program of liberal education?

We say that particular religious beliefs cannot be taught or dealt with in the public school because someone in the community will object to them or the way in which they are being handled. But if everything else to which someone might possibly object were to be eliminated from the public school program how much would be left? And if the history, literature, institutions, and achievements of religion cannot be dealt with in the same objective, exploratory manner as economics, political science, ethics, and philosophy, then what chance has religion to survive at all in the liberal scientific climate of modern education? By seeking to protect religion we may actually discredit it and discard it.

Of course, such an open-minded, scientific approach to religion is out of harmony with the dogmatic and intolerant attitude which characterizes authoritarian and transmissive religious teaching. This is, however, a truly Protestant approach. But probably the great majority of our churches do not have the courage or the confidence in their own cherished convictions to allow public education to make this approach. This solution awaits a much fuller development of Protestantism along the lines of its basic principles than has yet been achieved. Relatively few Protestants are as yet really Protestant enough for it.

Aren't moral and spiritual values sufficient?

The approach to our problem which has received most attention from public school authorities in recent years is that of emphasizing the moral and spiritual values available within the public school itself without involving the relationship between church and school. The Educational Policies Commission of the National Education Association and the American Association of School Administrators has issued a highly significant report on *Moral and Spiritual Values in the Public Schools.*[10] The report affirms that "a great and continuing purpose of education has been the development of moral and spiritual values."

Among ten "lines of good procedure" in seeking these values in the public school program, the following specifically mention religion as such:

"*Public schools should be friendly toward the religious beliefs of their students.* Although the public school teacher is obligated by the canons of his profession not to attempt to indoctrinate his personal sectarian creeds and opinions, the attitude of the public school toward the religious beliefs of the children in their care should be sympathetic. The teacher's words and attitudes should reassure each child that his religious

10 *Moral and Spiritual Values in the Public Schools,* Educational Policies Commission, 1201 Sixteenth Street, Washington, D.C., 1951. See also the extensive evaluation of this report by fifteen religious leaders in *Religious Education,* Chicago, The Religious Education Association, Vol. XLVI, No. 4, July-August, 1951, from which summary given here is quoted.

beliefs are considered right *for him*, so that he will feel comfortable with his own creed or lack of creed.

"The atheist and the bigot may object to even the most objective presentation of the facts about the role of religion in American life. But such views should not deter schools from teaching a decent respect for the religious opinions of mankind.

"*The public schools should continue to guard religious freedom.* ... The public school may certainly not teach sectarian religion, but teaching against religion is equally intolerant and intolerable. The science teacher, for example, who tells youth that religious faith is 'unscientific' is taking professional advantage of their immaturity and exhibiting his own.

"*The public schools should teach about religion.* This can be done without advocating or teaching any religious creed. To omit from the classroom all references to religion and its institutions is to neglect an important part of American life. Knowledge about religion is essential for a full understanding of our culture, literature, art, history, and current affairs.

"That religious beliefs are controversial is not an adequate reason for excluding teaching *about* religion from the public schools. Economic and social information is taught in the schools on the sensible theory that students need to learn how to face issues and to form sound judgments. Teaching about religion should be approached in the same spirit.

"*Moral values are built by a partnership among many agencies.* The school is an important source of moral and spiritual values, but it must always be a partner of the homes and the churches."

While the report implies that the grounds of moral and spiritual values available in public school teaching are naturalistic, it recognizes that a theistic basis may be supplied by religious institutions: "The churches and other organized institutions of religion play a major role in the development of moral and spiritual values. The great systems of religious belief reject a mechanistic view of the nature of man. They teach that a power exists above the material universe. They deny that man is merely another educable animal, whose behavior can be fully explained and rightly directed by science alone. They seek to understand and teach the relation of man to God. They grapple with the enduring problems of the meaning of human life, aspiration, suffering, and death. In these transcendental terms, religion adds a unique emphasis to moral and spiritual values."

This Report is a heartening and significant document. Its widespread influence can confidently be expected to contribute substantially toward the solution of our American problem in education. But it does not present the complete solution. It makes a contribution toward defining the respective fields and responsibilities of school and church, but it does not show how these partners are to be brought into more effective co-operation. The lines of procedure suggested leave many unanswered questions: When the public school is guiding its students into thinking critically and weighing values in all other fields, can it be satisfied to "reassure each child that his religious beliefs are considered right *for him,* so that he will feel comfortable with his own creed or lack of creed" no matter how inconsistent it may be with many other things which he is learning? Isn't refusal to encourage sound thinking in religion really discrimination against religion? Yet, is there any other really neutral position?

Can the public schools teach *about religion* and yet avoid regarding religion as sanction for moral conduct? Is it possible for a religious person to achieve the degree of objectivity which this viewpoint assumes on the part of the teacher? Can the *study* of religion really be separated from the *teaching* of religion?

Can a system of moral and spiritual values which are developed on a purely humanistic basis, avoiding transcendental terms, receive emphasis by merely adding these religious terms as reinforcement? Either moral and spiritual values have a theistic foundation or they have not. If they have, why not recognize it from the beginning? If they have not, why seek the co-operation of home and church to add them as "emphasis"? The fact that a minority who deny the religious grounds of morality and truth prevent the schools from affirming these grounds for all the rest, is but a restatement of our basic problem.

Is not the family responsible?

Since the family is the primary source and agency of religious nurture, is not this problem of incorporating religion in the total growing experience of children a responsibility of the family? In upholding the right of parents to send their children to parochial schools in lieu of public schools, and to request release of public school time so that their children may participate in weekday church schools, the courts have invariably asserted the parents' final authority over, and primary responsibility for, the education of his child. Does this not place definitely upon the parents the responsibility for providing children with a well-rounded education which includes such religious teachings and viewpoints as the parents desire? Isn't the problem of integrating into a unified and consistent total philosophy of life for each child, those experiences which are provided by home, church, school, and community, a problem which is up to the home? What teacher, other than the parent, is in such a favorable position to guide and help his child to "see life steadily and see it whole"?

Theoretically this is by far the most obvious solution to our problem. But unfortunately, for several generations past, trends in American family life have been in the opposite direction. Technological developments, making for an industrialized and urbanized society, have encouraged the family to give to specialized agencies function after function in economic, vocational, educational, health, and recreational activities. This might have set the family free from its traditional load of providing economic and physical welfare, to specialize even more fully in the realm of moral and spiritual nurture. Such ultimately might be the outcome of technology and specialization.

But, so far, the trend seems to have been for the family increasingly to abdicate its moral and religious role, and to look to specialized agencies like church, school, and club to provide for these functions also.

At the present time, therefore, we would find the majority of families both indisposed and incompetent to undertake this basic function of integrating the total experience of growing persons around the spiritual values which are inherent and indispensable in our American culture. Any policy and program for the Christian education of Protestants in America must provide for the family to play effectively its primary role in Christian nurture. But because Christian education for family life has been so neglected and is at present so inadequately provided, our American educational problem cannot in this generation be laid at the door of the family. The family itself is a major part rather than a solution of the problem. School and church must work together directly upon the problem itself, and also they must strive to qualify families in another generation to play a more effective part in its solution.

Can vacation religious education help?

Among the most important recent developments in our American program of religious education is the fruitful use of blocks of vacation time. The vacation church school, for persons from pre-school through junior high school grades, conducts an intensive program five days a week for a period of two to six weeks. The sessions are usually three-hour forenoon sessions, sometimes supplemented by afternoon playground activities. The program is much richer and more diversified than the Sunday school program, including in addition to worship and Bible study, such elements as dramatics, craft work, creative art work, and supervised play. By far the best results are obtained in the longer terms of from four to six weeks. The larger blocks of time in daily sequence provide an intensity of interest and cumulative experience not possible in the Sunday school or in weekday religious education. A good vacation church school provides as much time as a full year of Sunday school work, and is conducted under conditions which produce proportionately greater results.

The camp and conference program is another highly fruitful use of vacation time. While junior and junior high camps are multiplying, the camp movement has served especially the senior high school and college age groups. The prevalent camping period is a week, but the entire time is well organized and fruitfully used so that an experience of remarkable significance is provided. Not infrequently young people think of their week at camp as literally a Kingdom of God experience. The entire life of the group — from worship and courses in Bible study, missions, and Christian living to creative play and camp administration — is organized and directed as curriculum in Christian experience.

A potentially significant type of camp is the family camp in which the administrative and program unit is not the individual but the whole family.[11] The purpose is to provide the family as such with an intensive experience of Christian living and to lift family life to a higher level of spiritual insights and religious significance. It seems that expansion of the family camp movement might make a much larger contribution than would be made by extending indefinitely the development of age group camping, which but adds one more occasion for separating the family and limiting family building experiences.

Vacation religious education represents perhaps the greatest unused resource for enriching our American program of Christian education — unused because, so far, these potentially rich opportunities are being provided to only a small fraction of the church's constituency. Up to now public education has left the summer period fairly free. But among progressive educational leaders there is talk of adopting the eleven or twelve month school year in order to use the time which now, for the vast majority of our school population, is wasted educationally.

[11] *Planning the Family Camp*, Chicago, Division of Education, National Council of Churches, 1943.

Religious leaders and agencies should vigorously push into this vacation time with a religious program which will preempt some of it for religious purposes. A church which is not systematically using blocks of vacation time is neglecting one of its major educational opportunities.

What are the essentials of a solution?

Because the religious homogeneity and backgrounds of various sections of the country and of different communities varies, probably no one clearly defined approach can be nation-wide. The indigenous and locally autonomous character of both our public schools and church schools should be preserved. No national solution can be achieved and handed down. We can note, however, certain general or essential factors that should enter into whatever plan may be developed.

Any truly American plan of education must provide for incorporating our religious heritage and the spiritual values which characterize our culture within the total educational experience. This must be done in such a manner as to preserve full religious freedom with complete respect for the rights of religious minorities. It should harmonize the principle of the co-operation with that of the separation of church and state.

The principle provision for education should be made by public schools under state supervision. This is the necessary provision for a universally qualified democratic citizenship, community minded and public spirited. The program of the public schools should not be sectarian in any sense, but it must on the other hand avoid presenting a completely secular view of life and the universe, for this would be as untrue to our American heritage and culture as would a sectarian bias. This means that the public school in its personnel and program should be appreciative and positive in its attitude toward religion and religious institutions. It should be ready to co-operate with the churches in every way which will be consistent with neutrality toward their peculiarities or differences, treating all with fairness and equality.

A truly American system of education will recognize the place and desirability of private schools and parochial schools alongside the public school system, wherever there is sufficient patronage desirous of the spiritual plus which such schools may provide, and when the regular educational standards of the public schools are met. Such private schools should indicate no reflection upon, or lack of support for, our public school system, and they should never seek support from public school funds. They represent a wholesome expression of free enterprise in education and provide some safeguard against the misuse of public education in extending political control in the direction of the totalitarian state, if such a trend should arise. It is to be expected, however, that by far the major load of education in America will be carried by the tax-supported public educational system.

While the principal provisions for specifically religious education must be made by the churches, these provisions must be such as to bear a close and consistent relationship with education as a whole. The dualism in administration must cease to mean dualism in the educational experience of growing persons by which religion becomes isolated from education and from life as a whole. Religious education must come to be as scientific in its reverence for facts and discovery of new truth, as unbiased and objective in its handling of its subject matter, and as sincere and openminded in its dealing with differences of opinion as is the liberating, creative type of education which characterizes our best public schools. When religious education becomes truly Protestant by its creative, objective, liberating spirit, it will become consistent and continuous with our best general education; it will tend to make religion integral to education as a whole.

As our churches come increasingly to take this liberating, objective, scientific attitude in their own educational programs, they will be willing to have religion dealt with in this same objective manner in the public schools. It will then be unnecessary for public education to discriminate against the religious element in our culture and history by excluding it. Religious literature, institutions, and practices can be as frankly and constructively faced as are other phases of our culture in which diversities exist. This will go a long way toward correcting the secularizing tendencies in public education.

As our church school programs become less concerned about denominational indoctrination and more concerned about liberating the young into their total spiritual heritage and fellowship, those divisive concerns which hinder the co-operation of school and church will give way to common interests and values which will make co-operation easier. Our dual system of public schools and church schools can then so well integrate their programs as to present a fairly unified educational experience without the infringement of religious freedom or the introduction of sectarian influences into public education.

The co-operative relationships between public schools and the church should, then, reflect the realization that:

Widespread development of weekday religious education on released-time with mutual co-operation to make the most effective use of this time, in interdenominational church schools, is desirable.

A lively interest on the part of the churches in the religious character and attitude of public school personnel is needed. It would, in the long run, be both un-American and detrimental to school-church relationships for any one church or denomination to try to exert political influence upon the school board or in school elections in its own interests. But for the churches together to let their concern be felt regarding the attitude of public school personnel toward religion and the churches as a whole, is nothing short of a religious and civic obligation.

The churches of the community should be so closely related to each other that they could deal as a unit with the public school administration in working out co-operative arrangements as to schedule and shared activities. The programs of the churches which affect school children should be planned so as to leave the child's school time free of interference. On the other hand, the school should carefully avoid encroaching upon week end time and weekday evening time lest the churches have difficulty in conducting their programs. When the churches work together and synchronize their own programs, it is usually possible to arrange with the school administration to keep school activities from interfering with regularly scheduled church activities like choir practice and regular midweek meetings. Unless the churches do synchronize their programs and make a united approach to the school authorities, it is difficult for the school to avoid some interference with church programs.

The churches should see that effective use is made of a significant part of the summer vacation period for religious education. If they do this they have a right to expect the schools to avoid projecting school activities into this period.

The churches should give their full and hearty support to the public schools of their communities. Church leaders should be familiar with what goes on in the school because the children with whom they work are deeply affected by that program. Churches may well observe American Education Week in November each year with sermons and discussion on the importance of our public educational program.

Since the school exerts its greatest moral and spiritual influence through the personalities of its teachers, the church has a deep concern that these teachers shall be Christians. The best way to insure this is for the church to encourage many of its finest young people to dedicate their lives to the teaching profession as one of the best fields of Christian service. School boards can do a much better job of providing the school with Christian teachers if there is a good supply available.

It is clear that much of the solution of our American educational problem is up to the churches. In the degree that churches appreciate and seek to preserve our American tradition of religious freedom, and in the degree that they wish to see incorporated into the educational experience of each generation the spiritual values so characteristic of our American culture, the churches will reconstruct their own programs and policies in the direction of these essentials of a solution to our problem.

Though the problem is complex there is reason for encouragement, for real progress is being made. There is a more widespread awareness among the responsible leaders, churchmen, school men, and other public servants, than ever before. Well qualified agencies are open-mindedly attacking the problem. The work of the Educational Policies Commission of the National Educational Association; the American Council on Education; the Danforth Foundation; the Special Committee on Religion and Public Education of the National Council of Churches of Christ in America and the Religious Education Association are among the agencies whose work underlies the foregoing analysis, and whose continuing efforts insure competent guidance to church leaders.

CHAPTER 10

What Are the Growing Edges
of the Movement?

*As a movement the growing edges of Christian educa-
tion represent in some measure the "lag" between the
leadership and literature of the program and the prevalent
practice in local churches. The fulfillment of the present
promises of the movement will be accompanied and characterized by the following developments: The family will
assume a far larger and more effective role. Adult education will become the forefront of the movement and the
means by which it will succeed all along the line. A really
extensive and effective program for the discovery, enlistment, qualification, and motivation of the hosts of indispensable lay leaders will develop. Supervision, recognized
as the function of a professional worker, either the pastor
or an educational specialist, will lift the spiritual quality of
the work done by lay leaders. Like public education,
Christian education will again become a community movement as it was during the rise of the Sunday school, and
on an educational level equal to that of public education.
It will integrate religious learning with social action
around the unfinished tasks of the Kingdom of God. Indispensable to all these achievements will be the development and maintenance of the venturesome spirit.*

What does this movement mean?

Christian education in the life of the church today means much
more than it did at the beginning of this century. Probably

this growing concept and this expanding program constitute the most important development in the Protestant churches since the turn of the century. Modern Christian education is indeed a "movement." It is in no sense settled or in its final form. In fact, one of its characteristics is the great variety of expressions which this new educational concern takes. Practice in different churches of the same denomination or in the same community varies widely. Some Sunday schools resemble those of fifty years ago. In other cases an entire local congregation has organized its program to embody the educational ideal and procedure. Predominantly the actual program in the local church lags far behind that contemplated and advocated by the supervisory agencies and the literature of the movement. But it is a growing, changing movement. As such it has certain "growing edges" which indicate directions, which cope with the problems involved in the movement, and which promise much for the future. We can take courage as we look at these growing edges.

Will the family resume its primary educational role?

All studies and all authorities in the field bear testimony to the unique potential religious influence and personality-forming power of the family. When Christian education is conceived as centering in the experiences of growing persons, seeking through qualifying these experiences to develop Christlike persons as the primary outcome, the relative importance of the family is greatly increased. The family is the inevitable cradle of personality. Even though school, church, and community have their roles to play, the family largely conditions the effectiveness of those roles. While the predominant tendency in recent decades has been for the family to abdicate many of the family functions in favor of specialized agencies, it would seem that, in the realm of Christian nurture at least, the family should expand rather than further limit its responsibility and its conscious role. It seems probable that the whole religious educational movement will succeed in its most basic sense in about the degree that it succeeds in making family life a primary and widely prevalent means of Christian nurture. It might even be said that if the church enables its families properly to discharge their essential function of Christian nurture, any other educational service the church might render would be of quite secondary importance. Conversely, it might be said that if the church fails to enable and motivate its families to do their task of Christian nurture well, any other educational service it may render will be of quite limited significance. What are some of the implications of recognizing this primary role of the family?

The first change will be in the way in which home and church regard each other. The present typical attitude of even the Christian home toward the church is that religion is the church's business; that just as the public school takes over general education, so the church school should be expected to take over Christian education; and that the only responsibility of the home is to see that children get to the church school with reasonable regularity and punctuality. Even this responsibility is usually taken less seriously than is the corresponding responsibility in connection with public school attendance. Even Christian families will make plans which interfere with church school attendance more readily than they will those which mean public school absence. In spite of the very limited time which the church schedules for its job, punctuality and regularity of attendance fall far below those of the public school for the same children. Thus, after defining its responsibiliy in the minimum terms of merely co-operating with the church in its program for their children, the average family falls far below a serious discharge of even that responsibility.

The typical attitude of church school leaders toward the family tends to support rather than correct this minimum responsibility concept of parents. Home visitation, such as there is of it, and the meager materials supplied parents to interpret the program of Christian education, usually imply that the program centers in the church, that the major responsibility rests there, and that all that is requested of parents is their co-operation with the church in putting over *its* program. Parents and teachers agree then, and support one another, in the concept that Christian education is primarily a church function and the role of the family is secondary, supplementary, and more or less optional.

But all the relevant facts proclaim this interpretation as utterly unrealistic and subversive of any thorough provision for Christian nurture. If church and family are to operate in accordance with the known conditions of Christian growth, these attitudes need thorough reconstruction. It is much more realistic to say that the family is the basic and primary agency of Christian nurture, whereas the role of the church is supplementary and secondary. In fact, the basic role of the church should be, not to take over the job, but to qualify the family for doing it. The church's program can and should provide important corporate experiences and special age-group features which the family cannot well supply. The church can offer specialized leadership. The church can and must try to make up for homes which do not function religiously, at least until it can improve their functioning. These provisions will call for a larger instead of a more limited program than the typical church now offers. But rather than pretending to do the whole job, this program will be supplementary to the basic provisions which are family-centered.

Home and church will regard each other as partners in an inevitably shared task, each having its distinctive role to play and neither seeking to supplant the other. The church school is perhaps best regarded as a "parental co-operative" in which parents pool their resources to do collectively a part of the job which is still fully as much their own responsibility. This means that the church in all its work will think of the family rather than the individual as a basic administrative unit. Many more church activities will be planned to keep the family together rather than always to divide it into graded categories. The church will be as deeply concerned about, and make as careful provision for, those religious activities which go on in the homes of its people as for those which go on in the church.

The program of Christian education will be one jointly operative in home and church. Re-education of the attitudes of both parents and teachers is necessary to bring this about.

One of the greatest changes involved will be in the curricular materials of Christian education, and this change is already under way. A study made of the curricular materials of denominational publishing houses in 1944 [1] revealed that only in the lower grades were any materials whatever provided for use by parents or in the home. Such as there were clearly interpreted the program as centering in the church (except in the case of nursery materials) and regarded the parental role as purely supplementary and co-operative. In other words, curricular materials expressed and supported the existing attitudes of home and church toward each other. A plea was made to curriculum makers that a new kind of curriculum be undertaken, a curriculum developed from the ground up for the joint use of home and church, giving as careful attention to materials for the group experiences of the ungraded family as for those of the graded church groups; a curriculum in which there would be full correlation between the two fields of experience because the beginning point is in the primary family group rather than in the secondary graded church group.

The "practical and realistic answer" to such a proposal is that, if there were such a curriculum available, not ten per cent of even Christian families would be either qualified or disposed to use it. Very well. But as long as curricular materials clearly imply that the role of the home is purely supplementary, what chance is there of getting even ten per cent of the parents to take any more significant role? And even if they wanted to, how could they with no materials to work with? Teachers in the church school are provided with a ready made education set-up. Some of them have a little training for the job. Yet how far would they get if we placed in their hands curricular materials as meager as those available for the job of the home?

[1] Harry C. Munro, "A Family-Centered Curriculum," *Religious Education*, Chicago, The Religious Education Association, XXXIX, No. 3 (May-June, 1944), 161-168.

We are not going to improve the participation of parents in Christian education until the curricular materials provided their children imply that they have a basic role to play as teachers, and give them resource and guidance materials for playing that role comparable with what are provided the church teachers for their part of the program in the church. The indispensable approach to more satisfactory parental participation is curricular materials which assume and depend upon that participation and which provide the necessary resources for it.

Fortunately, the most recent curriculm developments show a decided tendency in that direction. Home and church are assumed to be partners in the program. Rich and attractive materials are provided for reading and for guided activities in the home. Initial parent-teacher conferences are specified as essential in introducing each curriculum unit, and continued home-church relationships are assumed. The curriculum is organized by "vertical" unifying themes rather than by the fragmentizing strata of the traditional graded curriculum. This does not impose uniformity. It simply leads to a harmonization of the principles of gradation and of unity, and a recognition of the significance of experiences in both graded and ungraded groups. It enables home and church to work together without the pattern of either being imposed upon the other.

These significant curriculum trends must be supported by a much more vigorous and comprehensive program of family life education in and through the church. Such a program involves every age-group and can be outlined from any beginning point. Suppose we start with the setting up of the Christian home through marriage. There are available today well-standardized techniques and rich guidance and resource materials on premarital counselling by ministers. Yet, except in two or three denominations where some form of premarital counselling is prerequisite to performing the marriage ceremony, a minister with any thoroughgoing policy and program in this function is rare indeed. The opportunity is almost staggering in its possibilities as a means of stabilizing and Christianzing marriage. If competent practice on the part of the Protestant ministry could become general in this field, it might well be the church's greatest contribution toward conserving and improving the American home. A natural sequence of such counselling is family guidance during the early years of the marriage when family patterns are being crystallized and the family's creative power of character formation is at its maximum.

The help which the family would receive in its religious functions as a result of the type of curriculum noted above would be considerable, but the church could and should do even more. The church should have regular classes especially for parents, and, through proper planning, help and guidance on family life should be made to flow naturally from its sermons, pastoral work, and special observances. Furthermore, young people should receive systematic guidance and enrichment in the fields of boy and girl relationships and of preparation for marriage previous to specific premarital counselling. In all its efforts toward achieving throughout its program a recognition and enrichment of family life, the church would be helped immeasurably by thinking of itself always as *a family of families* rather than merely as an organization of individuals.

The church may well regard the family unit as an effective means of building the church. But if that represents its principal regard for the family it is exploiting rather than serving the family. The church is never an end to be served. It is always a means to serving higher ends. The quality of family life is one of those higher ends. When the church measures its relationship to its families, not by the contribution which they can make to the church, but by the contributions which the church can make to ever richer and more creative family life, then the church will see its true spiritual objectives far nearer realization.

Can Christian education become lifelong?

In the past Christian education has characteristically been interpreted as the church's program for children and youth. There are several reasons why that limited concept is no longer tenable. The concept of education has broadened to include all learningful experience, and of course the religious experiences of adults, as well as those of youth, are educationally significant. So the church's total program, including its activities for whatever age, becomes an educational program. We do not say the church *has* a school. We think of the church *as* a school. Christian education is as broad as the whole church program and applies equally to all ages.

A vast adult education movement has developed, bearing testimony to the fact that, in our rapidly changing social order, education cannot terminate with schooling but must continue throughout life as an adjustment process to ever new demands which life makes upon us. Technological unemployment is but one dramatic expression of this fact. Adults are often compelled to acquire new skills or enter an entirely new vocation late in life because some new technological development has wiped out their earlier job and rendered obsolete their past skills and experience. This is only a sample of the adjustments which have to be made throughout life in such a day as ours. Education in early life could once prepare the young for living in a predictable future world. Today the best it can do is to prepare them for resourceful adjustment throughout life to an unpredictable world. So, all true education has necessarily become lifelong.

Unless religious education also becomes a lifelong process, it involves one in continuous maladjustments; for religious thinking, practices, and experiences are as subject to the disturbing influences of a rapidly changing social and cultural order as are any other phases of life. Only a growing religious experience is adequate to keep one in vital and creative relationships with his total social and spiritual environment. The low religious vitality and lack of spiritual motivation of multitudes today is due to the fact that their religious experience has become compartmentalized and stagnant while the rest of life has developed and matured. An immature, childish faith is inadequate for the intellectual requirements and the moral demands of a mature life. Only lifelong Christian education will keep one's religious thinking abreast of his other thinking and relate his religious convictions to the responsibilities of adulthood in a world like ours.[2]

Furthermore, to interpret true Christian experience as consisting chiefly of one conversion event followed by a lifetime of backward-looking stagnation is to see only its caricature. Religious vitality requires continuous religious growth. The climax is somewhere ahead as the goal of venturesome living and courageous thinking. Only such a conception of adult religious experience provides the basis for a vital, functional religious faith. In fact, the church's major educational job may be at the adult level rather than in earlier life.

This conception of Christian education as both lifelong and "lifewide" calls for pretty thorough reconstruction of the traditional church program, much of which seems calculated to keep people the way they already are rather than to effect continuous change in them. It calls for a serious, well-organized curriculum of adult study which will equip men and women with religious insights and understanding in the various complex areas of experience such as personal faith, family life, churchmanship, vocational relationships, social and community issues, and world relationships. It must provide also for a working mastery of the Bible and of church history and Christian doctrine as a means of knowing the Christian implications and obligations of living in the many complex areas of experience. The church's preaching program, which represents its heaviest investments in adult program, must be placed on an educational basis so as actually to promote religious growth and vital Christian living. The church's whole organizational and promotional life will need to be administered with the primary purpose of promoting growth in the lives of those who participate. These changes are directed toward conceiving the whole church itself as a "disciplehood," a school in Christian living. Specialized provision is needed to deal

[2] J. B. Phillips, *Your God Is Too Small* (New York: The Macmillan Company, 1952).

with four particular adult groups: "neo-adults," those in transition from youth into adulthood; parents; the non-participating church member; and those of retirement age, the "golden age" or "fulfillment years."

Can lay persons teach religion?

Teaching religion is the climax of all teaching. To do it effectively requires the finest teaching art. When we observe how frequently courses in literature or history or mathematics result, not in a lifelong interest and desire for further learning in these fields, but rather in a distaste for them, we realize the hazards of unskillful teaching. We know that it takes more than courses in religion to produce vital, continuously growing religious persons. It takes competent and effective leadership. We in the Protestant churches depend upon voluntary, largely untrained lay personnel for this most exacting of all teaching jobs. Under such leadership have we any hope of real success?

The conviction that teaching religion requires more than lay competence led at least one minister to abolish his Sunday school and arrange to teach all of his people, young and old, in separate age-groups on a staggered Sunday and week-day schedule. [3] Others have proposed that we have larger classes like the public school, using fewer and better teachers. There has been experimentation with paying church school teachers a modest honorarium as a basis for requiring more responsibility and setting definite standards of qualification and performance. Certainly, if really effective Christian teaching requires any of these means, we ought not to hesitate at either the cost or the necessary adjustments. Shall we continue in the Protestant churches to look to a relatively large, lay teaching staff, mostly untrained, and with only the motive of voluntary Christian service, to carry the exacting and highly important teaching load?

[3] Elmer G. Homrighausen, "A Man Who Abolished His Sunday School," *International Journal of Religious Education*, XI, No. 2 (October, 1934), 9.

Actually, the prevalent practice is far more true to Protestant principles than are any of the proposed improvements. Our Protestant churches supposedly are founded on individual believers' personal testimony to their own experience of God and salvation, and on the conviction that every believer is not only his own priest but his brother's priest as well. If such churches cannot staff their educational program with qualified lay, volunteer teachers, their own principles are being violated. Does a church which cannot produce such teachers have any real Protestant message to teach? Will not the professionalizing of its teaching staff destroy their teaching competence as Protestants? Qualified and responsible leadership is basic to our teaching program. But we must solve the problem of providing it within the framework and spirit of our Protestant faith and not by resort to some inconsistent expedient.

We may begin with the conviction that the church has all the potential leadership it needs for the job. Within any normal group individual differences will account for the presence of a sufficient number of persons who have the inherent capacity to provide all the lay leadership the group needs. The solution of our problem is not in wishing for leadership personnel which is not there. Rather, it is in developing the resources which are available. A systematic, continuous, long-range program by which each church could provide for its leadership needs would include four processes:

(1) The *discovery* of its potential leadership. This process should be continuous in all groups, but should be especially emphasized in later childhood and early adolescence. The method used in classes and departments should be such as to disclose this potential leadership and give it opportunity for expression. One of the great weaknesses of the transmissive educational pattern is that lack of participation on the part of learners prevents the emergence of leadership tendencies and abilities. Many adult classes, as we have previously noted, are so conducted as to discourage development of leadership skill by anyone but the teacher. The creative pattern of learning

through participation and the carrying of responsibility will almost automatically reveal and develop the potential leadership available in any group.

(2) The *enlistment* of leaders. The motive of service is usually high during middle adolescence. This is the time to enlist boys and girls in assistant or apprentice work, and in responsibilities within their reach and under careful guidance, through which they will receive the satisfaction of achievement and motivation for lifelong service commitment. In connection with vocational choice, Christian youth ought always to be confronted by the claims of Christ for their full time service. Whatever the vocation chosen, it should be interpreted as primarily an opportunity for Christian service, with voluntary leadership in the church's program as a matter for deliberate and consecrated commitment. Such commitments made and recognized at this time will hold steady through later periods when service motivation might otherwise be obscured by the adjustments involved in early adulthood. Enlistment for Christian service at any time should be an experience far more impressive and momentous than a mere agreement to "teach a class because we are short of teachers and can't get any one else." Enlistment and dedication to this kind of voluntary service should be dignified and hallowed by an appropriate commitment experience.

(3) The *qualification* of leaders. The church's general program should provide the spiritual qualifications needed, but there are skills and insights which call for special leadership development provisions. Training classes should be operating as a continuous and integral part of the regular educational program, and not merely as spasmodic and fragmentary interjections. Advantage should be taken of community training schools, summer conferences, laboratory schools, and the visits of specialists. Although any kind of remuneration for the actual service rendered by lay leaders in the church is highly questionable, the cost of securing the necessary training and of needed books and magazines is clearly an obligation of the church. In-

vestments here will be more wholesome and will go much farther than similar investments in direct remuneration, and they will probably increase rather than impair desirable motivation.

(4) The *motivation* and *continued guidance* of leaders. The teaching of religion is almost the same as the teaching of motives, for religion is power to live as well as guidance in living. Consequently, the motives which cause Christian teachers to devote effort and ability to their labor of love are of the very essence of their qualifications. The conditions under which they work, and the relationships involved, should be such as to inspire the deepest self-effacement and self-giving. So the church's provision for leadership should give special attention to the motives which are operative.

The outcome of such a comprehensive leadership program for the church should provide competent personnel for every task within the church's program. It should also develop churchmen who are competent and disposed to provide Christian leadership for many community agencies and activities which lie outside the church's own program.

One of the most significant of the growing edges of the movement is in this field of leadership recruitment and qualification. It calls for a function which is yet in its infancy in the movement, but which is begining to emerge. We must deal with this as the next of these growing edges.

How can the quality of Christian teaching be lifted?

The Christian educational program involves three principal jobs. Its cutting edge is *teaching* where leaders and learners meet in shared experiences. Teaching is conditioning and guiding others as they learn. In the Protestant churches it is a lay, voluntary job. The second job is *administration*. This function sets up and maintains the learning-teaching situation. It operates the educational machinery. It maintains the school as a social organism and provides for its smooth functioning. Administration also is a lay task. It requires no skill or insight beyond what lay personnel can well develop out of natural ability and vocational experience.

But the outcomes of these lay functions depend upon their quality. It is not the actual forms which learning activities take in the church school which determines their significance. It is the spiritual quality of the experiences involved. It is quite possible for the operations of the church school or class to proceed according to form and schedule but seldom or never to reach a really religious level. A Bible story can be dealt with and fail to produce a religious experience in the group. Religious quality cannot be insured through curricular materials or administrative regulations. How can we be assured that the program of a given church school actually reaches a religious level? This presents the need for a third function, that which is called in general education, *supervision*. It is the purpose of supervision to raise the quality of the learning-teaching process. In religious education it is the responsibility of supervision to see that the program reaches a religious level. Of course the supervisor has to work through teachers and administrators. His job is to enable and motivate them to raise their work in its spiritual quality until it reaches the necessary level. In a sense, the significance of all they do depends upon the success of the supervisory function.

This qualitative process is difficult and exacting. It requires insight into the nature of religious experience, the learning-teaching process, the resources and methods available, and the desired outcomes. Such insight lies beyond what can properly be expected of a lay voluntary worker. Supervision is a professional job. Training for it must be more comprehensive and thorough than can be expected of lay workers. The delicate relationships involved imply a professional rank on the part of the supervisor. The indispensable improvement needed throughout the educational program of the Protestant churches can be provided only by the introduction or extension of professional supervision.

In the larger churches where a staff of specialists can be

employed, one of these is usually a minister or director of religious education. His job should be this one of professional supervision. It is important that churches able to employ educational specialists should understand that this should be the function, so that the specialist may be held responsible for doing it, so that the lay staff shall expect it, and also so that the specialist will not be loaded with other activities which should be carried by lay workers.

In the great majority of churches which employ only one professional leader, this must become a principal function of the minister. Only as he is qualified to discharge this responsibility and is expected to do it as one of his major tasks, have these churches any chance of such a service. Obviously this involves considerable revision in the seminary training of these ministers and also in what their churches expect of them.

The techniques and resources to be used in this function are beyond the scope of this text. They will of course consist chiefly in ways of improving the lay leadership. The launching and operation of the whole systematic program for the discovery, enlistment, qualification, and motivation of the leadership staff, already outlined, will be the principal approach. The minister will thus become chiefly a leader of leaders, multiplying and projecting his own personality, skills, and purposes through many lay workers. This reinterpretation of the minister's job does not merely add another burden to his already heavy load. Rather, it gives him fresh resources for carrying that part of the load which is truly professional and for shifting to competent lay shoulders much of the load which he might otherwise continue to carry. Such an interpretation of the task of the church's professional leadership is the principal hope for developing an educational program of the required quality in Protestant churches.

Can the religious community become a reality?

Education in America is a community function. The early Sunday school movement, through Sunday school unions and associations, spread as a community movement. While the denominationalizing of the movement in the early part of this century was designed to raise the quality of the program and leadership and provide a better curriculum, it largely destroyed the community character of the movement. That community character greatly needs to be restored. Neighboring churches need to face their shared task of Christian education together at the community level. Denominational supervision of the local church program cannot improve it enough in quality to compensate for isolating it from participation with its neighboring churches in a community-wide and community-centered program of religious education.

For a local church to look exclusively to its denominational agencies for program materials and guidance and for fellowship in its task is to imply that the needs of its people are different from those of the people in its neighboring churches, but that they are the same as those of people of that same denomination in other communities across the nation. This assumption underlying the exclusively denominational relationship of the local church is absurd. The reverse is nearer the truth. If Christian education is to be in any sense life-centered and socially functional, the help needed by persons engaged in it is determined more by the total community conditions under which they work than by the denomination with which they happen to be affiliated.

Suppose we think of the boys and girls who comprise the junior department in a given church school. Suppose half a dozen other nearby churches each has also a group of juniors. The junior boys and girls of all these neighboring churches constitute one community group of junior age boys and girls. They go to the same public schools and there associate on a community rather than a denominational basis. They see the same advertising, magazine stands, taverns, and pool halls. They attend the same movies. They live under the same political regime, they share the same playgrounds. They live in the same general type of homes. In fact the only time they divide into these particular denominational groupings is when they go to church. In its general background of experience, any of these church groups of juniors has more in common with each of the other neighboring church junior groups than it has with any group of juniors in any other community, even if that group be of its own denomination. To treat this junior group in curriculum and supervision as though it had needs identical with widely scattered junior groups of this denomination, but different from those of junior groups in neighboring churches, is to caricature any life-centered, socially relevant Christian educational approach.

What intelligent, educationally minded leaders are doing, both locally and denominationally, to correct this critical defect in prevalent Christian educational practice involves both a new relationship among neighboring churches at the community level and basic changes in the policies and practices of denominational agencies. The inevitably shared tasks, working conditions, limitations, resources, and needs of neighboring churches in the same community as they face their educational responsibility are being recognized and corporately approached through local councils of churches. A local council of churches is a voluntary partnership of neighboring churches at the points of their common interests, responsibilities, and resources. A council in no way impairs the autonomy of a local church or compromises its doctrinal position. Rather, it places it in relationships which enable it to make its distinctive testimony and contribution to the whole religious community, while joining its neighboring churches at points of common testimony, need, and responsibility, as they face corporately the total community within which together they constitute the only embodiment of Christ's spirit and purpose. Such a council is the one hope for a corporate impact of the churches of a community upon its total life.

Interchurch fellowship, consultation, and common program planning enable the churches to maintain effective co-operative relationships with the public schools and with civic and welfare agencies. Such policies facilitate the relating of church activities and emphases to community movements, developments, and needs, and enable the churches to enlist and share resources which would not be available for any church acting separately. Such inter-church co-operation opens the only possibility for an efficient and thorough approach to the unchurched people of the community. Best of all, it creates in the community a spiritual climate of good will and mutual aid which enables every church to do a far more successful work within its own constituency. Support of such a council, both by full participation in all the commonly planned and sponsored activities and by sharing in its budget, is not contributing to an "outside agency," but is a way of making a part of the church's resources far more fruitful than they would otherwise be. It is, in short, the best way for a church to get certain parts of its work done.

The change required in denominational practices and policies to make such council work possible and effective is a recognition by denominational agencies and leaders that each church is a part of such a religious community and must be free to relate itself thereto. Denominational field plans and promotional policies, then, must take into account the priority which a church's community relationships frequently require. Denominational plans, schedules, promotional drives, and field services must be sufficiently flexible to enable the local church to operate as a part of the local religious community and yet maintain its denominational relationships and standing.

Furthermore, the council movement must be co-extensive with denominational field and national agencies, so that denominational plans and schedules can be synchronized in their approach to local communities. This calls for interdenominational planning and clearance at each geographical level from local to national. Denominational field secretaries and agencies in religious education must be in continuous consultation on regional, state, and national levels in order to effect such synchronization and co-ordination of promotional and field service plans. We will not have an efficient, comprehensive, intelligent program of field supervision in religious education until these channels for co-operative planning are open and effective at every level. When they are, the approach of denominational agencies to the local churches will be so synchronized and co-ordinated that they will support each other and encourage local churches to work together at their common task in the community, and at the same time carry out the plans of their denomination, for these interests will have been brought into harmony with each other. Unless denominational programs are thus brought into a common pattern designed to work through the whole religious community, the local church is torn between following its superimposed denominational program and functioning as a part of its religious community. This will impair both its denominational and its community relationship, in most cases particularly the latter.

Such councils are developing rapidly both in numbers and in effectiveness in some parts of the country. In other parts, particularly the deep south, denominational policies are still prevalently isolationist, and the development of religious educational programs on anything like a community basis is correspondingly retarded.

Nationally, the denominational agencies of religious education of some forty denominations, including about eighty-five per cent of American Protestantism, have been, since 1922, well organized for this co-operative approach to their task through the International Council of Religious Education. The International Council became in 1950 an integral part of the comprehensive National Council of the Churches of Christ in the U. S. A., which is church-wide and community-wide in its functions. As the denominations increasingly trust their co-operative agencies with larger and more important functions and resources, Protestant Christianity in Ameirca will be increasingly competent to face its responsibilities at each geographical level from the community to the nation at large.

Can religious education become socially effective?

With the Protestant emphasis upon the individual, it is not surprising that the religious educational movement has been largely preoccupied with individual goals and processes. We have already noted the interdependence of the individual and the social outcomes of any truly vital Christian education. One of the earliest prophets of the modern religious education movement gave an able exposition of this theme. [4] It has been recognized in the curriculum theory underlying our denominational programs. It has characterized such interdenominational plans as the United Christian Youth Movement and the United Christian Adult Movement. But this emphasis still awaits vital embodiment in the curricular materials which denominational agencies provide their local churches and in the operational policies and plans of those local churches.

The preceding section indicated one way in which Christian education will be enabled to become much more effective socially. The tasks of social action and social redemption with which vital Christian education must be concerned exist at the community level. It is only as neighboring churches join hands to undertake them that the full influence of the Christian community can be exerted upon the larger community. Local churches operating in isolation from each other are not apt to undertake any very significant social action enterprises. Any church which does is more likely to be suspected and criticized than to be supported by its neighboring nonparticipating churches. Under such conditions the social influence of the churches is negligible. But let the churches face their responsibility together and pool their resources through an effective council of churches, and their influence becomes something to reckon with. The council movement will be one of the most important ways in which this growing edge of social effectiveness will succeed.

[4] George Albert Coe, *A Social Theory of Religious Education* (New York: Charles Scribner's Sons, 1917).

The tendency in the past has been for social action and Christian education to be the concern of separate agencies and groups. Such dualism impairs both. Those unfinished tasks of the Kingdom of God with which social action is concerned provide the very experiences which growing persons need in a vital, experience-centered program of Christian education. Christian education provides the information, the careful and critical judgment, the constructive procedures, and the well-considered long-range goals which are needed by the program of social action if it is to be intelligent, steady, constructive. Particularly at the level of young people and adults, the educational program needs to become well identified with the social action program so that they constitute one unified program of effective Christian living. When increasingly our denominational programs and materials embody in actual practice what our denominational leaders have worked out cooperatively in theory in the United Christian Youth Movement and the United Christian Adult Movement, the Christian education movement itself will become the most effective way of harnessing our human potential to these unfinished tasks for getting God's will done on earth as it is in heaven.

Can the program become extensive enough?

If Christian education in America is to meet effectively the vast challenge of rampant secularism, materialism, and militarism, it must avail itself of every resource of time and program opportunity. This means that each local church and community must consider the various program provisions which are available, not as alternatives one to another but, rather, as all equally essential to any program sufficiently comprehensive and vigorous to do the job. The various sessions or programs which the churches can carry out need to be so planned and related as to constitute one systematic whole.

We need to make a larger use of Sunday. Expanding the programs for children from one to two hours has been demonstrated as a practical and fruitful enrichment of the Sunday program. More effective use of vesper or Sunday evening time for educational purposes is desirable for youth and adults. The church must maintain the strongest possible hold upon its one Holy Day lest it become a mere holiday of doubtful or negative moral and spiritual value.

But a Sunday program is not enough. Already, with our lengthening week end, our American mores are making a predominantly vacational and recreational use of Sunday. There is so much of potential good in week end family outings that the church can hardly condemn them. We may as well recognize that our best answer to the encroachment of secular interests upon Sunday time may, in most cases, be an increased use of weekday time for religious purposes. This means that wherever we can, we will conduct weekday religious education on a community-wide basis on released public school time. We will work for better relationships with public education so that the public school experience of our children will be as favorable as possible to a religious view of life and the universe. We will also in many cases find it advisable to expand religious education into weekday time by using free time, that is, time before or after public school time on one or more weekdays. There is extremely fruitful experience, for example, with a three-hour program for juniors after public school on Wednesday afternoon, which provides thorough Bible study, craft work, club work, music, and supper. Such a program can be made interesting enough that juniors will gladly participate regularly. Obviously it provides a great enrichment of what can be done on Sunday and secures greater regularity of attendance and a closer relationship with the public school without requiring any adjustments to its work.

A very much richer use should also be made of vacation time in this expanded program. Every child should be offered the opportunity each summer of three or four weeks of vacation church school program which would be sufficiently in the vacation spirit and pattern not to seem like just so much more school work. Every young person should be provided with several seasons of Christian camping or conference experience as an integral part of his local church educational program. Experiences can be provided and results secured thus that cannot be found in any other way. Adult camps and family camps offer unique opportunities. Vacation religious education ought not to be incidental or optional but integral to the church's regular educational program.

We have already noted the possibilities for greatly enriching the program by making the family more effective as a religious unit. This likewise is not an alternative to a richer church program. In fact, the expanded church program will be an important means of helping to develop the expanded family program, and vice versa. We have already lost so much ground through inadequate religious education in America that we face the necessity of a vigorous intensification of the program during the next generation by using to the full every resource and means which has been suggested. We are working in an unfavorable climate, and the best we can do will be none too good.

Can we keep the venturesome spirit?

These frontiers of the present religious educational movement in America call for the spirit of experimentation and of adventure. The creative, life-centered type of Christian education which we have been interpreting as the true expression of Protestant Christianity will embody this venturesome experimental spirit. As that spirit pushes out these growing edges of the movement, American Christianity will measure up to its tremendous responsibility in this confusing and momentous day. Only such a Christian education for Protestants can match this day.

Index

Index